COLLECTED WORKS OF RENÉ GUÉNON

THE REIGN OF QUANTITY
AND THE SIGNS OF THE TIMES

RENÉ GUÉNON

THE REIGN
OF QUANTITY

AND THE SIGNS
OF THE TIMES

Translator
Lord Northbourne

SOPHIA PERENNIS

HILLSDALE NY

Originally published in French as
Le Règne de la Quantité et les Signes des Temps
© Éditions Gallimard 1945
Fourth, revised edition 2001
Second Impression 2004
Third edition, Sophia Perennis, Ghent, 1995
Second edition, Penguin Books, Baltimore, 1972
First edition, Luzac & Co., London, 1953
English translation © Sophia Perennis 2001
All rights reserved

Series editor: James R. Wetmore

For information, address:
Sophia Perennis, P.O. Box 611
Hillsdale NY 12529
sophiaperennis.com

Library of Congress Cataloging-in-Publication Data

Guénon, René
[Règne de la quantité et les signes des temps. English]
The reign of quantity and the signs of the times / René Guénon ;
translated by Lord Northbourne—4th, rev. ed.

p. cm. — (Collected works of René Guénon)
Includes index.
ISBN 0 900588 67 5 (pbk: alk. paper)
ISBN 0 900588 68 3 (cloth: alk. paper)
1. Materialism—Miscellanea. 2. Civilization, Modern—Philosophy—
Miscellanea. I. Title.
BD701.G813 2001
291.2—dc21   2001001097

CONTENTS

EDITORIAL NOTE

THE PAST CENTURY HAS WITNESSED an erosion of earlier cultural values as well as a blurring of the distinctive characteristics of the world's traditional civilizations, giving rise to philosophic and moral relativism, multiculturalism, and dangerous fundamentalist reactions. As early as the 1920s, the French metaphysician René Guénon (1886–1951) had diagnosed these tendencies and presented what he believed to be the only possible reconciliation of the legitimate, although apparently conflicting, demands of outward religious forms, 'exoterisms', with their essential core, 'esoterism'. His works are characterized by a foundational critique of the modern world coupled with a call for intellectual reform; a renewed examination of metaphysics, the traditional sciences, and symbolism, with special reference to the ultimate unanimity of all spiritual traditions; and finally, a call to the work of spiritual realization. Despite their wide influence, translation of Guénon's works into English has so far been piecemeal. The *Sophia Perennis* edition is intended to fill the urgent need to present them in a more authoritative and systematic form. A complete list of Guénon's works, given in the order of their original publication in French, follows this note.

The Reign of Quantity gives a concise but comprehensive view of the present state of affairs in the world, as it appears from the point of view of the 'ancient wisdom', formerly common both to the East and to the West, but now almost entirely lost sight of. The author indicates with his fabled clarity and directness the precise nature of the modern deviation, and devotes special attention to the development of modern philosophy and science, and to the part played by them, with their accompanying notions of progress and evolution, in the formation of the industrial and democratic society which we now regard as 'normal'. Guénon sees history as a descent from Form (or Quality) toward Matter (or Quantity); but after the Reign of Quantity—modern materialism and the 'rise of the masses'—

Guénon predicts a reign of 'inverted quality' just before the end of the age: the triumph of the 'counter-initiation', the kingdom of Antichrist. This text is considered the *magnum opus* among Guénon's texts of civilizational criticism, as is *Symbols of Sacred Science* among his studies on symbols and cosmology, and *Man and His Becoming according to the Vedānta* among his more purely metaphysical works.

Guénon often uses words or expressions set off in 'scare quotes'. To avoid clutter, single quotation marks have been used throughout. As for transliterations, Guénon was more concerned with phonetic fidelity than academic usage. The system adopted here reflects the views of scholars familiar both with the languages and Guénon's writings. Brackets indicate editorial insertions, or, within citations, Guénon's additions. Wherever possible, references have been updated, and English editions substituted.

The present translation is a revised version of that made by Lord Northbourne for the original edition, and the publisher would like to thank Christopher James Northbourne, the translators's son, for his help, encouragement, and permission to work from his father's text. For additional editorial help and proofreading, thanks go to John Ahmed Herlihy, Brian Latham, and Allan Dewar; and for Arabic transliterations, to Prof S. H. Nasr. A special debt of thanks is owed to Cecil Bethell, who revised and proofread the text at several stages and provided the index. Cover design by Michael Buchino and Gray Henry, based on a drawing of a shell disk preserved in the Peabody Museum, by Guénon's friend and collaborator Ananda K. Coomaraswamy.

THE WORKS
OF RENÉ GUÉNON

INTRODUCTION

SINCE THE TIME WHEN *The Crisis of the Modern World* was written, the march of events has only served to confirm, all too completely and all too quickly, the validity of the outlook on the present situation that was adopted in that book, although the subject matter was then dealt with independently of all preoccupation with immediate 'actuality' as well as of any intention toward a vain and barren 'critique'. Indeed, it goes without saying that considerations of that order are worth nothing except insofar as they represent an application of principles to certain particular circumstances; and it may also be noted in passing that if those who have formed the truest judgment of the errors and insufficiencies of the mentality of our times have generally maintained toward them a purely negative attitude, or have only departed from that attitude to propose virtually insignificant remedies quite inadequate to cope with the growing disorder in all domains, it is because a knowledge of true principles has been just as lacking in their case as it has been in the case of those who have persisted in admiring a so-called 'progress' and in deluding themselves as to its fatal outcome.

Besides, even from a purely disinterested and 'theoretical' point of view, it is not enough to denounce errors and to show them up for what they really are; useful though that may be, it is still more interesting and instructive to explain them, that is to say to investigate how and why they have come about; for everything that has any kind of existence, even error, has necessarily its reason for existence, and disorder itself must in the end find its place among the elements of universal order. Thus, whereas the modern world considered in itself is an anomaly and even a sort of monstrosity, it is no less true that, when viewed in relation to the whole historical cycle of which it is a part, it corresponds exactly to the conditions pertaining to a certain phase of that cycle, the phase that the Hindu tradition specifies as the final period of the *Kali-Yuga*. It is these conditions, arising as a consequence of the development of the cycle's manifestation, that have determined its peculiar characteristics, and from this point of view it is clear that the present times could not be otherwise than they actually are. Nonetheless, it is evident that if disorder is to be seen as an element of order, or if error is to be reduced to a partial and distorted aspect of some truth, it is necessary to place oneself above the level of the contingencies of the domain to which that disorder and those errors as such belong; similarly, in order to grasp the true significance of the modern world in the light of the cyclical laws governing the development of the present terrestrial humanity, it is necessary to be entirely detached from the mentality that is its special characteristic and to avoid being affected by it in the least degree. This is the more evident in that the said mentality implies of necessity, and as it were by definition, a complete ignorance of the laws in question, as well as of all other truths which, being more or less directly derived from transcendent principles, are essentially part of traditional knowledge; all characteristically modern conceptions are, consciously or unconsciously, a direct and unqualified denial of that knowledge.

For some time past the author has had it in mind to follow up the *Crisis of the Modern World* with a work of a more strictly 'doctrinal' character, in order to set out with more precision certain aspects of the explanation of the present period given in the earlier book, in conformity with the strictly traditional point of view, which will always be adhered to; in the present case it is, for the very reasons already given, not merely the only valid point of view, but it might even be said to be the only point of view possible, since no such explanation could be imagined apart from it. Various circumstances have delayed the realization of that project up till now, but this is beside the point for anyone who is sure that everything that must happen necessarily happens in its due time, and often in ways both unforeseen and completely independent of our will. The feverish haste with which our contemporaries approach everything they do is powerless against this law and can produce only agitation and disorder, that is to say effects which are wholly negative; but would these people still be 'moderns' if they were capable of understanding the advantages of following the indications given by circumstances that, far from being 'fortuitous'—as their ignorance leads them to suppose—are basically nothing but more or less particularized expressions of the general order, an order at the same time both human and cosmic, with which we are compelled to integrate ourselves either voluntarily or involuntarily?

Among the features characteristic of the modern mentality, the tendency to bring everything down to an exclusively quantitative point of view will be taken from now on as the central theme of this study. This tendency is most marked in the 'scientific' conceptions of recent centuries; but it is almost as conspicuous in other domains, notably in that of social organization—so much so that, with one reservation the nature and necessity of which will appear hereafter, our period could almost be defined as being essentially and primarily the 'reign of quantity'. This characteristic is chosen in preference to any other, not solely nor even principally because it is one of the most evident and least contestable, but above all because of its truly fundamental nature, for reduction to the quantitative is strictly in conformity with the conditions of the cyclic phase at which humanity has now arrived; and also because it is the particular tendency in question that leads logically to the lowest point of the 'descent' that proceeds continuously and with ever-increasing speed from the beginning to the end of a *Manvantara*, that is to say throughout the whole course of the manifestation of a humanity such as ours. This 'descent', as has often been pointed out on previous occasions, is but a gradual movement away from the principle, which is necessarily inherent in any process of manifestation; in our world, by reason of the special conditions of existence to which it is subject, the lowest point takes on the aspect of pure quantity, deprived of every qualitative distinction; it goes without saying that this point represents strictly speaking a limit, and that is why it is not legitimate to speak otherwise than of a 'tendency', for, during the actual course of the cycle, the limit can never be reached since it is as it were outside and beneath any existence, either realized or even realizable.

We come now to a matter of particular importance which must be established from the outset, both in order to avoid possible misconceptions and in order to dispose in advance of a possible source of delusion, namely the fact that, by virtue of the law of analogy, the lowest point is as it were the obscure reflection or the inverted image of the highest point, from which follows the consequence, paradoxical only in appearance, that the most complete absence of all principle implies a sort of 'counterfeit' of the principle itself, something that has been expressed in a 'theological' form in the words 'satan is the ape of God.' A proper appreciation of this fact can help greatly toward the understanding of some of the darkest enigmas of the modern world, enigmas which that world itself denies because though it carries them in itself it is incapable of per-ceiving them, and because this denial is an indispensable condition for the maintenance of the special mentality whereby it exists. If our contemporaries as a whole could see what it is that is guiding them and where they are really going, the modern world would at once cease to exist as such, for the 'rectification' that has often been alluded to in the author's other works could not fail to come about through that very circumstance; on the other hand, since this 'recti-fication' presupposes arrival at the point at which the 'descent' is completely accomplished, where 'the wheel stops turning'—at least for the instant marking the passage from one cycle to another—it is necessary to conclude that, until this point is actually attained, it is impossible that these things should be understood by men in gen-eral, but only by the small number of those who are destined to pre-pare, in one way or in another, the germs of the future cycle. It is scarcely necessary to say that everything that the author has set out in this book and elsewhere is intended to be addressed exclusively to these few, without any concern for the inevitable incomprehension of the others; it is true that these others are, and still must be for a certain time to come, an immense majority, but then it is precisely in the 'reign of quantity', and only then, that the opinion of the majority can claim to be taken into consideration at all.

However that may be, it is particularly desirable before going any further to apply the principle outlined above to a more limited sphere than that to which it has just been applied. It must serve to dispel any confusion between the point of view of traditional sci-ence and that of profane science, especially as certain outward simi-larities may appear to lend themselves to such confusion. These similarities often arise only from inverted correspondences; for whereas traditional science envisages essentially the higher of the corresponding terms and allows no more than a relative value to the lower term, and then only by virtue of its correspondence with the higher term, profane science on the other hand only takes account of the lower term, and being incapable of passing beyond the domain to which it is related, claims to reduce all reality to it. Thus, to take an example directly connected with the subject of this book, the Pythagorean numbers, envisaged as the principles of things, are by no means numbers as understood by the moderns, whether mathematicians or physicists, just as principial immutability is by no means the immobility of a stone, nor true unity the uniformity of beings denuded of all their qualities; nonetheless, because numbers are in question in both cases, the partisans of an exclusively quantitative science have not failed to reckon the Pythagoreans as among their 'precursors'. So as not unduly to anticipate developments to follow, only this much need be said here, namely that this is but one more instance of the fact that the profane sciences of which the modern world is so proud are really and truly only the degenerate 'residues' of the ancient traditional sciences, just as quantity itself, to which they strive to reduce everything, is, when considered from their special point of view, no more than the 'residue' of an existence emptied of everything that constituted its essence; thus these pretended sciences, by leaving aside or even intentionally eliminating all that is truly essential, clearly prove themselves incapable of furnishing the explanation of anything whatsoever.

Just as the traditional science of numbers is quite a different thing from the profane arithmetic of the moderns, including all the algebraic or other extensions of which the latter is capable, so there is also a 'sacred geometry' no less profoundly different from the 'academic' science nowadays designated by the same name. There is no need to insist at length on this point, for those who have read the author's earlier works, in particular *The Symbolism of the Cross*, will call to mind many references to the symbolical geometry in question, and they will have been able to see for themselves how far it lends itself to the representation of realities of a higher order, at least to the extent that those realities are capable of being represented in a form accessible to the senses; and besides, are not geometrical forms fundamentally and necessarily the very basis of all figured or 'graphic' symbolism, from that of the alphabetical and numerical characters of all languages to that of the most complex and apparently strange initiatic *yantras*? It is easy to understand that this kind of symbolism can give rise to an indefinite multiplicity of applications; and it should be equally clear that such a geometry, very far from being related only to pure quantity, is on the contrary essentially qualitative. The same can be said of the true science of numbers, for the principial numbers, though they must be referred to as numbers by analogy, are situated relatively to our world at the pole opposite to that at which are situated the numbers of common arithmetic; the latter are the only numbers the moderns know, and on them they turn all their attention, thus taking the shadow for the reality, like the prisoners in Plato's cave.

The present study is designed to provide a further and more complete demonstration of what, in a very general sense, is the true nature of these traditional sciences, thus bringing into prominence the abyss separating them from the profane sciences, which are something like a caricature or parody of them. This in turn will make it possible to measure the extent of the decadence undergone by the modern mentality in passing from one to the other; it will also indicate, by correctly situating the objects taken into account by each science, how this decadence follows strictly the downward movement of the cycle now being passed through by our humanity. Let it be clear however that these are questions nobody can ever claim to treat completely, for they are by their very nature inexhaustible; but an attempt will be made to say enough to enable anyone to draw the necessary conclusions so far as the determination of the 'cosmic moment' corresponding to the present period is concerned. If, however, a proportion of the matters to be dealt with nevertheless continues to appear obscure to some people, that will only be because the point of view adopted fails to conform to their mental habits, and is too foreign to everything that has been inculcated into them by the education they have received and by the environment in which they live; nothing can be done about this, for there are things for which a symbolical mode of expression properly so called is the only one possible, and which will consequently never be understood by those for whom symbolism is a dead letter. It must also be remembered that a symbolical mode of expression is the indispensable vehicle of all teaching of an initiatic character; but, without even considering the profane world and its evident and in a sense natural lack of comprehension, it is enough to glance at the vestiges of initiation that still persist in the West in order to see what some people, for lack of intellectual 'qualification', make of the symbols proffered for their meditation. One may be quite sure that these people, with whatever titles they may be endowed and whatever initiatic degrees they may have received 'virtually', will never get so far as to penetrate to the real meaning of the smallest fragment of the mysterious geometry of 'the Great Architects of the Orient and of the Occident'.

As the West has just been alluded to, one further remark is called for: however far afield the state of mind that has been specifically designated as 'modern' may have spread, especially in recent years, and however strong may be the hold it has taken and that it exercises ever more completely — at least externally — over the whole world, this state of mind remains nevertheless purely Western in origin: in the West it had its birth, and the West was for a long time its exclusive domain; in the East its influence will never be anything but a Westernization. However far that influence may extend in the course of events still to be unfolded, its extension can never be held to contradict what has been said about the difference between the spirit of the East and that of the West, and this difference is none other than that between the traditional spirit and the modern spirit; for it is all too clear that to the extent that a man 'Westernizes' himself, whatever may be his race or country, to that extent he ceases to be an Easterner spiritually and intellectually, that is to say from the one point of view that really holds any interest. This is not a simple question of geography, unless that word be understood in a sense other than its modern one, for there is also a symbolical geography; indeed, in this connection, there is a very significant correspondence between the domination of the West and the end of a cycle, for the West is the place where the sun sets, that is to say where it arrives at the end of its daily journey, and where, according to Chinese symbolism, 'the ripe fruit falls to the foot of the tree'. As to the means whereby the West has come to establish that domination, of which the 'modernization' of a more or less considerable number of Easterners is only the latest and most vexing consequence, it has been made sufficiently clear in the author's other works that these means are based on material strength alone, which amounts to saying that Western domination is itself no more than an expression of the 'reign of quantity'.

Thus, from whatever side one looks at things, one is always brought back to the same considerations and constantly sees them verified in all possible applications. There ought not to be anything surprising in this, for truth is necessarily coherent; but that certainly does not mean that truth is 'systematic', as profane philosophers and scholars all too readily imagine, confined as they are within narrowly limited conceptions to which alone the word 'systems' can properly be applied, and which merely reflect the insufficiency of individual minds left to their own devices; this is so even when the minds in question belong to those conventionally called 'men of genius', for all the most vaunted speculations of such people are certainly not equal in value to a knowledge of the smallest traditional truth. Enough has been said on that subject in another place, for it has previously been found necessary to denounce the errors of 'individualism', for that again is one of the characteristics of the modern spirit; here it may be added that the false unity of the individual, conceived as constituting in himself a complete whole, corresponds in the human order to the false unity of the so-called 'atom' in the cosmic order: both the one and the other are merely elements that are regarded as 'simple' from a purely quantitative point of view, and as such are supposed to be capable of a sort of indefinite repetition, which is strictly speaking an impossibility since it is essentially incompatible with the very nature of things; in fact, this indefinite repetition is nothing but the pure multiplicity toward which the present world is straining with all its might, without however being able ever to lose itself entirely therein, because pure multiplicity is situated beneath the level of manifested existence, and represents the extreme opposite of principial unity. The descending cyclic movement must therefore be considered as taking place between these two poles, starting from unity, or rather from the point closest to unity in the domain of manifestation, relatively to the state of existence envisaged, and gradually tending toward multiplicity, that is to say toward multiplicity considered analytically and without reference to any principle, for it goes without saying that in the principial order all multiplicity is synthetically comprehended in unity itself. It might appear that there is, in a sense, multiplicity at the two extreme points, in the same way as there is correlatively, as has just been pointed out, unity on the one side and 'units' on the other; but the notion of inverse analogy applies strictly here too, so that while the principial multiplicity is contained in metaphysical unity, arithmetical or quantitative 'units' are on the other hand contained in the other and inferior multiplicity. Incidentally, does not the mere possibility of speaking of 'units' in the plural show clearly enough how far removed the thing so spoken of is from true unity? The multiplicity of the lower order is by definition purely quantitative, it could be said to be quantity itself, deprived of all quality; on the other hand the multiplicity of the higher order, or that which can be called so analogically, is really a qualitative multiplicity, that is to say the integrality of the qualities or attributes that constitute the essence of beings and of things. So it can be said that the descent referred to tends away from pure quality toward pure quantity, both the one and the other being limits situated outside manifestation, the one above it and the other beneath. In relation to the special conditions of our world or of our state of existence, these limits are an expression of the two universal principles that have elsewhere been referred to as 'essence' and 'substance', and they are the two poles between which all manifestation is produced. This is a point that must be explained more fully before going any further, for it provides an indispensable key to the better understanding of the considerations to be developed later in this study.

1

QUALITY
AND QUANTITY

QUALITY AND QUANTITY are fairly generally regarded as complementary terms, although the profound reason for their complementarism is often far from being understood, this reason lying in the 'polar' correspondence referred to toward the end of the introduction to this book. This, the first of all cosmic dualities, is a starting-point, for it is situated at the very principle of existence or of universal manifestation, and without it no manifestation would be possible in any mode whatsoever: it is the duality of *Purusha* and *Prakriti* according to the Hindu doctrine, or to use another terminology, that of 'essence' and 'substance'. Its two terms must be envisaged as universal principles, and as being the two poles of all manifestation; but, at another level, or rather at a number of different levels (for there are many levels, corresponding to the more or less particularized domains that can be envisaged in the interior of universal manifestation), these two terms can also be used analogically and in a relative sense to designate that which corresponds to the two principles, or most directly represents them with reference to a particular more or less limited mode of manifestation. Thus it is that essence and substance can be spoken of in relation either to a world, that is to say to a state of existence determined by certain special conditions, or in relation to a being considered as a separate entity, or even to each of the states of that being, that is to say, to its manifestation in each of the degrees of existence; in this last case, there is naturally a correspondence between what essence and substance represent in the microcosm and what they represent, considered from a macrocosmic point of view, in the world in which the manifestation of the being is situated; in other words, they are then only particularizations of the relative principles that are the determinations of universal essence and substance in relation to the conditions of the world in question.

Understood in this relative sense, and especially with reference to particular beings, essence and substance are in effect the same as the 'form' and 'matter' of the scholastic philosophers; but it is better to avoid the use of these latter terms because, doubtless owing to an imperfection of the Latin language in this connection, they only convey rather inaccurately the ideas they ought to express,[1] and also because they have lately become even more equivocal by reason of the quite different meaning commonly assigned to them in current speech. However that may be, to say that every manifested being is a composite of 'form' and 'matter' amounts to saying that its existence necessarily proceeds simultaneously from both essence and substance, and consequently that there is in each being something corresponding both to the one and to the other of these two principles, in such a way that the being is as it were a resultant of their union, or to speak more exactly, a resultant of the action exercised by the active principle, Essence, on the passive principle, Substance; and if consideration is confined to the special case of individual beings, the 'form' and the 'matter' that constitute those beings are respectively identical with what the Hindu tradition designates as *nāma* and *rūpa*. While on the subject of concordances between different terminologies, thus perhaps incidentally enabling some people to translate the explanations given into a language to which they are more accustomed, it may be added that the Aristotelian designations 'act' and 'potency' also correspond to essence and substance. Aristotle's terms are susceptible of a more extended application than are the terms 'form' and 'matter', but to say that there is in every being a mixture of act and potency comes back to the same thing in the end, for act is that in him by which he participates in essence, and potency is that in him by which he participates in substance; pure

1. These words translate in a rather unsatisfactory way the Greek terms εἶδος and ὕλη employed in the same sense by Aristotle. These terms will be referred to again later.

act and pure potency could not exist anywhere in manifestation, since they are true equivalents of universal essence and substance.

Provided that this is clearly understood, it is possible to speak of the Essence and of the Substance of our world, that is, of the world that is the domain of the individual human being, and it can be said that in conformity with the particular conditions that define this world as such, these two principles appear in it under the aspects of quality and of quantity respectively. This may appear evident at first sight so far as quality is concerned, since essence is the principial synthesis of all the attributes that belong to a being and make that being what it is, and since attributes and qualities are really synonymous: and it may be observed that quality, considered as the content of Essence, if such an expression be allowable, is not exclusively confined to our world, but is susceptible of a transposition that universalizes its significance. There is nothing remarkable in this, since Essence represents the superior principle; but in any such universalization quality ceases to be the correlative of quantity, for quantity, unlike quality, is strictly linked up with the special conditions of our world; furthermore, from a theological point of view, is not quality in some way brought into relation with God himself when his attributes are spoken of, whereas it would be manifestly inconceivable to pretend to assign to him any sort of corresponding quantitative determination.[2] To this the objection might perhaps be raised that Aristotle ranks quality as well as quantity among his 'categories', which are only special modes of the being and not coextensive with it; he does so however without effecting the transposition previously mentioned, indeed he has no need to effect it, for the enumeration of his 'categories' relates only to our world and to its conditions, in such a way that quality cannot be and is not really meant to be understood otherwise than in a sense that is more immediate for us in our state as individuals, the sense in which, as explained earlier, it appears as a correlative of quantity.

It is of interest to note on the other hand that the 'form' of the scholastics is what Aristotle calls εἶδος, and that this latter word is

2. It is possible to speak of *Brahma saguna* or 'qualified', but there can be no possible question of Brahma 'quantified'.

also used to mean 'species', which is properly speaking a nature or an essence common to an indefinite multitude of individuals. Specific nature is of a purely qualitative order, for it is truly 'innumerable' in the strict sense of the word, that is to say it is independent of quantity, being indivisible and entire in every individual belonging to the species, so that it is quite unaffected by the number of those individuals, 'plus' or 'minus' not being applicable to it. Moreover, εἶδος is etymologically the 'idea', not only in the modern psychological sense, but also in an ontological sense nearer than is ordinarily supposed to the sense in which Plato uses it, for whatever may be the real differences in this connection between the conceptions of Plato and of Aristotle, as so often happens they have been greatly exaggerated by disciples and commentators. The Platonic ideas are also essences; Plato gives expression chiefly to the transcendent aspect and Aristotle to the immanent aspect, but this does not imply incompatibility; independently of any conclusions to which the 'systematic' spirit may lead, it is only a matter of a difference of level; in any case, they are always considering 'archetypes' or the essential principles of things, such principles representing what may be called the qualitative side of manifestation. Furthermore, the Platonic ideas, under another name and by direct filiation, are the same thing as the Pythagorean numbers; and this shows clearly that although the Pythagorean numbers are, as already indicated, called numbers analogically, they are in no way numbers in the ordinary quantitative sense of the word; they are on the contrary purely qualitative, corresponding inversely on the side of essence to what the quantitative numbers are on the side of substance.[3]

On the other hand, when Saint Thomas Aquinas says that *numerus stat ex parte materiae* he is speaking of quantitative number, thereby affirming decisively that quantity has an immediate connection with the substantial side of manifestation. The word

---

3. It may be observed that the name of a being, insofar as it is an expression of its essence, is properly speaking a number understood in this qualitative sense; and this establishes a close link between the conception of the Pythagorean numbers — and consequently that of the Platonic ideas — and the use of the Sanskrit word *nāma* to denote the essential side of a being.

'substantial' is used here because *materia* in the scholastic sense is not by any means the same as 'matter' as understood by modern physicists, but is properly 'substance', whether that word be taken in its relative meaning, as when it is put into correlation with *forma* and referred to particular beings, or whether it be taken, when *materia prima* is in question, as the passive principle of universal manifestation, that is, as pure potentiality, and so as the equivalent of *Prakriti* in the Hindu doctrine. However, as soon as 'matter' is in question, in whatever sense the word be taken, everything becomes particularly obscure and confused, and doubtless not without reason;[4] and therefore, while it has been possible to give an adequate account of the relation of quality to essence without developing a long argument, it will be necessary to go more deeply into the relation between quantity and substance in order to present a clear picture of the various aspects assumed by the Western conception of 'matter' even before the advent of the modern deviation in which this word was destined to play so great a part: and it is all the more necessary to do so because this question is in a sense at the very root of the principal subject of this study.

4. It must be pointed out, in connection with essence and substance, that the scholastics often translate as *substantia* the Greek word οὐσία, which on the contrary means properly and literally 'essence', and this contributes not a little to the growth of linguistic confusion; hence such expressions as 'substantial form' for instance, this expression being very ill adapted to convey the idea of that which really constitutes the essential side of a being and not its substantial side.

2

MATERIA SIGNATA QUANTITATE

THE SCHOLASTICS gave the name *materia*, generally speaking, to what Aristotle had called ὕλη; but this *materia*, as has already been said, must in no way be identified with the 'matter' of the moderns, for the idea of 'matter', complex and even in some ways contradictory as it is, seems to have been as strange to the ancient Westerners as it still is to Easterners. Even admitting that *materia* can become 'matter' in certain special cases, or rather to be more accurate, that the more recent conception can be made to fit into the earlier one, *materia* nevertheless includes many other things at the same time, and it is these other things that must be carefully distinguished from 'matter'; but for the purpose of naming them as a group by some comprehensive term like ὕλη or *materia*, we have no better word at our disposal in Western languages than the word 'substance'. In any case, ὕλη, as a universal principle, is pure potency in which nothing is distinguished or 'actualized', and it constitutes the passive 'support' of all manifestation; it is therefore, taken in this sense, precisely *Prakriti* or universal substance, and everything that has been said elsewhere about *Prakriti* applies equally to ὕλη thus understood.[1] Substance, understood in a relative sense as being that

---

1. The primary meaning of the word ὕλη is related to the vegetative principle; here there is an allusion to the 'root' (in Sanskrit *mūla*, a term applied to *Prakriti*) which is the starting-point of manifestation; in this can be seen some connection

which represents analogically the substantial principle and plays its part in relation to a more or less narrowly restricted order of existence, furnishes the term ὕλη with a secondary meaning, particularly when this term is correlated with εἶδος to designate the two sides, essential and substantial, of particular existences.

The scholastics, following Aristotle, distinguish these two meanings by speaking of *materia prima* and *materia secunda*, so that it can be said that their *materia prima* is universal substance and their *materia secunda* is substance in the relative sense; but, since terms become susceptible of multiple applications at different levels as soon as the relative is considered, what is *materia* at a certain level can become *forma* at another, and inversely, according to the more or less particularized hierarchy of the degrees of manifested existence under consideration. In no case is a *materia secunda* pure potency, although it may constitute the potential side of a world or of a being; universal substance alone is pure potency, and it is situated not only beneath our world (*substantia*, from *sub stare*, is literally 'that which stands beneath', a meaning also attached to the ideas of 'support' and 'substratum'), but also beneath the whole of all the worlds and all the states comprised in universal manifestation. In addition, for the very reason that it is potentiality, absolutely 'undistinguished' and undifferentiated universal substance is the only principle that can properly be said to be 'unintelligible', not merely because we are not capable of knowing it, but because there is actually nothing in it to be known; as for relative substances, insofar as they participate in the potentiality of universal substance, so far do they also participate in its 'unintelligibility'. Therefore the explanation of things must not be sought on the substantial side, but on the contrary it must be sought on the essential side; translated into terms of spatial symbolism, this is equivalent to saying that every explanation must proceed from above downward and not from below upward; and this observation has a special relevance at this

which does in fact plunge its roots into that which constitutes the obscure support of our world, substance indeed being in a way the tenebrous pole of existence, as will appear more clearly later on.

point, for it immediately gives the reason why modern science actually lacks all explanatory value.

Before going further it should be noted here that the physicists' 'matter' can in no case be anything but a *materia secunda*, since the physicists regard it as being endowed with properties, on the nature of which they are incidentally not entirely in agreement, so that their 'matter' is not potentiality and 'indistinction' and nothing else besides; moreover, as the physicists' conceptions relate to the sensible world and do not go beyond it, they would not know what to do with the conception of a *materia prima*. Nonetheless, by a curious confusion, they talk all the time of 'inert matter', without noticing that if it were really inert it would have no properties and would not be manifested in any way, so that it could have no part in what their senses can perceive; nevertheless they persist in pronouncing everything that comes within range of their senses to be 'matter', whereas inertia can actually only be attributed correctly to *materia prima*, because it alone is synonymous with passivity or pure potentiality. To speak of the 'properties of matter' while asserting at the same time that 'matter is inert' is an insoluble contradiction; and, by a strange irony, modern 'scientism', which claims to eliminate all 'mystery', nonetheless appeals in its vain attempts at explanation only to the very thing that is most 'mysterious' in the popular sense of the word, that is to say most obscure and least intelligible!

The question now arises, after setting aside the supposed 'inertia of matter' as being really no more than an absurdity, whether 'matter', endowed as it is with the more or less defined qualities that enable it to be manifested to our senses, is the same thing as the *materia secunda* of our world as understood by the scholastics. Doubt will at once arise as to the validity of any such assimilation, if it be noted that the *materia secunda* in question, if it is to play a part in relation to our world analogous to that played by *materia prima* or universal substance in relation to all manifestation, must in no way be manifested in this world itself, but can only serve as 'support' or 'root' to whatever is manifested therein, and that in consequence, sensible qualities cannot be inherent in it, but on the contrary must proceed from 'forms' implanted in it; and this again amounts to saying that anything that is quality must necessarily be referred to essence. Here a new confusion makes its appearance: modern physicists, in their efforts to reduce quality to quantity, have arrived by a sort of 'logic of error' to the point of confusing the two, and thence to the attribution of quality itself to their 'matter' as such; and they end by assigning all reality to 'matter', or at least all that they are capable of recognizing as reality: and it is this that constitutes 'materialism' properly so called.

Nevertheless, the *materia secunda* of our world cannot be devoid of all determination, for if it were so it would be inseparable from the *materia prima* itself in its complete 'indistinction'; neither can it be a sort of generalized *materia secunda*, for it must be determined in accordance with the special conditions of this world, in such a way that it can effectively play the part of substance in relation to this world in particular, and not in relation to anything else. The nature of this determination must then be specified, and this is what Saint Thomas Aquinas does when he defines this particular *materia secunda* as *materia signata quantitate*; quality is therefore not inherent in it and is not that which makes it what it is, even if quality is considered only in relation to the sensible order; its place is taken by quantity, which thus really is *ex parte materiæ*. Quantity is one of the very conditions of existence in the sensible or corporeal world; it is the condition that belongs most exclusively of all to that world; therefore, as might have been expected, the definition of the *materia secunda* in question cannot concern anything other than this world, but it must concern this world as a whole, for everything that exists in this world is necessarily subject to quantity. The definition given is therefore fully sufficient, and there is no need to attribute to *materia secunda*, as has been done to modern 'matter', properties that can in no way really belong to it. It can be said that quantity, regarded as constituting the substantial side of our world, is as it were its 'basic' or fundamental condition: but care must be taken not to go too far and attribute to it an importance of a higher order than is justifiable, and more particularly not to try to extract from it the explanation of this world. The foundation of a building must not be confused with its superstructure: while there is only a foundation there is still no building, although the foundation is indispensable to the building; in the same way, while there is only quantity there is still no sensible manifestation, although sensible manifestation has its very root in quantity. Quantity, considered by itself, is only a necessary 'presupposition', but it explains nothing; it is indeed a base, but nothing else, and it must not be forgotten that the base is by definition that which is situated at the lowest level, so that the reduction of quality to quantity is intrinsically nothing but a 'reduction of the higher to the lower', and some have very rightly attributed this very character to materialism: to claim to derive the 'greater' from the 'lesser' is indeed one of the most typical of modern aberrations.

One further question presents itself: we meet with quantity under diverse modes, and in particular as discontinuous quantity, which is nothing but number,[2] and as continuous quantity, which is principally represented by spatial and temporal magnitudes; among all these modes, which is the one that can most accurately be called pure quantity? This question has its importance, all the more so because Descartes, whose place is at the starting-point of many specifically modern philosophical and scientific conceptions, tried to define matter in terms of extension, and to make his definition the principle of a quantitative physics, which though not yet quite 'materialism', was at least 'mechanism', and it might be tempting to draw the conclusion that extension, as being directly inherent in matter, represents the fundamental mode of quantity. On the other hand, Saint Thomas Aquinas, when he says that *numerus stat ex parte materiae*, seems rather to suggest that number constitutes the substantial basis of this world, and therefore that it is number that must properly be looked on as pure quantity; and the attribution of a 'basic' character to number is in perfect agreement with the fact that in the Pythagorean doctrine number is taken, by inverse analogy, as the symbol of the essential principles of things. It should be

---

2. The pure idea of number is essentially that of whole number, and it is evident that the sequence of the whole numbers constitutes a discontinuous series; all the extensions that have been applied to this idea, and that have given rise to the notions of fractional numbers and incommensurable numbers, are real alterations, and only in fact represent the efforts that have been made to reduce as far as possible the intervals in the numerical discontinuity, so as to lessen the imperfection inherent in the application of number to continuous magnitudes.

noted too that the 'matter' of Descartes is no longer the *materia secunda* of the scholastics; it is on the other hand an example, perhaps the earliest in point of date, of the modern physicists' 'matter', although Descartes' notion did not then include all that his successors were gradually to incorporate in it in order to arrive at the most recent theories of the 'constitution of matter'. There is therefore reason to suspect that there may be some error or confusion in the Cartesian definition of matter, and that some element not of a purely quantitative order must have slipped into it at that stage, perhaps unsuspected by its originator: the nature of his error will be made clear in chapter 4, where we shall see that extension, although it is obviously quantitative in character, like everything else belonging to the sensible world, cannot be regarded as pure quantity. It may also be observed that the theories which go farthest in the direction of a reduction to the quantitative are generally 'atomistic' in one way or another, that is to say they introduce discontinuity into their notion of matter in such a way as to bring it into much closer relation to the nature of number than to that of extension; and the very fact that the material from which bodies are formed cannot in any case be conceived otherwise than as extended is never anything but a source of contradictions in all 'atomism'. Another cause of confusion is the habit that has grown up of considering 'body' and 'matter' as nearly synonymous; actually, bodies are in no sense *materia secunda*, which is not met with anywhere in the manifested existences of this world, bodies only proceeding from it as from their substantial principle. But number, like *materia secunda*, is never perceived directly and in a pure state in the corporeal world, and it is number that must without doubt be considered primarily as constituting the fundamental mode in the domain of quantity; the other modes of quantity are only derived from number, that is to say they are so to speak only quantity by virtue of their participation in number: and this is implicitly recognized whenever it is maintained, as in fact it always is, that everything quantitative must be expressible in terms of number. In these other modes, even when quantity is the predominant element, it always appears as more or less mixed with quality; thus it is that the conceptions of space and of time, despite the efforts of modern mathematicians, can never be exclusively quantitative, unless indeed it be accepted that they must be reduced to entirely empty notions, without contact with any kind of reality; and is not the science of today in actual fact made up to a large extent of such empty notions, purely 'conventional' in character and without the least effective significance? This last question must be more fully dealt with, especially so far as it concerns the nature of space, for this aspect of the question is very closely connected with the principles of geometrical symbolism, while at the same time it provides an excellent example of the degeneration that traditional conceptions must undergo in order to become profane conceptions; the procedure will be to examine first of all how the conception of 'measure', the very foundation of geometry, can be transposed, in a traditional sense, in such a way as to give it a significance quite other than that which modern scientists attach to it, for they only see in 'measure' a means for getting as near as they can to their topsy-turvy 'ideal', which seeks to bring about by degrees the reduction of all things to quantity.

3

MEASURE
AND MANIFESTATION

THE USE OF THE WORD 'matter', except where modern conceptions are being specially examined, will henceforth be avoided for preference; and it must be understood that the reason for this lies in the confusions to which it inevitably gives rise, since it is impossible to use the word without at once evoking, even in those who are aware of the different meaning attached to the word by the scholastics, the idea of that which modern physicists call 'matter', for this last acceptation is the only one that holds good in current language. The idea in question, as we have seen, is not met with in any traditional doctrine whether it be Eastern or Western; this indicates at least that, even to the extent that it might legitimately be admitted after clearing it of certain incongruous and even flatly contradictory elements, it contains nothing that is really essential and is related only to one highly particularized way of looking at things. At the same time, since the idea is very recent, it cannot be implicit in the word itself, which is far older, so that the original meaning of the word must be quite independent of its modern meaning. It must however be admitted that the true etymological derivation of this word is very difficult to determine — as if a more or less impenetrable obscurity must inevitably envelop everything that has to do with 'matter' — and it is scarcely possible in this connection to do more than distinguish certain conceptions associated with its root; this will be by no means without interest, although it is impossible to specify exactly which of the various conceptions is the closest to the primitive meaning of the word.

The connection that seems to have been noticed most often is that which relates *materia* to *mater*, and this fits in well with the idea of substance as the passive principle and as symbolically feminine; it can be said that *Prakriti* plays the 'maternal' part in relation to manifestation and *Purusha* the 'paternal'; and the same is true at all the levels at which a correlation of essence and substance can be envisaged analogically.[1] On the other hand, it is also possible to relate this same word *materia* to the Latin verb *metiri* 'to measure' (and it will appear later that there is in Sanskrit a form still closer to it): 'measure' however implies determination, and determination cannot be applied to the absolute indetermination of universal substance or the *materia prima*, but must rather be related to some other more restricted notion, a point we propose to now examine more closely.

Ananda K. Coomaraswamy has said on this subject:

For everything that can be conceived or perceived (in the manifested world) Sanskrit has only the expression *nāma-rūpa*, the two terms of which correspond to the 'intelligible' and the 'sensible', considered as two complementary aspects referred respectively to the essence and to the substance of things.[2] It is true that the word *mātra*, which literally means 'measure', is the etymological equivalent of *materia*; but that which is thus 'measured' is not the physicists' 'matter', it is the possibilities of manifestation inherent in the spirit (*Ātmā*).[3]

---

1. This also agrees well with the original meaning of the word ὕλη which was given above: the plant is so to speak the 'mother' of the fruit that comes forth from it and is nourished from its substance, but the fruit is only developed and ripened under the vivifying influence of the sun, the sun being thus in a sense its 'father'; and as a result the fruit itself is symbolically assimilated to the sun by 'co-essentiality', if it be permissible to use this expression, as may also be understood by reference to explanations given elsewhere of the symbolism of the *Ādityas* and other similar traditional notions.

2. These two terms, 'intelligible' and 'sensible', used in this way as correlatives, properly belong to the language of Plato; it is well known that the 'intelligible world' is for Plato the domain of 'ideas' or of 'archetypes', which, as we have seen, are actually essences in the proper sense of the word; and, in relation to this intelligible world, the sensible world, which is the domain of corporeal elements and proceeds from their combinations, is situated on the substantial side of manifestation.

3. 'Notes on the Kaṭa Upaniṣad,' *New Indian Antiquary* (Bombay) 470 (1938): pt.2.

The idea of 'measure', brought in this way into direct relation with manifestation itself, is very important, and is moreover far from being peculiar to the Hindu tradition, which Coomaraswamy had particularly in view here. It can indeed truthfully be said that the idea is found in all the traditional doctrines in one form or another, and, while it is naturally impossible to attempt to enumerate all the relevant concordances that could be pointed out, enough can perhaps be said to justify this statement, and at the same time to clarify, as far as it is possible to do so, the symbolism of 'measure', which plays so important a part in certain initiatic forms.

Measure, understood in the literal sense, is principally concerned with the domain of continuous quantity, that is to say, it is concerned most directly with things that have a spatial character (for time, though no less continuous than space, can only be measured indirectly, by as it were attaching it to space through movement as intermediary, thus establishing a relation between the two). This amounts to saying that measure is specifically concerned either with extension itself, or with what is conventionally called the 'matter of physics', by reason of the character of extension that this last necessarily possesses: but this does not mean that the nature of matter can, as Descartes claimed, be reduced simply to extension and nothing more. In the first case, measure is correctly said to be 'geometrical'; in the second case, it would more usually be called 'physical' in the ordinary sense of the word; but in reality the second case becomes merged in the first, for it is only by virtue of the fact that bodies are situated in extension and occupy a certain defined part of it that they are directly measurable, whereas their other properties are not susceptible of measurement, except to the degree that they can in some way be related to extension. We are at this point, as was foreseen, a long way from the *materia prima*, which in its absolute indistinction, can neither be measured in any way nor be used as a measure of anything else; but it is necessary to enquire whether the notion of measure be not more or less closely linked with whatever it is that constitutes the *materia secunda* of our world, and it turns out that a linkage exists through the fact that the *materia secunda* is *signata quantitate*. Indeed, if measure directly concerns extension and what is contained therein, it is only by the quantitative aspect of this extension that measure is made possible;

but continuous quantity as such is, as explained, only a derived mode of quantity, that is to say it is only quantity by virtue of its participation in pure quantity, which in its turn is inherent in the *materia secunda* of the corporeal world; and besides, just because continuity is not pure quantity, measure always carries a certain degree of imperfection in its numerical expression, as the discontinuity of number makes a fully adequate application of number to the determination of continuous magnitudes impossible. Number is indeed the basis of all measurement, but, so long as number is considered by itself there can be no question of measurement, for measurement is the application of number to something else. An application of this kind is always possible within certain limits, but only after taking into account the 'inadequacy' just referred to, and this applies to everything subject to the quantitative condition, in other words, to everything belonging to the domain of corporeal manifestation. Only—and here the idea expressed by Coomaraswamy recurs—it must be most carefully noted that, despite certain prevalent misuses of ordinary language, quantity is never really that which is measured, it is on the contrary that by which things are measured; and furthermore, it can be said that the relation of measure to number corresponds, in an inversely analogical sense, to the relation of manifestation to its essential principle.

It is evident that in order to carry the idea of measure beyond the limits of the corporeal world, it must be analogically transposed. The manifestation of the possibilities of the corporeal order takes place in space, so that space may be made use of to represent the whole domain of universal manifestation, which otherwise would not be 'representable'; thus the idea of measure, when it is applied to this comprehensive domain, is an essential part of the spatial symbolism that is so frequently employed. Fundamentally then, measure is an 'assignation' or a 'determination' necessarily implied in all manifestation, in every order and under every mode; as a determination, it naturally conforms to the conditions of each state of existence, and it is even in a certain sense identified with those conditions themselves, it being truly quantitative only in our world since quantity, like space and time, is no more than one of the special conditions of corporeal existence. But there is in every world a determination that can be symbolized for us by the quantitative determination we know as measure, because it is the determination corresponding in other worlds to measure in our own, in accordance with the difference of conditions in each; and it can be said that through this determination these other worlds, together with all that they contain, are realized or 'actualized' as such, since it is inherent in the very process of manifestation. Coomaraswamy remarks that 'the Platonic and Neoplatonic concept of "measure" (μέτρον) agrees with the Indian concept: the "non-measured" is that which has not yet been defined; the "measured" is the defined or finite content of the universe, that is, of the "ordered" universe; the "non-measurable" is the Infinite, which is the source both of the indefinite and of the finite, and remains unaffected by the definition of whatever is definable,' that is to say by the realization of the possibilities of manifestation which it carries in itself.

It is clear from this that the idea of measure is intimately connected with that of 'order' (in Sanskrit *rita*), and 'order' is in turn related to the production of the manifested universe, the universe being, according to the etymological meaning of the Greek word κόσμος, a production of 'order' out of 'chaos', the latter being the indefinite in the Platonic sense, and the 'cosmos' the definite.[4] The production of 'order' is also assimilated in all traditions to an 'illumination' (the *Fiat Lux* of Genesis), the 'chaos' being symbolically identified with darkness: 'chaos' is the potentiality from which as starting-point manifestation will be 'actualized', that is to say, it is in effect the substantial side of the world, which is therefore described as the tenebrous pole of existence, whereas essence is the luminous pole since it is the influence of essence that illuminates the 'chaos' in order to extract from it the 'cosmos'; all this is in agreement with the inter-relation of the different meanings implicit in the Sanskrit word *srishti*, which designates the production of manifestation, and

4. The Sanskrit word *rita* is related by its root to the Latin *ordo*, and it is scarcely necessary to point out that it is related even more closely to the word 'rite': a rite is, etymologically, that which is accomplished in conformity with 'order', and which consequently imitates or reproduces at its own level the very process of manifestation; and that is why, in a strictly traditional civilization, every act of whatever kind takes on an essentially ritual character.

contains simultaneously the ideas 'expression', 'conception', and 'luminous radiation'.[5] The solar rays make apparent the things they illumine so that they become visible, the rays thus being said symbolically to 'manifest' them; and if a central point in space is considered, together with the radii emanating from it, it can also be said that these radii 'realize' space by causing it to pass from virtuality to actuality, and that their effective extension is at any instant the measure of the space realized. These radii correspond to the directions of space properly so called (these directions being often represented by the symbolism of 'hair', a similar symbolism being used in connection with the solar rays); space is defined and measured by the three-dimensional cross, and in the traditional symbolism of the 'seven solar rays', six of those rays arranged in two opposite pairs form the cross, while the 'seventh ray', the ray that passes through the 'solar gate', can only be represented graphically by the center itself. All this is perfectly coherent, and is linked together as rigorously as could be; and it may be added that, in the Hindu tradition, the 'three steps' of *Vishnu*, whose 'solar' character is well-known, measure the 'three worlds', which amounts to saying that they 'effectuate' the totality of universal manifestation. We know too that the three elements that constitute the sacred monosyllable *Om* are designated by the term *mātra*, showing that they also respectively represent the measure of the three worlds; and by the mediation of these *mātras*, the being realizes in itself the corresponding states or degrees of universal existence and so becomes itself the 'measure of all things'.[6]

The Sanskrit word *mātra* has as its exact equivalent in Hebrew the word *middah*; and the *middoth* are assimilated in the Kabbalah to the divine attributes, by which God is said to have created the worlds, and this conception is also brought directly into relation with the symbolism of the central point and the directions of space.[7] In this connection the Biblical statement may be recalled, according to which God has 'arranged all things by measure and

5. Cf. A. K. Coomaraswamy, ibid.
6. Cf. *Man and His Becoming according to the Vedānta*, chap. 17.
7. Cf. *The Symbolism of the Cross*, chap. 4.

number and weight';[8] these three categories clearly represent diverse modes of quantity, but they are only literally applicable as such to the corporeal world and to nothing else, though by an appropriate transposition they may nevertheless also be taken as an expression of universal 'order'. The same is also true of the Pythagorean numbers, but the mode of quantity that is primarily associated with measure, namely, extension, is the mode that is most often and most directly brought into relation with the process of manifestation itself, by virtue of a certain natural predominance of spatial symbolism in this connection, arising from the fact that space constitutes the 'field' (in the sense of the Sanskrit *kshetra*) within which corporeal manifestation is developed, corporeal manifestation being inevitably taken as the symbol of the whole of universal manifestation.

The idea of measure immediately evokes the idea of 'geometry', for not only is every measurement essentially 'geometrical' as we have already seen, but also geometry itself can be called the science of measurement; but it goes without saying that geometry understood primarily in a symbolic and initiatic sense is here in question, profane geometry being merely a degenerate vestige thereof, deprived of its original deep significance, which is entirely lost to modern mathematicians. Such is the essential foundation of all conceptions in which divine activity, conceived as producing and ordering the worlds, is assimilated to 'geometry', and consequently also to architecture, for the two are inseparable;[9] and it is known that these conceptions have been preserved and transmitted in uninterrupted succession from Pythagorism (which was itself only an 'adaptation' and not really 'original') down to what still remains of the Western initiatic organizations, however unconscious these organizations may now be of the nature of the conception in question. Related to this very point is Plato's statement that 'God geometrizes always' (ἀεὶ ὁ Θεὸς γεωμέτρει), recourse to the neologism 'geometrizes' being

---

8. *Omnia in mensura, numero et pondere disposuisti* (Wisd. of Sol. 11:20).

9. In Arabic, the word *hindesah*, of which the primary meaning is 'measure', serves to denote both geometry and architecture, the latter being really an application of the former.

inevitable in order to translate this exactly, as there is no authentic word to describe the activity of the geometrician; and the corresponding inscription said to have been put on the door of his school is: 'Let none but a geometrician enter here,' implying that his teaching, at least on its esoteric side, could only be truly and effectively understood through an 'imitation' of the divine activity itself. A sort of last echo of this in modern philosophy (modern as to its date, but really in reaction against specifically modern ideas) is found in this statement of Leibnitz: 'while God calculates and practices His cogitation [that is to say, sets out his plans] the world is made' (*dum Deus calculat et cogitationem exercet, fit mundus*), but, all these things had a far more precise significance for the men of old, for in the Greek tradition the 'geometrician God' was none other than the hyperborean Apollo, and thus we are brought back once more to the 'solar' symbolism, and at the same time to a fairly direct derivation from the primordial tradition; but that is another question, which could not be developed here without getting entirely off the subject; all that can be done now is to give, as opportunity occurs, a few glimpses of the traditional knowledge that is so completely forgotten by our contemporaries.[10]

10. Coomaraswamy has called attention to a curious symbolical drawing by William Blake representing the 'Ancient of Days', appearing in the solar orb, whence he points toward the outside a compass held in his hand, all of which might illustrate the following words from the *Rg-Veda* (viii.25.18): 'With his ray he hath measured [or determined] the bounds of Heaven and of Earth' (and among the symbols of certain Masonic grades is found a compass, the head of which is formed of a sun with rays). Here it is a case of the figuration of that aspect of the Principle that Western initiations call the 'Great Architect of the Universe', who becomes too in certain cases the 'Great Geometrician of the Universe', and who is identical with *Vishvakarma* of the Hindu tradition, the 'Spirit of Universal Construction'; his terrestrial representatives, that is to say those who in some way 'incarnate' this Spirit in the case of each distinct traditional form, are what has earlier been called, for this very reason, the 'Great Architects of the Orient and of the Occident'.

4

SPATIAL QUANTITY
AND QUALIFIED SPACE

IT HAS ALREADY BEEN MADE CLEAR THAT EXTENSION is not
purely and simply a mode of quantity; in other words, while it is
undoubtedly legitimate to speak of quantity as extended or spatial,
this does not necessarily imply that extension can be treated as
quantity and nothing more. This must be insisted on again, because
it is particularly important in that it reveals the insufficiency of Cartesian 'mechanism' and of the other physical theories derived more
or less directly from it in modern times. The first thing to be noticed
in this connection is that if space were purely quantitative it would
have to be entirely homogeneous, and its parts would have to be
indistinguishable one from another by any characteristic other than
their respective sizes; this would amount to conceiving it as no
more than a container without content, that is to say as something
which cannot have an independent existence in manifestation, for
the relation of container to content necessarily presupposes, by its
very nature as a correlation, the simultaneous presence of both of
its terms. The question may be put, at least with some appearance
of reason, as to whether geometrical space can be conceived as
endowed with some such homogeneity, but whatever may be the
answer to that question no such conception of homogeneity is compatible with physical space, with the space that contains bodies, for
the presence of those bodies suffices to determine qualitative differences between the parts of space they occupy — and Descartes was
undoubtedly thinking of physical space, for otherwise his theory
would not mean anything, since it would then not be applicable in

any real sense to the world of which it claims to provide the explanation.[1] It would be useless to object that 'empty space' is only the starting-point of his theory because, in the first place, this would lead back to the conception of a container without content, implying an emptiness that can have no place in the manifested world, emptiness as such not being a possibility of manifestation;[2] and, in the second place, since Descartes reduces the whole nature of bodies to extension, he is compelled thenceforth to suppose that their presence adds nothing to what space itself already is. Indeed the diverse properties of bodies are no more in his eyes than mere modifications of extension; but if that be so, whence can these properties come, unless they are in some way inherent in extension itself, and how can they be so inherent if the nature of extension is lacking in any qualitative elements? Here there is something very like contradiction; indeed it would be difficult to maintain that this contradiction, and a good many others like it, is not implicit in the work of Descartes; for he, like the more recent materialists who surely have ample reason to proclaim themselves his followers, seem really to be trying to extract the 'greater' from the 'lesser'. To say that a body is nothing but extension in a purely quantitative sense, is really the same as to say that its surface and its volume, which measure the portion of extension actually occupied by it, are the body itself with all its properties, which is manifestly absurd; therefore some other interpretation must be sought, and it becomes impossible to avoid the admission that extension itself is in some way qualitative, but if it is so, it cannot serve as the basis of an exclusively 'mechanistic' theory.

1. It is true that Descartes, at the beginning of his physics, only claims to construct a hypothetical world on the basis of certain assumptions, which can be reduced to extension and movement; but, since he is at pains to demonstrate later that the phenomena that would be produced in such a world are precisely those of which we are aware in our own, it is clear that, in spite of his purely verbal precaution, he intends to conclude that our world is in fact constituted like the world he began by imagining.

2. This argument is equally applicable against atomism, which by definition admits no positive existence other than that of atoms and their combinations, and is thus necessarily led to posit a void between the atoms for them to move about in.

Now although these considerations show that Cartesian physics cannot be valid, they are still not sufficient to establish firmly the qualitative character of extension; indeed it might well be argued that, although it is true that the nature of bodies cannot be reduced to extension alone, yet this is just because they derive nothing from extension other than their quantitative elements. But at this point the following observation becomes pertinent: among the corporeal determinations which are undeniably of a purely spatial order, and which can therefore rightly be regarded as modifications of extension, there is not only the size of bodies, but also their situation; is situation itself therefore also purely quantitative? The partisans of a reduction to quantity will doubtless reply that the situation of a plurality of bodies is defined by their distances, and that distance is certainly a quantity — the quantity of extension that lies between them, just as their size is the quantity of extension that they occupy; but is distance sufficient by itself to define the situation of bodies in space? There is something else that cannot possibly be left out of account, and that is the direction along which distance must be measured; but, from a quantitative point of view, direction cannot but be a matter of indifference, because space cannot be considered as other than homogeneous in this respect, and this implies that particular directions in space are in no way distinguished one from another; so if direction is an effective element in situation, and if it is a purely spatial element, as it evidently is, and no less so than distance, then there must be something qualitative in the very nature of space.

In order to leave no room for doubt, physical space and bodies can be left out of the picture, nothing then remaining to be considered but a space that is in the strict sense purely geometrical, and this surely does represent what may be called space reduced to itself alone; in studying such a space, does geometry really take nothing into account but strictly quantitative conceptions? Let it be clearly understood that only the profane geometry of the moderns is now under consideration; and the question may at once be asked whether, if there proves to be anything in profane geometry that cannot be reduced to quantity, does it not immediately follow that it is even less possible and less legitimate to claim to reduce everything in the domain of the physical sciences to quantity? Even the question of situation can be left out here, because it only plays a really conspicuous part in certain special branches of geometry, which might perhaps be regarded as not constituting a strictly integral part of pure geometry:[3] but in the most elementary geometry, not only has the size of figures to be taken into account, but also their shape; and would any geometrician, however deeply imbued with modern conceptions, dare to maintain for example that a triangle and a square of equal area are one and the same thing? He would only say that they are 'equivalent', but he would clearly be leaving out as being understood the words 'in respect of size', and he would have to recognize that in another respect, namely that of shape, there is something that differentiates them; and the reason for which equivalence in size does not carry with it similitude of shape is that there is something in shape that precludes its being reduced to quantity. But this is not all: for there is a whole section of elementary geometry to which quantitative considerations are strange, namely the theory of similar figures; similarity is in fact defined exclusively by shape and is wholly independent of the size of figures, and this amounts to saying that it is of a purely qualitative order.[4] If we now care to enquire into the essential nature of spatial shape, it will be found to be definable as an assemblage of directional tendencies: at every point in a line its directional tendency is specified by a tangent, and the assemblage of all the tangents defines the shape of the line. In three-dimensional geometry the same is true of surfaces, straight line tangents being replaced by plane tangents; it is moreover evident that the shape of all bodies, as well as that of simple geometrical figures, can be similarly defined, for the shape of a body is the shape of the surface by which its volume is delimited. The conclusion toward which all this leads could be foreseen when the situation of bodies was being discussed, namely, that it is the notion of direction that without doubt represents the real qualitative element inherent in the very nature of space, just as the

3. Such are, for instance, descriptive geometry, and the geometry to which certain mathematicians have given the name of *analysis situs*.

4. This is just what Leibnitz expressed by the formula: *Aequalia sunt ejusdem quantitatis; similia sunt ejusdem qualitatis.*

this very confusion seems to have its own 'logic', since for several centuries, during which it has assumed many different forms, it has always tended in the same direction; but this 'logic' really resides in a conformity with the development of the human cycle, itself in turn the result of current cosmic conditions. This leads directly to considerations connected with the nature of time, and with what may be called, in opposition to the purely quantitative conceptions of the 'mechanists', the qualitative determinations of time.

5

THE QUALITATIVE
DETERMINATIONS
OF TIME

IF SPACE IS NOT PURE QUANTITY, time appears to be still less so: temporal magnitudes as well as spatial magnitudes can be spoken of, and in both cases continuous quantity is involved (for there is no occasion to pause to consider the strange conception of Descartes, according to which time is constituted of a series of discontinuous instants, so that it becomes necessary to assume a constant repetition of the act of 'creation', the world otherwise always vanishing away during the intervals of temporal discontinuity); nevertheless, there is a big distinction to be made between the two cases, arising from a fact to which attention has already been called, namely that space can be measured directly, whereas time can only be measured by relating it back in some way to space. What is measured is never really a duration, it is the space covered in a certain length of time in the course of a movement of which the law is known; and as any such law expresses a relation between time and space, it is possible, when the amount of the space covered is known, to deduce therefrom the amount of time occupied in covering it; and whatever may be the artifices employed, there is actually no other way than this whereby temporal magnitudes can be determined.

Another observation leading to the same conclusion is the following: the only phenomena that are situated in space as well as in time are those that are properly called corporeal; phenomena belonging to the mental order, such as are studied by 'psychology' in the ordinary sense of the word, have no spatial character, though, like other phenomena, they are developed in time; and the mental, since it belongs to subtle manifestation, is, within the individual domain, necessarily nearer to essence than is the corporeal; the nature of time thus being such that it can reach into the subtle domain and therein condition mental manifestations, the conclusion must be that the nature of time is more qualitative than that of space. While on the subject of mental phenomena, it may be added that, once they are seen to be akin to that which represents essence in the individual, it is quite useless to look for quantitative elements in them, and it is still more useless to try to reduce them to quantity; the things which the 'psycho-physiologists' determine quantitatively are not really in themselves mental phenomena, as is imagined, but only some of their corporeal concomitants; in such investigations there is nothing that comes anywhere near to contact with the intrinsic nature of the mental, and so nothing that can explain it in the smallest degree; the absurd idea of a quantitative psychology surely represents the fullest development of the modern 'scientistic' aberration.

All this being so, if it is right to speak of 'qualified' space, it is all the more right to speak of 'qualified' time, which means that there must be fewer quantitative determinations and more qualitative determinations in time than in space. 'Empty time', moreover, has no more an effective existence than has 'empty space', and in this connection everything that has been said about space could be repeated about time: outside this world there is no time, just as there is no space, and inside it, realized time contains all events, just as realized space contains all bodies. In certain respects there is something like a symmetry between space and time, so that they can often be alluded to in terms that are more or less parallel; but this symmetry, which is not found with respect to the other conditions of corporeal existence, arises rather on the qualitative than on the quantitative side, as is indicated by the difference already pointed out between the determination of spatial magnitudes and temporal magnitudes, as well as by the absence, in the case of time, of a quantitative science of an order comparable to that of the geometry of space. Moreover, on the qualitative side symmetry is conspicuously apparent in the correspondence existing between spatial symbolism and temporal symbolism, of which many examples have been given elsewhere; in fact it goes without saying that whenever symbolism is in question the essential part is played by considerations of quality and not of quantity.

It is evident that periods of time are qualitatively differentiated by the events unfolded within them, just as the parts of space are differentiated by the bodies they contain; it is not therefore in any way justifiable to regard as being really equivalent durations of time that are quantitatively equal when they are filled by totally different sequences of events; it is indeed a matter of current observation that quantitative equality disappears completely from the mental appreciation of duration in the face of qualitative difference. Someone may perhaps argue that qualitative difference is not inherent in duration itself, but only in what happens within it; it therefore becomes necessary to enquire whether there be not something in the qualitative determination of events that originates from time itself; and it seems that such is recognized to be the case, at least implicitly, when, as constantly happens in ordinary speech, the particular conditions of this or that period are referred to. This seems indeed to be even more obvious in the case of time than in that of space, although, as explained, qualitative elements are far from being negligible when the situation of bodies is in question; and it could even be said, in the final analysis, that a particular body cannot be situated indifferently in any place, any more than a particular event can happen indifferently at any time; but here the symmetry is not perfect, because the situation of a body in space can vary through the occurrence of movement, whereas that of an event in time is rigidly determined and strictly 'unique', so that the essential nature of events seems to be much more rigidly tied to time than that of bodies is to space; and this again confirms that time must have in itself the more markedly qualitative character.

The truth is that time is not something that unrolls itself uniformly, so that the practice of representing it geometrically by a straight line, usual among modern mathematicians, conveys an idea of time that is wholly falsified by over-simplification; we shall see later that a tendency toward a pernicious simplification is yet another characteristic of the modern spirit, and also that it inevitably accompanies a tendency to reduce everything to quantity. The correct representation of time is to be found in the traditional conception of cycles, and this conception obviously involves a 'qualified' time; besides, whenever the question of geometrical representation arises, whether in fact it be set out graphically or only expressed through the use of an appropriate terminology, it is clear that a spatial symbolism is being made use of; all this may suggest that an indication of some kind of correlation may well be discovered between the qualitative determinations of time and those of space. A correlation can in fact be found: in the case of space, these determinations consist essentially in the directions; and the cyclical figuration effectively establishes a correspondence between the phases of a temporal cycle and the directions of space. In order to satisfy oneself of this, it is enough to consider an example chosen from among those that are simplest and most immediately accessible, that of the annual cycle, which, as is well enough known, plays a very important part in traditional symbolism,[1] wherein the four seasons are made to correspond with the four cardinal points.[2]

A more or less complete exposition of the doctrine of cycles cannot be entered upon here, although that doctrine is naturally implicit in and fundamental to the whole of this study; if the limits

1. It will suffice at this point to call attention, on the one hand, to the extent of the use of the symbolism of the zodiac, especially from a strictly initiatic point of view, and on the other hand, to the direct applications in the field of ritual to which the unfolding of the annual cycle gives rise in most traditional forms.

2. While on the subject of the qualitative determinations of space and time and their correspondences, it would be a pity not to mention a testimony which is certainly not suspect, as being that of an 'official' orientalist, Marcel Granet, who has devoted to such traditional notions a whole section of his book entitled La Pensée chinoise [Paris: A. Michel, 1988]. It goes without saying that he cannot see in these notions anything but singularities, which he is at pains to explain exclusively in terms of 'psychology' and 'sociology', but there is no need to pay any attention here to such interpretations, for they are the inevitable outcome of the prejudices of modernity in general and of the universities in particular, only the noting of the fact being relevant here; from this point of view, a striking picture can be found in the book in question of the antithesis presented by a traditional civilization, on the one hand (and this would be no less true for any such civilization other than the Chinese) and the 'quantitative' civilization of the modern West on the other.

of the available space are not to be overstepped, it must suffice for the present to formulate a few observations more directly connected with the subject of this book taken as a whole, referring wherever necessary in later chapters to relevant matters connected with the doctrine of cycles. The first of these observations is as follows: not only has each phase of a temporal cycle, of whatever kind it may be, its peculiar quality that influences the determination of events, but the speed with which events are unfolded also depends on these phases, and is therefore of a qualitative rather than of a quantitative order. Therefore, in speaking of the speed of events in time, by analogy with the speed of displacement of a body in space, a certain transposition of the notion of speed has to be effected, for speed in time cannot be reduced to quantitative expression, as can be done in mechanics when speed properly so called is in question. What this means is that, according to the different phases of the cycle, sequences of events comparable one to another do not occupy quantitatively equal durations; this is particularly evident in the case of the great cycles, applicable both to the cosmic and to the human orders, the most notable example being furnished by the decreasing lengths of the respective durations of the four *Yugas* that together make up a *Manvantara*.[3] For that very reason, events are being unfolded nowadays with a speed unexampled in the earlier ages, and this speed goes on increasing and will continue to increase up to the end of the cycle; there is thus something like a progressive 'contraction' of duration, the limit of which corresponds to the 'stopping-point' previously alluded to; it will be necessary to return to a special consideration of these matters later on, and to explain them more fully.

The second observation is connected with the descending direction of the cyclical movement, insofar as this movement is regarded as the chronological expression of a process of manifestation that

---

3. The decrease is known to be proportionate to the numbers 4, 3, 2, 1, their total, 10, comprising the entire cycle; human life itself is moreover well known to be considered as growing shorter from one age to another, which amounts to saying that life passes by with ever-increasing rapidity from the beginning to the end of a cycle.

implies a gradual separation from the principle, a point we have referred to often enough that further insistence on it can be dispensed with. It is only mentioned again here because, taken in connection with what has just been said, it gives rise to a spatial analogy of considerable interest. The increase in the speed of events, as the end of the cycle draws near, can be compared to the acceleration that takes place in the fall of heavy bodies: the course of the development of the present humanity closely resembles the movement of a mobile body running down a slope and going faster as it approaches the bottom; and even though certain reactions operating in a contrary sense complicate the matter to some extent (within the limits of the possibility of such reactions), nonetheless this comparison gives a very accurate picture of the cyclical movement looked at in a general way.

Here, then, is a third and final observation. The descending movement of manifestation, and consequently that of the cycle of which it is an expression, takes place away from the positive or essential pole of existence toward its negative or substantial pole, and the result is that all things must progressively take on a decreasingly qualitative and an increasingly quantitative aspect; and that is why the last period of the cycle must show a very special tendency toward the establishment of a 'reign of quantity'. Moreover, the statement that this must be so for all things does not merely imply that it must be so as seen from a human point of view, but also that a real modification of the 'environment' itself is involved. Each period of the history of humanity corresponds specifically to a determinate 'cosmic moment', so that there must necessarily be a constant correlation between the state of the world itself, or of what is called 'nature' in the usual sense of the word and more especially of the terrestrial environment, and the state of mankind, whose existence is evidently conditioned by that environment. It may be added that total ignorance of such cosmic modifications is not least among the causes of the incomprehension of modern science whenever anything beyond certain limits is concerned; itself born of the very special conditions of the present period, this science is all too obviously incapable of conceiving other and different conditions, incapable even of the mere admission that anything of the kind could exist; thus the point of view that constitutes the definition of modern science establishes 'barriers' in time, which it is as impossible for science to break down as it is for a short-sighted person to see clearly beyond a certain distance; a true 'intellectual myopia' is indeed thoroughly characteristic in all respects of the modern and 'scientistic' mentality. Later developments of this theme will lead to a better understanding of the nature of these modifications of the environment, which can only be alluded to now in quite a general way; but it may already have occurred to the reader that many things nowadays regarded as 'fabulous' were not at all so for the ancients, and even that they may still not be so for those who have retained, not only the possession of certain aspects of traditional knowledge, but also an outlook that allows them to reconstitute the shape of a 'lost world', as well as to foresee, at least in its broad outlines, what will be the shape of a future world. For no other reason than that manifestation is ruled by cyclical laws, the past and the future are in analogical correspondence, so much so that, whatever the ordinary person may think, previsions of this kind have not really any 'divinatory' character whatever, but are founded entirely on what have been called the qualitative determinations of time.

6

THE PRINCIPLE
OF INDIVIDUATION

THE NATURES OF SPACE AND TIME have now been dealt with adequately for the purpose in view, but it is necessary to return to the subject of 'matter' in order to examine a question not so far mentioned, in such a way as to shed a fresh light on certain aspects of the modern world. The scholastics looked on *materia* as constituting the *principium individuationis*; what was their reason for looking at things in that way, and how far was it justified? In order to understand what is involved in this question it is sufficient, without in any way going beyond the limits of our world (for no principle is here involved of a transcendent order with respect to this world) to envisage the relation of individuals to species; in this relation species is on the side of 'form' or essence, and individuals, or more exactly that which distinguishes individuals of the same species one from another, are on the side of 'matter' or substance.[1] There is nothing surprising in this, bearing in mind what has been said above about the meaning of the word εἶδος, which is at once both 'form' and 'species', and about the purely qualitative character of

---

1. It should be pointed out that there is a difficulty in this connection, at least in appearance: in the hierarchy of kinds, if one considers the relation of one particular kind to a second less general kind, which is as it were a species in relation to the first, the first plays the part of 'matter' and the second the part of 'form'; thus at first sight the relation appears to apply in a reverse direction, though actually it is not comparable to the relation of species to individuals; moreover, it is envisaged from a purely logical point of view, as if it were the relation of a subject and an attribute, the subject corresponding to the designation of the kind and the attribute to that of the 'specific difference'.

the latter; but the point needs some further elucidation, particularly, in the first place, in order to eliminate various terminological uncertainties likely to arise.

It has already been explained why the word 'matter' can give rise to misunderstandings; the word 'form' is perhaps even more liable to do so, because its usual meaning is quite different from that which it bears in scholastic language; it was used in its usual meaning when the consideration of form in geometry was alluded to above, but if scholastic language had been used instead, it would have been necessary to say 'figure' and not 'form'; to have done so would however have been unduly contrary to established usage, of which account must inevitably be taken if misunderstanding is to be avoided, and that is why the word 'form' is always used in this book in its ordinary meaning, except when it is used with particular reference to scholasticism. For instance, the word is used in its ordinary meaning in the statement that, of all the conditions of a state of existence, form is the one that specifically characterizes that state as individual; it goes without saying that form in this sense must in no way be conceived as endowed with a spatial character, for it is so endowed only in our world, because it is there combined with another condition, namely space, and space belongs to the domain of corporeal manifestation alone. But this question then arises: does not form thus understood, rather than 'matter' (or if preferred, quantity), represent the true 'principle of individuation', since individuals are what they are by virtue of the fact that they are conditioned by form? So stated, this question represents a misunderstanding of what the scholastics in fact mean when they speak of a 'principle of individuation'; in no sense are they referring to that which defines a state of existence as an individual state, for they seem never to have attained to a conception quite of that order; and in any case, from this point of view, species itself must be regarded as being within the individual order, for it is in no way transcendent with regard to the state so defined. The same point can be made in another way, by making use of the geometrical representation described elsewhere, and in that case, the whole hierarchy of kinds must be envisaged as extending horizontally and not vertically.

The real question of the 'principle of individuation' has a much more restricted range, and can be reduced to this: the individuals of any one species all participate in a common nature, which is that of the species itself, and is in all of them equally; how then does it come about that, in spite of this community of nature, these individuals are distinct beings, or even that they are in any way distinguishable one from another? It must be understood that individuals are now being considered only insofar as they belong to a species, independently of anything else that may be peculiar to them under other headings; the question could therefore well be formulated in this way: of what order is the determination which is added to specific nature so that individuals may become separate beings while remaining within the species? It is this determination that the scholastics relate to 'matter', that is to say ultimately to quantity, according to their definition of the *materia secunda* of our world; and thus 'matter' or quantity appears distinctly as a principle of 'separativity'. It can also be said that quantity is a determination added to species, as species is exclusively qualitative and so is independent of quantity, but such is not the case with individuals owing to the fact that they are 'incorporated'; and in this connection the greatest care must be taken to note that, despite an erroneous opinion only too widespread among the moderns, species must in no way be conceived as a 'collectivity', the latter being nothing but an arithmetical sum of individuals; a 'collectivity' is, unlike species, entirely quantitative. Confusion between the general and the collective is yet another consequence of the tendency that leads the moderns to see nothing anywhere other than quantity; it is this tendency which is constantly reappearing as a factor underlying all the conceptions characteristic of their particular mentality.

The conclusion is this: quantity will predominate over quality in individuals to the extent that they approach a condition in which they are, so to speak, mere individuals and nothing more, and to the extent that they are thereby more separate one from another; and it must be emphasized that this does not mean that they are more differentiated, for there is also a qualitative differentiation, which is properly speaking the opposite of that quantitative differentiation in which the separation in question consists. This separation turns individuals into so many 'units', and turns their collectivity into quantitative multiplicity; at the limit, these individuals would be no more than something comparable to the imagined 'atoms' of the physicists, deprived of every qualitative determination; and although this limit can never in fact be reached, it lies in the direction which the world of today is following. A mere glance at things as they are is enough to make it clear that the aim is everywhere to reduce everything to uniformity, whether it be human beings themselves or the things among which they live, and it is obvious that such a result can only be obtained by suppressing as far as possible every qualitative distinction; but it is particularly to be noted that some people, through a strange delusion, are all too willing to mistake this 'uniformization' for a 'unification', whereas it is really exactly the opposite, as must appear evident in the light of the ever more marked accentuation of 'separativity' implied. It must be insisted that quantity can only separate and cannot unite; everything that proceeds from 'matter' produces nothing but antagonism, in many diverse forms, between fragmentary 'units' that are at a point directly opposite to true unity, or at least are pressing toward that point with all the weight of a quantity no longer balanced by quality; but 'uniformization' constitutes so important an aspect of the modern world, and one so liable to be wrongly interpreted, that another chapter must be devoted to a fuller development of this subject.

7

UNIFORMITY
AGAINST UNITY

IF THE DOMAIN OF MANIFESTATION that constitutes our world is considered as a whole, it can be said that the existences contained therein, as they gradually move away from the principial unity, become progressively less qualitative and more quantitative. Principial unity, which contains synthetically within itself all the qualitative determinations of the possibilities of this domain, is in fact its essential pole, whereas its substantial pole, which evidently must become nearer as the other becomes more remote, is represented by pure quantity, with the indefinite 'atomic' multiplicity it implies, and with the exclusion of any distinction between its elements other than the numerical. This gradual movement away from essential unity can be envisaged from a twofold point of view, that of simultaneity and that of succession; this means that it can be seen as simultaneous in the constitution of manifested beings, where its degrees determine for their constituent elements, or for the corresponding modalities, a sort of hierarchy; or alternatively as successive in the very movement of the whole of manifestation from the beginning to the end of a cycle: needless to say it is to the second point of view that attention will chiefly be directed in this book. In all cases however the domain in question can be represented geometrically by a triangle of which the apex is the essential pole, which is pure quality, while the base is the substantial pole, which in our world is pure quantity, symbolized by the multiplicity of the points comprised in the base, and contrasted with the single point which is the apex; and if lines are drawn parallel to the base to represent different degrees of remoteness from the apex, it becomes clear that multiplicity, which symbolizes the quantitative, will be all the more accentuated as the base is approached and the apex left behind. Nevertheless, to make the symbol as exact as possible, the base must be supposed to be indefinitely remote from the apex, firstly because the domain of manifestation is in itself truly indefinite, and secondly so that the multiplicity of the points in the base may be, so to speak, brought to its maximum; this would also indicate in addition that the base, that is to say pure quantity, can never be reached in the course of the development of manifestation, though manifestation tends always more and more toward it; it would also indicate that from below a certain level the apex, that is to say essential unity or pure quality, would be more or less lost to view, and this corresponds precisely to the existing condition of our world.

It was said earlier that in pure quantity the 'units' are only distinguished one from another numerically, there being indeed no other category in which a distinction can be made; but this alone makes it clear that pure quantity is really and necessarily beneath all manifested existence. It is useful to recall here what Leibnitz referred to as the 'principle of indiscernibles', by which he meant that there cannot exist anywhere two identical beings, that is to say, two beings alike in every respect. As has been pointed out elsewhere, this is an immediate consequence of the limitlessness of universal possibility, which carries with it the absence of all repetition in particular possibilities; it can indeed be said that if two beings are assumed to be identical they would not really be two, but, as coinciding in every respect, they would actually be but one and the same being; conversely, in order that beings may not be identical or indiscernible there must always be some qualitative difference between them, and their determinations can never be purely quantitative. Leibnitz expresses this by saying that it is never true that two beings, whatever they may be, differ *solo numero*, and this, in its application to bodies, overrides 'mechanistic' conceptions such as those of Descartes; and Leibnitz goes on to say that if they did not differ qualitatively 'they would not even be beings,' but something like divisions, exactly resembling each other, of a homogeneous space and time; such divisions have no real existence, but are only what the scholastics called *entia rationis*. In this connection it may be remarked that

Leibnitz himself does not seem to have had an adequate idea of the nature of space and time, for when he defines space simply as an 'order of coexistence' and time as an 'order of succession' he is only considering them from a purely logical point of view, thereby reducing them to homogenous containers quite without quality and so with no effective existence, and he is taking no account whatever of their ontological nature, that is to say, of the real nature of space and time as manifested in our world, wherein they really exist as conditions determining the special mode of existence distinguished as corporeal existence.

The conclusion that emerges clearly from all this is that uniformity, in order that it may be possible, presupposes beings deprived of all qualities and reduced to nothing more than simple numerical 'units'; also that no such uniformity is ever in fact realizable, while the result of all the efforts made to realize it, notably in the human domain, can only be to rob beings more or less completely of their proper qualities, thus turning them into something as nearly as possible like mere machines; and machines, the typical product of the modern world, are the very things that represent, in the highest degree attained up till now, the predominance of quantity over quality. From a social viewpoint, 'democratic' and 'egalitarian' conceptions tend toward exactly the same end, for according to them all individuals are equivalent one to another. This idea carries with it the absurd supposition that everyone is equally well fitted for anything whatsoever, though nature provides no example of any such 'equality', for the reasons already given, since it would imply nothing but a complete similitude between individuals; but it is obvious that, in the name of this assumed 'equality', which is one of the topsy-turvy 'ideals' most dear to the modern world, individuals are in fact directed toward becoming as nearly alike one to another as nature allows—and this in the first place by the attempt to impose a uniform education on everyone. It is no less obvious that differences of aptitude cannot in spite of everything be entirely suppressed, so that a uniform education will not give exactly the same results for all; but it is all too true that, although it cannot confer on anyone qualities that he does not possess, it is on the contrary very well fitted to suppress in everyone all possibilities above the common level; thus the 'leveling' always works downward: indeed, it could not work in any other way, being itself only an expression of the tendency toward the lowest, that is, toward pure quantity, situated as it is at a level lower than that of all corporeal manifestation—not only below the degree occupied by the most rudimentary of living beings, but also below that occupied by what our contemporaries have a habit of calling 'lifeless matter', though even this last, since it is manifested to our senses, is still far from being wholly denuded of quality.

The modern Westerner is moreover not content only to impose an education of that sort at home; he also wants to impose it on other peoples, together with the whole gamut of his own mental and bodily habits, so as to make all the world uniform, while at the same time he imposes uniformity on the outward aspect of the world by the diffusion of the products of his industry. The consequence, paradoxical only in appearance, is that to the extent that more uniformity is imposed on it, the world is by so much the less 'unified' in the real sense of the word. This is really quite natural, since the direction in which it is dragged is, as explained already, that in which 'separativity' becomes more and more accentuated; and here the character of 'parody', so often met with in everything that is specifically modern, makes its appearance. In fact the imposition of uniformity, while actually leading in a direction exactly opposite to that of true unity, since it tends to realize that which is most remote therefrom, takes shape as a sort of caricature of unity, and it does so because of the analogical relation whereby, as was pointed out very early in this book, unity itself is inversely reflected in the 'units' that constitute pure quantity. It is this inversion that justified the earlier reference to a topsy-turvy 'ideal', and it can be seen that these words must in fact be understood in a very precise sense; nevertheless, it is by no means suggested that a rehabilitation of that word 'ideal' is in any way desirable, for it serves indifferently almost any purpose nowadays, and particularly that of masking the absence of all true principle; it is indeed so misused that it has by now come to be almost devoid of meaning. It is tempting however to observe that, according to its actual derivation, it ought to denote a certain tendency toward the 'idea' understood more or less in the

Platonic sense, that is to say toward essence and toward the qualitative, however vaguely these may be conceived, whereas most frequently, as in the case in question, it is used to designate their exact opposite.

The existing tendency to impose uniformity not only on human individuals but also on things has already been alluded to: indeed the men of today boast of the ever growing extent of the modifications they impose on the world, and the consequence is that everything is thereby made more and more 'artificial', for this is the very result that these modifications are calculated to produce, since all their activity is directed toward a domain as strictly quantitative as possible. Besides, as soon as the desire to produce a purely quantitative science arose, it became inevitable that the practical applications derived from that science should share its character; these applications as a whole are generally designated by the name of 'industry', and modern industry can be said to represent from all points of view the triumph of quantity, because its operations do not demand any knowledge other than quantitative, and because the instruments of which it makes use, that is to say machines properly so called, are developed in such a way that qualitative considerations come in to the least possible extent, while the men who work them are themselves limited to activity of an entirely mechanical kind—quality also being completely sacrificed to quantity in the actual products of industry. A few more observations can usefully be made in order to cover this subject adequately, but before proceeding with them, a question which will be returned to later may be interpolated: whatever may be thought about the value of the results of the action that modern man applies to the world, it is a fact, independently of any estimation of values, that this action succeeds, and that at least to a certain extent, it reaches the ends at which it aims; if the men of another period had acted in the same way (but this is a wholly 'theoretical' and unrealistic supposition, in view of the actual mental differences between these men and those of today) would the results have been the same? In other words, in order that the terrestrial environment may be suitable for such action, must it not be in some way predisposed thereto by the cosmic conditions of the cyclic period in which we now are; that is, must there not be something in that environment which, with reference to earlier periods, has undergone a change? It would be premature to go fully into the nature of that change at this point, or to do more than characterize it as being necessarily of the nature of a qualitative diminution, allowing a firmer hold to everything that springs from quantity; but what has been said about the qualitative determinations of time at least makes the possibility of a change of this kind conceivable and renders understandable the idea that the artificial modifications of the world, in order that they may come about, must presuppose natural modifications to which they merely correspond or conform in one way or another, by virtue of the correlation that invariably exists in the cyclical movement of time between the cosmic order and the human order.

8

ANCIENT CRAFTS
AND MODERN INDUSTRY

THERE IS A GREAT CONTRAST between what the ancient crafts used to be and what modern industry now is, and it presents in its essentials another particular case and at the same time a practical application of the contrast between the qualitative and quantitative points of view, which predominate in the one and in the other respectively. In order to see why this is so, it is useful to note first of all that the distinction between the arts and the crafts, or between 'artist' and 'artisan', is itself something specifically modern, as if it had been born of the deviation and degeneration which have led to the replacement in all fields of the traditional conception by the profane conception. To the ancients the *artifex* was indifferently the man who practised an art or a craft; but he was, to tell the truth, something that neither the artist nor the artisan is today, if those words are used in the modern sense (moreover the word 'artisan' tends more and more to disappear from contemporary language); he was something more than either the one or the other because, at least originally, his activity was bound up with principles of a much more profound order. If the crafts used to comprehend in one way or another the arts properly so called, since the two were not then separated by any essential characteristic, it is because the nature of the crafts was truly qualitative, for nobody can refuse to admit that such is the nature of art, more or less by definition. Nevertheless the moderns, for that very reason, narrowly restrict their conception of art, and relegate it to a sort of closed domain having no connection with the rest of human activity, that is, with what they regard as constituting 'reality', using the word in the very crude sense it bears for them; and they go so far as freely to attribute to art, thus robbed of all practical significance, the character of a 'luxury', a term thoroughly characteristic of what could without any exaggeration be called the 'silliness' of our period.

In every traditional civilization, as there has often been occasion to point out, every human activity of whatever kind is always regarded as derived essentially from principles. This is conspicuously true for the sciences, and it is no less true for the arts and the crafts, and there is in addition a close connection between them all, for according to a formula postulated as a fundamental axiom by the builders of the Middle Ages, *ars sine scientia nihil*; the science in question is of course traditional science, and certainly not modern science, the application of which can give birth to nothing except modern industry. By this attachment to principles human activity could be said to be as it were 'transformed', and instead of being limited to what it is in itself, namely, a mere external manifestation (and the profane point of view consists in this and nothing else), it is integrated with the tradition, and constitutes for those who carry it out an effective means of participation in the tradition, and this is as much as to say that it takes on a truly 'sacred' and 'ritual' character. That is why it can be said that, in any such civilization, 'every occupation is a priesthood';[1] but in order to avoid conferring on this last word a more or less unwarrantable extension of meaning, if not a wholly false one, it must be made clear that priesthood is not priesthood unless it possesses something that has been preserved in the sacerdotal functions alone, ever since the time when the previously non-existent distinction between the sacred and the profane arose.

To see what is meant by the 'sacred' character of the whole of human activity, even only from an exterior or, if preferred, exoteric point of view, it is only necessary to consider a civilization like the Islamic, or the Christian civilization of the Middle Ages; it is easy to see that in them the most ordinary actions of life have something 'religious' in them. In such civilizations religion is not something

---

1. A.M. Hocart, *Les Castes* (Paris: P. Geuthner, 1938), p 27. [*Caste: A Comparative Study* (New York: Russell and Russell, 1968).]

restricted, narrowly bounded and occupying a place apart, without effective influence on anything else, as it is for modern Westerners (at least for those who still consent to admit religion at all); on the contrary it penetrates the whole existence of the human being, or better, it embraces within its domain everything which constitutes that existence, and particularly social life properly so called, so much so that there is really nothing left that is 'profane', except in the case of those who for one reason or another are outside the tradition, but any such case then represents no more than a mere anomaly. Elsewhere, where the word 'religion' cannot properly be applied to the form of the civilization considered, there is nonetheless a traditional and 'sacred' legislation that plays an equivalent part though it has a different character, similar considerations thus applying to all traditional civilizations without exception. But there is something more: looking at esoterism rather than exoterism (these words being used for convenience although they do not strictly apply to all cases in the same way) it becomes clear that there exists, generally speaking, an initiation linked to the crafts and taking them as its base or its 'support';[2] these crafts must therefore be capable of a superior and more profound significance if they are to provide effectively a way of access to the initiatic domain, and it is evidently by reason of their essentially qualitative character that such a thing is possible.

The notion that helps most toward an understanding of this point is that which the Hindu doctrine calls *svadharma*. In itself this notion is entirely qualitative, since it implies the accomplishment by every being of an activity conformable to its own particular essence or nature, and thereby eminently conformable to 'order' (*rita*) in the sense already explained; and it is this same notion, or rather its absence, that indicates so clearly where the profane and modern conception fails. Indeed, according to the modern conception a man can adopt any profession, and even change it to suit his whim,

2. It may be noted that all that still persists in the way of authentically initiatic organizations in the West, whatever may be their present state of decadence, has no other origin than this. Initiations belonging to other categories disappeared completely a long time ago.

as if the profession were something wholly outside himself, having no real connection with what he really is, that by virtue of which he is himself and not anyone else. According to the traditional conception, on the other hand, each person must normally fulfil the function for which he is destined by his own nature, using the particular aptitudes essentially implicit in that nature as such;[3] he cannot fulfill a different function except at the cost of a serious disorder, which will have its repercussions on the whole social organization of which he is a part; and much more than this, if that kind of disorder becomes general, it will begin to have an effect on the cosmic environment itself, since all things are linked together by rigorous correspondences. Without developing this last point any further, although an application to modern conditions might well be made, what has been said so far can be summarized thus: according to the traditional conception, it is the essential qualities of beings that determine their activity; according to the profane conception on the other hand, these qualities are no longer taken into account, and individuals are regarded as no more than interchangeable and purely numerical 'units'. The latter conception can only logically lead to the exercise of a wholly 'mechanical' activity, in which there remains nothing truly human, and that is exactly what we can see happening today. It need hardly be said that the 'mechanical' activities of the moderns, which constitute industry properly so called and are only a product of the profane deviation, can afford no possibility of an initiatic kind, and further, that they cannot be anything but obstacles to the development of all spirituality; indeed they cannot properly be regarded as authentic crafts, if that word is to retain the force of its traditional meaning.

If the craft is as it were a part of the man himself and a manifestation or expansion of his own nature, it is easy to see how it can serve as a basis for an initiation, and why it is the best possible basis in a

---

3. It should be noted that the French word *métier* is etymologically derived from the Latin *ministerium*, and properly means 'function'. [The word *métier* is here translated as 'craft'. Its exact meaning is somewhere between 'craft' and 'vocation' as commonly understood today, and it does not appear to have a precise equivalent in modern English. TR.]

majority of cases. Initiation has in fact as its objective the surpassing of the possibilities of the human individual as such, but it is no less true that it can only take that individual such as he is as starting-point, and then only by taking hold as it were of his superior side, that is, by attaching itself to whatever in him is most truly qualitative; hence the diversity of initiatic paths, in other words, of the means made use of as 'supports' in order to conform to the differences of individual natures; these differences become, however, of less importance as time goes on, in proportion as the being advances on its path and thus approaches the end which is the same for all. The means employed cannot be effective unless they really fit the very nature of the being to whom they are applied; and since it is necessary to work from what is more accessible toward what is less so, from the exterior toward the interior, it is normal to choose them from within the activity by which its nature is manifested outwardly. But it is obvious that this activity cannot be used in any such way except insofar as it effectively expresses the interior nature; thus the question really becomes one of 'qualification' in the initiatic sense of the word; and in normal conditions, the very same 'qualification' ought to be a requirement for the practice of the craft itself. All this is also connected with the fundamental difference that separates initiatic teaching, and more generally all traditional teaching, from profane teaching. That which is simply 'learned' from the outside is quite valueless in the former case, however great may be the quantity of the notions accumulated (for here too profane 'learning' shows clearly the mark of quantity); what counts is, on the contrary, an 'awakening' of the latent possibilities that the being carries in itself (which is, in the final analysis, the real significance of the Platonic 'reminiscence').[4]

These last considerations make it understandable that initiation, using the craft as 'support', has at the same time, and as it were in a complementary sense, a repercussion on the practice of the craft. The craftsman, having fully realized the possibilities of which his professional activity is but the outward expression, and thus possessing the effective knowledge of that which is the very principle of

---

4. On this subject see particularly the *Meno* of Plato.

his activity, will thenceforth consciously accomplish what was previously only a quite 'instinctive' consequence of his nature; and thus, since for him initiatic knowledge is born of the craft, the craft in its turn will become the field of application of the knowledge, from which it will no longer be possible to separate it. There will then be a perfect correspondence between the interior and the exterior, and the work produced can then become the expression, no longer only to a certain degree and in a more or less superficial way, but the really adequate expression, of him who conceived and executed it, and it will then constitute a 'masterpiece' in the true sense of the word.

There is thus no difficulty in seeing how far removed true craft is from modern industry, so much so that the two are as it were opposites, and how far it is unhappily true that in the 'reign of quantity' the craft is, as the partisans of 'progress' so readily declare, a 'thing of the past'. The workman in industry cannot put into his work anything of himself, and a lot of trouble would even be taken to prevent him if he had the least inclination to try to do so; but he cannot even try, because all his activity consists solely in making a machine go, and because in addition he is rendered quite incapable of initiative by the professional 'formation'—or rather deformation—he has received, which is practically the antithesis of the ancient apprenticeship, and has for its sole object to teach him to execute certain movements 'mechanically' and always in the same way, without having at all to understand the reason for them or to trouble himself about the result, for it is not he, but the machine, that will really fabricate the object. Servant of the machine, the man must become a machine himself, and thenceforth his work has nothing really human in it, for it no longer implies the putting to work of any of the qualities that really constitute human nature.[5] The end of all this is what is called in present-day jargon 'mass-production', the

5. It may be remarked that the machine is in a sense the opposite of the tool, and is in no way a 'perfected tool' as many imagine, for the tool is in a sense a 'prolongation' of the man himself, whereas the machine reduces the man to being no more than its servant; and, if it was true to say that 'the tool engenders the craft', it is no less true that the machine kills it; the instinctive reactions of the artisans against the first machines thus explain themselves.

purpose of which is only to produce the greatest possible quantity of objects, and of objects as exactly alike as possible, intended for the use of men who are supposed to be no less alike; that is indeed the triumph of quantity, as was pointed out earlier, and it is by the same token the triumph of uniformity. These men who are reduced to mere numerical 'units' are expected to live in what can scarcely be called houses, for that would be to misuse the word, but in 'hives' of which the compartments will all be planned on the same model, and furnished with objects made by 'mass-production', in such a way as to cause to disappear from the environment in which the people live every qualitative difference; it is enough to examine the projects of some contemporary architects (who themselves describe these dwellings as 'living-machines') in order to see that nothing has been exaggerated. What then has happened to the traditional art and science of the ancient builders, or to the ritual rules by which the establishment of cities and of buildings was regulated in normal civilizations? It would be useless to press the matter further, for one would have to be blind to fail to see the abyss that separates the normal from the modern civilization, and no doubt everyone will agree in recognizing how great the difference is; but that which the vast majority of men now living celebrate as 'progress' is exactly what is now presented to the reader as a profound decadence, continuously accelerating, which is dragging humanity toward the pit where pure quantity reigns.

9

THE TWOFOLD
SIGNIFICANCE
OF ANONYMITY

IN CONNECTION WITH the traditional conception of the crafts, which is but one with that of the arts, there is another important question to which attention must be drawn: the works of traditional art, those of medieval art, for instance, are generally anonymous, and it is only very recently that attempts have been made, as a result of modern 'individualism', to attach the few names preserved in history to known masterpieces, even though such 'attributions' are often very hypothetical. This anonymity is just the opposite of the constant preoccupation of modern artists to affirm and to make known above all their own individualities; on the other hand, a superficial observer might think that it is comparable to the anonymity of the products of present-day industry, although the latter have no claim whatever to be called 'works of art'; but the truth is quite otherwise, for although there is indeed anonymity in both cases, it is for exactly contrary reasons. It is the same with anonymity as with many other things which by virtue of the inversion of analogy, can be taken either in a superior or in an inferior sense: thus, for example, in a traditional social organization, an individual can be outside the castes in two ways, either because he is above them (*ativarna*) or because he is beneath them (*avarna*), and it is evident that these cases represent two opposite extremes. In a similar way, those among the moderns who consider themselves to be outside all religion are at the extreme opposite point from those who, having penetrated to the principial unity of all the traditions, are no longer tied to any particular traditional form.[1] In relation to the conditions of the normal humanity, or to what may be called its 'mean', one category is below the castes and the other beyond: it could be said that one has fallen to the 'infra-human' and the other has risen to the 'supra-human'. Now, anonymity itself can be characteristic both of the 'infra-human' and of the 'supra-human': the first case is that of modern anonymity, the anonymity of the crowd or the 'masses' as they are called today (and this use of the highly quantitative word 'mass' is very significant), and the second case is that of traditional anonymity in its manifold applications, including its application to works of art.

In order to understand this properly, recourse must be had to the doctrinal principles that are common to all the traditions. The being that has attained a supra-individual state is, by that fact alone, released from all the limiting conditions of individuality, that is to say it is beyond the determinations of 'name and form' (*nāma-rūpa*) that constitute the essence and the substance of its individuality as such; thus it is truly 'anonymous', because in it the 'ego' has effaced itself and disappeared completely before the 'Self'.[2] Those who have not effectively attained to such a state must at least, as far as their capabilities permit, use every endeavour to reach it; and they must consequently and no less consistently ensure that their activity imitates the corresponding anonymity, so that it might be said to participate therein to a certain extent, and it will then furnish a 'support' for a spiritual realization to come. This is specially noticeable in monastic institutions, whether Christian or Buddhist, where what may be called the 'practice' of anonymity is always kept up, even if its deeper meaning is too often forgotten; but it would be wrong to suppose that the reflection of that kind of anonymity in the social order is confined to this particular case, for that would be

1. Such people could say with Muḥyi 'd-Dīn ibn al- 'Arabī: 'My heart has become capable of all forms: it is a pasture for gazelles and a monastery for Christian monks, and a temple for idols, and the *Kaabah* of the pilgrim, and the table of the *Thorah* and the book of the *Quran*. I am the religion of Love, whatever road his camels may take; my religion and my faith are the true religion.'

2. On this subject, see A.K. Coomaraswamy, '*Ākimchañña*: Self-Naughting', *New Indian Antiquary* (Bombay) 3 (1940).

to give way to the illusion of the distinction between 'sacred' and 'profane', a distinction which, let it be said once more, does not exist and has not even any meaning in strictly traditional societies. What has been said about the 'ritual' character of the whole of human activity in such societies explains this sufficiently, and, particularly as far as the crafts are concerned, it has been shown that their character was such that it was thought right to speak of 'priesthood' in connection with them; there is therefore nothing remarkable in the fact that in them anonymity was the rule, because it represents true conformity to the 'order' which the *artifex* must apply himself to realize as perfectly as possible in everything he does.

Here an objection might be raised: the craft must conform to the intrinsic nature of him who practices it, and we have seen that the product will then necessarily express his nature, and that when that expression is really adequate the product can be regarded as perfect of its kind, or as being a 'masterpiece'; now this nature is the essential aspect of the individuality, the aspect defined by the 'name'; is there not something here that seems to point toward the very reverse of anonymity? In order to answer this, it must first be pointed out that, despite all the false Western interpretations of notions such as those of *Moksha* and *Nirvana*, the extinction of the 'ego' is in no sense an annihilation of the being, on the contrary, it implies something like a 'sublimation' of its possibilities (without which, it may be remarked in passing, the very idea of 'resurrection' would have no meaning); doubtless the *artifex*, who is still in the individual human state, can do no more than tend toward such a 'sublimation', but the very fact that he keeps his anonymity will be for him the sign of this 'transforming' tendency. It can also be said that, in relation to society itself, it is not inasmuch as he is 'such and such a person' that the *artifex* produces his work, but inasmuch as he fulfils a certain 'function' that is properly 'organic' and not 'mechanical' (marking thus the fundamental difference between such work and modern industry), and he must identify himself as far as possible with this function in his work; and this identification, while it is the means of his own 'spiritual discipline', gives to some extent the measure of the effectiveness of his participation in the traditional organization, into which he is incorporated by the practice of his particular craft itself and in which he occupies the place truly suited to his nature. Thus, however one looks at the matter, anonymity appears to be in one way or another the normal thing; and even when everything that it implies in principle cannot be effectively realized, there must at least be a relative anonymity, in the sense that, particularly where there has been an initiation based on the craft, the profane or 'exterior' individuality known as 'such an one, son of such an one' will disappear in everything connected with the practice of the craft.[3]

If now we move to the other extreme, that represented by modern industry, we see that here too the worker is anonymous, but it is because his product expresses nothing of himself and is not really his work, the part he plays in its production being purely 'mechanical'. Indeed the worker as such really has no 'name', because in his work he is but a mere numerical 'unit' with no qualities of his own, and he could be replaced by any other equivalent 'unit', that is, by any other worker, without any change in what is produced by their work.[4] Thus, as was said earlier, his activity no longer comprises anything truly human, and so far from interpreting or at least reflecting something 'supra-human' it is itself brought down to the 'infra-human', and it even tends toward the lowest degree of that condition, that is to say, toward a modality as completely quantitative as any that can be realized in the manifested world. This 'mechanical' activity of the worker represents only a particular case (actually the most typical that can be found under present conditions, because

3. It will easily be understood from this why, in craft initiations such as Compagnonnage just as much as in religious orders, it is forbidden to designate an individual by his profane name; there is still a name, and therefore an individuality, but it is an individuality already 'transformed', at least virtually, by the very fact of initiation. [Regarding the Compagnonnage, see *Perspectives on Initiation*, chap. 5, n6; also *Studies in Freemasonry and the Compagnonnage*. ED.]

4. There could only be a quantitative difference, because one worker may work faster than another (and all the 'ability' that is demanded of him consists only in such speed), but from the qualitative point of view the product would always be the same, since it is determined neither by the worker's mental conception of the work nor by a manual dexterity directed to giving it its outward shape, but only by the performance of the machine, the man having nothing to do but to ensure its proper working.

industry is the domain in which modern conceptions have succeeded in expressing themselves most completely) of the way of life that the peculiar 'idealism' of our contemporaries seeks to impose on all human individuals in all the circumstances of their existence. This is an immediate consequence of the so-called 'egalitarian' tendency, in other words, of the tendency to uniformity, which demands that individuals shall be treated as mere numerical 'units', thus realizing equality by a leveling down, for that is the only direction in which equality can be reached 'in the limit', that is to say, in which it is possible, if not to reach it altogether (for as we have seen to do so is incompatible with the very conditions of manifested existence) at least to continue indefinitely to approach it, until the 'stopping point' that will mark the end of the present world is attained.

Anyone who wonders what happens to the individual in such conditions will find that, because of the ever growing predominance of quantity over quality in the individual, he is so to speak reduced to his substantial aspect, called in the Hindu doctrine *rūpa* (and in fact he can never lose form without thereby losing all existence, for form is what defines individuality as such), and this amounts to saying that he becomes scarcely more than what would be described in current language as 'a body without a soul', and that in the most literal sense of the words. From such an individual the qualitative or essential aspect has indeed almost disappeared ('almost', because the limit can never actually be reached); and as that aspect is precisely the aspect called *nāma*, the individual really no longer has any 'name' that belongs to him, because he is emptied of the qualities which that name should express; he is thus really 'anonymous', but in the inferior sense of the word. This is the anonymity of the 'masses' of which the individual is part and in which he loses himself, those 'masses' that are no more than a collection of similar individuals, regarded purely and simply as so many arithmetical 'units'. 'Units' of that sort can be counted, and the collectivity they make up can thus be numerically evaluated, the result being by definition only a quantity; but in no way can each one of them be given a denomination indicating that he is distinguished from the others by some qualitative difference.

It has been said that the individual loses himself in the 'masses' or at least that he tends more and more to lose himself; this 'confusion' in quantitative multiplicity corresponds, again by inversion, to 'fusion' in the principial unity. In that unity the being possesses all the fullness of his possibilities 'transformed', so that it can be said that distinction understood in the qualitative sense is there carried to its supreme degree, while at the same time all separation has disappeared;[5] in pure quantity, on the other hand, separation is at its maximum, since in quantity resides the very principle of separativity, and the being is the more 'separated' and shut up in himself the more narrowly his possibilities are limited, that is, the less his essential aspect comprises of quality; but at the same time, since he is to that extent less distinguished qualitatively from the bulk of the 'masses', he really tends to become confused with it. The word 'confusion' is particularly appropriate here because it evokes the wholly potential indistinction of 'chaos', and nothing less than chaos is in fact in question, since the individual tends to be reduced to his substantial aspect alone, which is what the scholastics would call a 'matter without form' where all is in potency and nothing in act, so that the final term, if it could be attained, would be a real 'dissolution' of everything that has any positive reality in the individual; and for the very reason that they are extreme opposites, this confusion of beings in uniformity appears as a sinister and 'satanic' parody of their fusion in unity.

5. This is the meaning of Eckhart's expression 'fused, but not confused', which A.K. Coomaraswamy, in the article mentioned earlier, very pointedly compares with the meaning of the Sanskrit expression *bhedabheda*, 'distinction without difference', that is, without separation.

10

THE ILLUSION
OF STATISTICS

RETURNING NOW TO THE CONSIDERATION of the more specifically 'scientific' point of view as the modern world understands it,
its chief characteristic is obviously that it seeks to bring everything
down to quantity, anything that cannot be so treated being left out
of account and is regarded as more or less non-existent. Nowadays
people commonly think and say that anything that cannot be 'put
into figures', or in other words, cannot be expressed in purely quantitative terms, for that reason lacks any 'scientific' value; and this
assumption holds sway not only in 'physics' in the ordinary sense of
the word, but in all the sciences 'officially' recognized as such in
these days, and as we have seen, even the psychological domain is
not beyond its reach. It has been made sufficiently clear in earlier
chapters that this outlook involves losing touch with everything
that is truly essential, in the strictest interpretation of the word; also
that the 'residue' that alone comes within the grasp of such a science
is in reality quite incapable of explaining anything whatever; but
there is one highly characteristic feature of modern science that
deserves further emphasis, for it indicates with particular distinct-
ness how far science deludes itself about what can be deduced from
mere numerical evaluations; this feature is moreover directly connected with the subject of the previous chapter.

The tendency to uniformity, which extends into the 'natural'
domain and is not confined to the human domain alone, leads to
the idea, which even becomes established as a sort of principle (only
it ought to be called a 'pseudo-principle'), that there exist repeti-
tions of identical phenomena; but this, by virtue of the 'principle of

indiscernibles', is no more than a sheer impossibility. A good example of this idea is afforded by the current assertion that 'the same causes always produce the same effects', and this, enunciated in that form, is inherently absurd, for there cannot in fact ever be the same causes or the same effects in a successional order of manifestation; is it not quite commonplace for people to go so far as to say that 'history repeats itself', whereas the truth is only that there are analogical correspondences between certain periods and certain events? It would be correct to say that causes that are comparable one to another in certain connections produce effects similarly comparable in the same connections; but, alongside the resemblances, which can if desired be held to represent a kind of partial identity, there are always and inevitably differences, because of the simple fact that there are by hypothesis two distinct things in question and not only one single thing. It is true that these differences, for the very reason that they represent qualitative distinctions, become less as the degree of manifestation of the things considered becomes lower, and that consequently there is then a corresponding increase of resemblance, so that in some cases a superficial and incomplete observation might give the impression of a sort of identity; but actually differences are never wholly eliminated, and this must be so in the case of anything that is not beneath the level of manifestation altogether. Even if there were no differences left other than those arising from the ever-changing influence of time and place, they could still never be entirely negligible; it is true however that this cannot be understood unless account is taken of the fact that real space and time are not, as modern conceptions would have them, merely homogenous containers and modes of pure quantity, but that on the contrary temporal and spatial determinations have also a qualitative aspect. However that may be, it is legitimate to ask how people who neglect differences, and as it were refuse to see them, can possibly claim that an 'exact' science has been built up; strictly and in fact there can be no 'exact' science but pure mathematics, which happens to be concerned with the domain of quantity alone. That being the case, all the rest of modern science is, and can only be, a tissue of more or less crude approximations, and that not only in its applications, in which everyone is compelled to acknowledge the inevitable imperfection of the means of observation and measurement, but even from a purely theoretical point of view as well: the unrealizable suppositions that provide almost the entire foundation of 'classical' mechanics, while these in turn provide the basis for the whole of modern physics, could be used to furnish a multitude of characteristic examples.[1]

The founding of a science more or less on the notion of repetition brings in its train yet another delusion of a quantitative kind, the delusion that consists in thinking that the accumulation of a large number of facts can be of use by itself as 'proof' of a theory; nevertheless, even a little reflection will make it evident that facts of the same kind are always indefinite in multitude, so that they can never all be taken into account, quite apart from the consideration that the same facts usually fit several different theories equally well. It will be said that the establishment of a greater number of facts does at least give more 'probability' to a theory; but to say so is to admit that no certitude can be arrived at in that way, and that therefore the conclusions promulgated have nothing 'exact' about them; it is also an admission of the wholly 'empirical' character of modern science, although, by a strange irony, its partisans are pleased to accuse of 'empiricism' the knowledge of the ancients, whereas exactly the opposite is the truth: for this ancient knowledge, of the true nature of which they have no idea whatever, started from principles and not from experimental observations, so that it can truly be said that profane science is built up exactly the opposite way round to traditional science. Furthermore, insufficient as 'empiricism' is in itself, that of modern science is very far from being integral, since it neglects or sets aside a considerable part of the evidence of experience, the very part that has a specifically qualitative character; for perceptual experience cannot, any more than any other kind of experience, have a bearing on pure quantity as its object, and the nearer is the approach to pure quantity the greater is the distance

1. Where, for example, has anyone ever seen a 'heavy material point', or a 'perfectly elastic solid', an 'unstretchable and weightless thread', or any other of the no less imaginary 'entities' with which this science is replete, though it is regarded as being above all else 'rational'.

from the reality which nevertheless is supposed to be grasped and to be explained; in fact it is not at all difficult to see that the most recent theories are also those that have the least relation to reality, and most readily replace it by 'conventions'. These conventions cannot be said to be wholly arbitrary, for it is not really possible that they should be so, since the making of any convention necessarily involves there being some reason for making it, but at least they are as arbitrary as possible; that is to say, they have as it were only a minimum of foundation in the true nature of things.

It has just been said that modern science, simply because it tries to be entirely quantitative, fails to take account of differences between particular facts even in cases where those differences are most accentuated, and such cases are naturally those in which qualitative elements have the greatest predominance over quantitative elements; and it can be said that this is why the greater part of reality eludes it, and why the partial and inferior aspect of truth that it can grasp in spite of all its failings (because total error could have no meaning other than that of pure negation) is reduced to almost nothing. This is more particularly the case when facts within the human order come under consideration, for these are the most qualitative of all those that modern science regards as included in its domain; science is determined nonetheless to treat them exactly like other facts, such as are concerned not only with 'organized matter' but even with 'matter in the raw', for it has in the end only one method, which it applies uniformly to the most diverse objects, precisely because, by reason of its special point of view, it is incapable of perceiving what are the essential differences between facts. And it is above all in the human order, whether in the field of history or 'sociology' or 'psychology' or any other kind of study that could be named, that the fallacious character of the 'statistics' to which the moderns attach so much importance becomes most apparent; here as elsewhere, statistics really consist only in the counting up of a greater or lesser number of facts that are all supposed to be exactly alike, for if they were not so their addition would be meaningless; and it is evident that the picture thus obtained represents a deformation of the truth, and the less the facts taken into account are alike or really comparable, or the greater is the relative importance and complexity of the qualitative elements involved, the worse is the deformation. Nonetheless, the setting out of figures and calculations gives to the statistician, as it is intended to give to other people, a kind of illusion of 'exactitude' that might be called 'pseudo-mathematical'; but in fact, without its being noticed and because of the strength of preconceived ideas, almost any desired conclusion is drawn indifferently from such figures, so completely without significance are they in themselves. The proof of this is that the same statistics in the hands of several experts, even though they may all be 'specialists' in the same line, often give rise, according to the respective theories of the experts, to quite different conclusions, which may even sometimes be diametrically opposed. That being the case, the self-styled 'exact' sciences of the moderns, to the extent that they make use of statistics and go so far as to extract from them predictions for the future (relying always on the supposed identicality of the facts taken into account, whether past or future), are really no more than mere 'conjectural' sciences, to use an expression freely employed by the promoters of a kind of modern astrology dubbed 'scientific'; and in employing this term they admit more freely than many other people what their astrology really consists in, for it certainly has only the vaguest and most remote connection, perhaps no more than that of a common terminology, with the true traditional astrology of the ancients, which is today as completely lost as all other knowledge of the same order. This 'neo-astrology' does actually make great use of statistics in its efforts to establish itself 'empirically' and without attaching itself to any principle, statistics indeed playing a preponderant part in it; and that is the very reason why it is thought right to adorn it with the epithet 'scientific', whereby the scientific character of the true astrology is implicitly denied, and this denial is again very significant and very characteristic of the modern mentality.

To assume that facts are identical when they are really only of the same kind, or comparable only in certain respects, while it contributes toward the illusion of an 'exact' science, as has already been explained, satisfies at the same time the desire for an excessive simplification, which is also strikingly characteristic of the modern mentality, so much so that this mentality could, without admitting any ironical intention, be qualified as 'simplistic' as much in its 'scientific' conceptions as in all its other manifestations. These ideas all hang together: the desire for simplification necessarily accompanies the tendency to reduce everything to the quantitative, and it reinforces that tendency, for obviously nothing can be simpler than quantity; if a being or a thing could successfully be shorn of all its distinctive qualities, the 'residue' thus obtained would indeed be endowed with a maximum of simplicity: at the limit this extreme simplicity would be such as can only belong to pure quantity, being then the simplicity of the exactly similar 'units' that constitute numerical multiplicity—a point important enough to warrant more detailed consideration.

11

UNITY
AND 'SIMPLICITY'

WE HAVE SEEN that a desire for simplification can become illegitimate or pernicious and that it has become a distinctive feature of the modern mentality; this desire is so strong that certain philosophers have given way to it in the scientific domain, and have gone to the length of presenting it as a sort of logical 'pseudo-principle', in the form of a statement that 'nature always takes the simplest course'. This is a perfectly gratuitous postulate, for there does not seem to be any reason why nature should work in that way and not in any other; many conditions other than simplicity can enter into its workings, and can outweigh simplicity to such an extent that nature seems, at least from our point of view, often to take a course that is extremely complicated. Indeed, this particular 'pseudo-principle' amounts to no more than a wish arising from a sort of 'mental laziness': it is desired that things should be as simple as possible, because if they really were so they would be so much the easier to understand; and all this is quite in accordance with the very modern and profane conception of a science that must be 'within the reach of all', but that is obviously only possible if it is so simple as to be positively 'infantile', and if all considerations of a superior or really profound order are rigorously excluded from it.

Even shortly before the beginning of modern times properly so called there can be found something like an early indication of this state of mind in the scholastic adage: *entia non sunt multiplicanda praeter necessitatem.*[1] All is well if the application of this adage is

1. This adage, like another according to which *nihil est in intellectu quod non prius fuerit in sensu* (and this is the first formulation of what was later to be called

limited to purely hypothetical speculations, but then it becomes of no interest whatever, except within the domain of pure mathematics, for there at least it is legitimate for anyone to confine himself to working on mental constructions without having to relate them to anything else; he can 'simplify' then as much as he likes, just because he is concerned only with quantity, for insofar as quantity is considered in itself and by itself, its combinations are not comprised in the effective order of manifestation. On the other hand, as soon as matters of fact need to be taken into account, it is quite another affair, and it becomes impossible not to recognize that 'nature' herself seems to go out of her way to multiply beings *praeter necessitatem;* what kind of logical satisfaction can anyone experience in contemplating, for instance, the multitude and the prodigious variety of the kinds of animals and plants that live around him? Surely this is a long way from the simplicity postulated by those philosophers who want to twist reality to suit the convenience of their own understanding and the understanding of the 'average' of their like; and if such is the case in the corporeal world, in itself a very limited domain of existence, how much more must it be the case in the other worlds; must it not indeed then be indefinitely much more so?[2] In order to cut short the discussion of this subject, it is only necessary to recall that, as has been explained elsewhere, everything that is possible is for that reason real in its own order and according to its own mode, and that since universal possibility is necessarily infinite everything that is other than a sheer impossibility has its

'sensualism') is among those that can be assigned to no particular author, and it is likely that they belong only to the period of decadence of scholasticism, that is, to a time that is in fact, despite current 'chronology', not so much the end of the Middle Ages as the beginning of modern times—provided that it is right, as has been suggested elsewhere, to date that beginning as far back as the fourteenth century.

2. In this connection the scholastic adage of the decadent period could be contrasted with the conceptions of Saint Thomas Aquinas himself concerning the angelic state, *ubi omne individuum est species infima.* This means that the differences between the angels are not analogous to the 'individual differences' of our world (the word *individuum* thus being not entirely correct here, as supra-individual states are in question), but to 'specific differences'; the true reason for this is that each angel represents as it were the expression of a divine attribute, as is shown clearly by the constitution of the names in the Hebrew angelology.

place therein: what else, then, but this same desire for a misconceived simplification drives philosophers, when evolving their 'systems', always to try to set a limit to universal possibility in one way
or another?[3]

It is a particularly strange fact that the tendency to simplicity
understood in this sense, together with the tendency to uniformity,
which in a sense runs parallel to it, is taken by people whom it
affects as a striving for 'unification'; but it is really 'unification'
upside down, like everything else that is directed toward the domain
of pure quantity, or toward the lower and substantial pole of existence; it is thus another example of that sort of caricature of unity
that has already been considered from other points of view. If true
unity is also to be described as 'simple', that word must be understood in quite a different sense, so that it conveys only the essential
indivisibility of true unity, and so as to exclude the idea that unity is
in any way 'composite', and this implies that it cannot rightly be
conceived as made up of parts of any kind. A sort of parody of the
indivisibility of unity may be found in the indivisibility that some
philosophers and physicists attribute to their 'atoms', but they fail to
see that it is not compatible with the nature of the corporeal, for a
body is by definition extended, and extension is indefinitely divisi-
ble, so that a body is of necessity always made up of parts, and it
does not make any difference how small it is or may be supposed to
be, so that the notion of indivisible corpuscles is self-contradictory;
but a notion of that kind evidently fits in well with a search for simplicity carried to such lengths that it can no longer correspond to
the lowest degree of reality.

On the other hand, although the principial unity is absolutely
indivisible, it can nevertheless be said to be of an extreme complexity, since it contains 'eminently' all that constitutes the essence or
qualitative side of manifested beings, when considered from the

---

3. That is why Leibnitz said that 'every system is true in what it affirms and false
in what it denies,' and this means that it contains an amount of truth proportional
to the amount of positive reality included in it, and an amount of error corresponding to the reality excluded; it is important to add that it is precisely the negative and limitative side of a 'system' that constitutes it as such.

point of view of a 'descent' into lower degrees. It is enough to go back to the explanation given above of the way in which the 'extinction of the ego' ought to be understood in order to see that unity is that wherein all quality subsists, 'transformed' and in its fullness, and that distinction, freed from all 'separative' limitation, is indeed carried therein to its highest level. As soon as the domain of manifested existence is entered, limitation appears in the form of the particular conditions that determine each state or each mode of manifestation; in the course of a descent to ever lower levels of existence limitation becomes ever narrower, and the possibilities inherent in the nature of beings become more restricted in range, which amounts to saying that the essence of these beings is correspondingly simplified; this simplification continues progressively toward a lower level than that of existence itself, that is to say toward the domain of pure quantity, where it is finally brought to its maximum through the complete suppression of every qualitative determination.

Thus it can be seen that simplification follows strictly the descending course which, in current terms as inspired by Cartesian dualism, would be described as leading from 'spirit' toward 'matter': inadequate as these terms may be as substitutes for 'essence' and 'substance', they can perhaps usefully be employed here for the sake of better understanding. It is therefore all the more extraordinary that anyone should attempt to apply this kind of simplification to things that belong to the 'spiritual' domain itself, or at least to as much of it as people are still able to conceive, for they go so far as to extend it to religious conceptions as well as to philosophical or scientific conceptions. The most typical example is that of Protestantism, in which simplification takes the form both of an almost complete suppression of rites, together with an attribution of predominance to morality over doctrine; and the doctrine itself becomes more and more simplified and diminished so that it is reduced to almost nothing, or at most to a few rudimentary formulas that anyone can interpret in any way that suits him. Moreover, Protestantism in its many forms is the only religious production of the modern spirit, and it arose at a time when that spirit had not yet come to the point of rejecting all religion, but was on the way toward doing so by virtue of the anti-traditional tendencies which are inherent in it and which really make it what it is. At the end-point of this 'evolution' (as it would be called today), religion is replaced by 'religiosity', that is to say by a vague sentimentality having no real significance; it is this that is acclaimed as 'progress', and it shows clearly how all normal relations are reversed in the modern mentality, for people try to see in it a 'spiritualization' of religion, as if the 'spirit' were a mere empty frame or an 'ideal' as nebulous as it is insignificant. This is what some of our contemporaries call a 'purified religion', but it is so only insofar as it is emptied of all positive content and has no longer any connection with any reality whatsoever.

Another thing worth noting is that all the self-styled 'reformers' constantly advertise their claim to be returning to a 'primitive simplicity', which has certainly never existed except in their imaginations. This may sometimes only be a convenient way of hiding the true character of their innovations, but it may also very often be a delusion of which they themselves are the victims, for it is frequently very difficult to determine to what extent the apparent promoters of the anti-traditional spirit are really conscious of the part they are playing, for they could not play it at all unless they themselves had a twisted mentality. Furthermore, it is difficult to see how the claim to primitive simplicity can be reconciled with the idea of 'progress', of which they simultaneously claim to be agents; the contradiction is enough by itself to indicate that there is something really abnormal in all this. However that may be, and confining attention to the idea of 'primitive simplicity', there seems to be no reason whatever why things should always begin by being simple and continue to get more complex: on the contrary, considering that the germ of any being must necessarily contain the virtuality of all that the being will be in the future, so that all the possibilities to be developed in the course of its existence must be included in the germ from the start, the conclusion that the origin of all things must really be exceedingly complex is inevitable. This gives an exact picture of the qualitative complexity of essence; the germ is small only in relation to quantity or substance, and by symbolically transposing the idea of 'size' it can be deduced through inverse analogy that what is least in quantity must be greatest in quality.[4] In a similar way every tradition at its origin contains the entire doctrine, comprehending in principle the totality of the developments and adaptations that may legitimately proceed from it, together with the totality of the applications to which they may give rise in all domains; human interventions can do nothing but restrict and diminish it, if they do not denature it altogether, and the work of all 'reformers' really consists in nothing more than that.

Another peculiar thing is that modernists of all sorts (taking into account not those of the West alone, but also those of the East, for the latter are in any case merely 'Westernized'), while they boast of doctrinal simplicity as representing 'progress' in the field of religion, often speak as if religion ought to have been made for idiots, or at least as if they supposed that the people they are speaking to must inevitably be idiots; do they really think that by asserting, rightly or wrongly, that a doctrine is simple they are suggesting to a man of the most moderate intelligence a valid reason for adopting it? This is in the end no more than a manifestation of the 'democratic' idea, in the light of which, as was said earlier, it is desired that science too shall be 'within the reach of all'. It is scarcely necessary to remark that these same 'modernists' are always, as a necessary consequence of their attitude, the declared enemies of all esoterism, for it goes without saying that esoterism, which is by definition only the concern of an elect, cannot be simple, so that its negation appears as an obligatory first stage in all attempts at simplification. As for religion properly so called, or more generally the exterior part of any tradition, it must admittedly be such that everyone can understand something of it, according to the range of his capacity, and in that sense it is addressed to all; but this does not mean that it must therefore be reduced to such a minimum that the most ignorant (this word not being used with reference to profane instruction, which has no importance here) or the least intelligent can grasp it: quite to

4. The Gospel parable of the mustard seed may be recalled here, as also the similar texts from the *Upanishads* quoted elsewhere (see *Man and His Becoming according to the Vedānta*, chap. 3), and it may also be added in this connection that the Messiah himself is called 'Seed' in a number of biblical passages.

the contrary, there must be in it something that is so to speak at the level of the possibilities of every individual, however exalted they may be, for thus alone can it furnish an appropriate 'support' to the interior aspect which, in any unmutilated tradition, is its necessary complement and belongs wholly to the initiatic order. But the modernists, in specifically rejecting esoterism and initiation, thereby deny that religious doctrines contain in themselves any profound significance; thus it is that, in their pretension to 'spiritualize' religion, they fall into its opposite, the narrowest and crudest 'literalism', in which the spirit is most completely lacking, thus affording a striking example of the fact that what Pascal said is often all too true—'He who tries to play the angel plays the beast.'

But that is not quite all that need be said about 'primitive simplicity', for there is at any rate one sense in which that expression can find a realistic application, and that is when the indistinction of 'chaos' is in question, for 'chaos' is in a way 'primitive' since it is 'in the beginning'; but it is not there by itself, since all manifestation necessarily presupposes simultaneously and correlatively both essence and substance, and 'chaos' only represents its substantial base. If that were what the partisans of 'primitive simplicity' meant there would be no need to disagree with them, for the tendency to simplification would reach its end-point in precisely that indistinction, if it could be realized up to the limit of its ultimate consequences; but it is necessary to point out that this ultimate simplicity, being beneath manifestation and not in it, would in no way correspond to a true 'return to origins'. In this connection and in order to resolve an apparent antinomy, a clear distinction must be made between the two points of view, which are respectively related to the two poles of existence: when it is said that the formation of the world started from 'chaos', then the point of view is solely the substantial, and the beginning must then be regarded as timeless, for obviously time does not exist in 'chaos' but only in the 'cosmos', so that if the order of development of manifestation is being taken into account (that order being reflected in the domain of corporeal existence, by virtue of the conditions which define that existence, as an order of temporal succession), the starting-point must not be the substantial pole, but the essential pole, the manifestation of which, in conformity with cyclic laws, takes the form of a continuous recession, or of a descent toward the substantial pole. The 'creation', inasmuch as it is a resolution of 'chaos', is in a sense 'instantaneous' and is properly the biblical *Fiat Lux*; but it is the primordial Light itself that is really the origination of the 'cosmos', and this Light is the 'pure spirit' in which are the essences of all things; such being its beginning, the manifested world cannot possibly do otherwise than move in a downward direction, getting ever nearer and nearer to 'materiality'.

12

THE HATRED
OF SECRECY

A point THAT HAS ONLY BEEN TOUCHED ON INCIDENTALLY in earlier chapters must now be elaborated. It is what may be called the tendency to 'popularization' (this word being another of those that are particularly significant as pointers to the nature of the modern mentality), in other words, the pretension to put everything 'within the reach of all', to which attention has already been drawn as being a consequence of 'democratic' conceptions, and that amounts in the end to a desire to bring all knowledge down to the level of the lowest intelligences. It would be only too easy to point out the multiple ineptitudes that result, generally speaking, from the ill-considered diffusion of an instruction that is claimed to be equally distributed to all, in identical form and by identical methods; this can only end, as has already been said, in a sort of leveling down to the lowest—here as elsewhere quality being sacrificed to quantity. It is no less true to say that the profane instruction in question has nothing to do with any kind of knowledge in the true sense of the word, and that it contains nothing that is in the least degree profound; but, apart from its insignificance and its ineffectuality, what makes it really pernicious is above all the fact that it contrives to be taken for what it is not, that it tends to deny everything that surpasses it, and so smothers all possibilities belonging to a higher domain; it even seems probable that it is contrived specially for that purpose, for modern 'uniformization' necessarily implies a hatred of all superiority.

A still more surprising thing is that some people these days think that they can expound traditional doctrines by adopting profane instruction itself as a sort of model, without taking the least account of the nature of traditional doctrines and of the essential differences that exist between them and everything that is today called by the names of 'science' and 'philosophy', from which they are separated by a real abyss; in so doing they must of necessity distort these doctrines completely by over-simplification and by only allowing the most superficial meaning to appear, for otherwise their pretensions must remain completely unjustified. In any case, by such means the modern spirit penetrates right into what is most opposed to it, radically and by definition; and it is not difficult to appreciate the dissolving effect of the results, though those who make themselves the instruments of this kind of penetration may not grasp their nature, and often act in good faith and with no clear intention. The decadence of religious doctrine in the West and the corresponding total loss of esoterism show well enough what may happen in the end if that way of looking at things were one day to become general even in the East as well; the danger is so serious that it must be clearly pointed out while there is yet time.

Most incredible of all is the main argument put forward in justification of their attitude by this new variety of 'propagandist'. One of them recently wrote to the effect that, while it is true that restrictions were formerly applied to the diffusion of certain sorts of knowledge, there is no longer any reason to observe them nowadays, because (the phrase that follows must be quoted word for word so that no suspicion of exaggeration can arise) 'the general level of culture has been raised, and the spirit of man has been made ready to receive the integral teaching.' Here may be seen as clearly as possible the confusion between traditional teaching and profane instruction, the latter being described by the word 'culture', which has become one of its most frequent designations in our day; but 'culture' is something that has not the remotest connection with traditional teaching or with the aptitude for receiving it, and what is more, since the so-called raising of the 'general level' has as its inevitable counterpart the disappearance of the intellectual elect, it can be said that 'culture' represents the exact opposite of a preparation for traditional teaching. There is good reason to wonder how a Hindu (for it is a Hindu who was quoted above) can be completely ignorant of our present position in the *Kali-Yuga*, and can go so far as to say that 'the time has come when the whole system of the *Vedānta* can be set forth to the public,' for the most elementary knowledge of cyclic laws compels the conclusion that the time is less favorable than it ever was. It has never been possible to place the *Vedānta* 'within the reach of the common man', for whom incidentally it was never intended, and it is all the more certainly not possible today, for it is obvious enough that the 'common man' has never been more totally uncomprehending. And finally, the truth is that everything that represents traditional knowledge of a really profound order, and therefore corresponds to what must be meant by 'integral teaching' (for if those words have really any meaning, initiatic teaching properly so called must be comprised in it), becomes more and more difficult of access, and becomes so everywhere; in face of the invasion of the modern and profane spirit it is clear that things could not be otherwise; how then can anyone be so far unaware of reality as to assert the very opposite, and as calmly as if he were enunciating the least contestable of truths?

In the case quoted as an example for the purpose of 'illustrating' a particular mentality, the reasons given to justify the special interest that the propagation of the Vedantic teaching might have nowadays are no less extraordinary. 'The development of social ideas and of political institutions' is first put forward in this connection; but even if it really is a 'development' (and it would in any case be desirable to specify in what direction), this too has no more connection with the understanding of metaphysical doctrine than has the diffusion of profane instruction; it is enough to look at the extent to which political preoccupations, wherever they have been introduced into any Eastern country, are prejudicial to the knowledge of traditional truths, in order to conclude that it would be more justifiable to speak of an incompatibility, at least in practice, than of a possible concordance between these two 'developments'. It is not easy to see what link 'social life', in the purely profane sense in which it is conceived today, could possibly have with spirituality, to which, on the other hand, it brings nothing but obstacles: such links obviously existed when social life was integrated into a traditional civilization, but it is precisely the modern spirit that has destroyed them, or that tries to destroy them wherever they still persist; what then can be expected of a 'development' of which the most characteristic feature is that it works in direct opposition to all spirituality?

The same author puts forward yet another reason: 'Besides,' says he, 'it is the same for the *Vedānta* as for the other truths of science; there are no longer today any scientific secrets; science does not hesitate to publish the most recent discoveries.' True enough, profane science is only made for 'the public at large', and since it came into being such has been the only justification for its existence; all too obviously it is really nothing more than it appears to be, for it keeps itself entirely on the surface of things, and it can be said to do so, not on principle, but rather through a lack of principle; certainly there is nothing in it worth the trouble of keeping secret, or more accurately, worth reserving to the use of an elite, and anyhow an elite would have no use for anything of that sort. In any case, what kind of assimilation can anyone hope to establish between the so-called 'truths' and 'most recent discoveries' of profane science and the teachings of a doctrine such as the *Vedānta* or any other traditional doctrine, even one that is more or less exterior? It is a case of the same confusion all the time, and it is permissible to ask to what extent anyone who perpetrates it with such insistence can have any understanding of the doctrine he wants to teach; there can really be no accommodation between the traditional spirit and the modern spirit, any concession made to the latter being necessarily at the expense of the former, since the modern spirit consists fundamentally in the direct negation of everything that constitutes the traditional spirit.

The truth is that the modern spirit implies in all who are affected by it in any degree a real hatred of what is secret, and of whatever seems to come more or less near to being secret, in any and every domain; and this affords an opportunity for a more precise explanation of the point. Strictly speaking it cannot even be said that 'popularization' of the doctrines is dangerous, at least so long as it is only a question of their theoretical side; for it would be merely useless, even if it were possible. But in fact truths of a certain order by their very nature resist all 'popularization': however clearly they are set out (it being understood that they are set out such as they are in their true significance and without subjecting them to any distortion) only those who are qualified to understand them will understand them, and for all others they will be as if they did not exist. This has nothing to do with 'realization' and the means appropriate to it, for in that field there is absolutely nothing that can have any effective value otherwise than from within a regular initiatic organization; from a theoretical point of view reserve can only be justified by considerations of mere opportunity, and so by purely contingent reasons, which does not mean that such reasons need be negligible. In the end, the real secret, the only secret than can never be betrayed in any way, resides uniquely in the inexpressible, which is by the same token incommunicable, every truth of a transcendent order necessarily partaking of the inexpressible; and it is essentially in this fact that the profound significance of the initiatic secret really lies, for no kind of exterior secret can ever have any value except as an image or symbol of the initiatic secret, though it may occasionally also be not unprofitable as a 'discipline'. But it must be understood that these are things of which the meaning and the range are completely lost to the modern mentality, and incomprehension of them quite naturally engenders hostility; besides, the ordinary man always has an instinctive fear of what he does not understand, and fear engenders hatred only too easily, even when a mere direct denial of the uncomprehended truth is adopted as a means of escape from fear; indeed, some such denials are more like real screams of rage, for instance those of the self-styled 'free-thinkers' with regard to everything connected with religion.

Thus the modern mentality is made up in such a way that it cannot bear any secret or even any reserve; since it does not know the reason for them, such things appear only as 'privileges' established for somebody's profit; neither can it bear any kind of superiority. Anyone who undertook to explain that these so-called 'privileges' really have their foundation in the very nature of beings would be wasting his time, for that is just what 'egalitarianism' so obstinately denies. Not only does the modern mentality boast, without any justification, of the suppression of all 'mystery' by its science and philosophy—exclusively rational as it is, and brought 'within the reach of all'—but the horror of 'mystery' goes so far in all domains as to extend also even into what is commonly called 'ordinary life'. Nonetheless, a world in which everything had become 'public' would have a character nothing short of monstrous. The notion is still hypothetical, because we have not in spite of everything quite reached that point yet, and perhaps it never will be fully attained because it represents a 'limit'; but it is beyond dispute that a result of that kind is being aimed at on all sides, and in that connection it may be observed that many who appear to be the adversaries of democracy are really doing nothing that does not serve further to emphasize its effects, if that be possible, simply because they are just as much penetrated by the modern spirit as are those whom they seek to oppose. In order to induce people to live as much as possible 'in public', it is not enough that they should be assembled in the 'mass' on every occasion and on any and every pretext, but they must in addition be lodged, not only in 'hives' as was suggested ear-lier, but literally in 'glass hives', and these must be arranged in such a way that they can only take their meals 'in common'. People who are capable of submitting themselves to such an existence have really fallen to a 'infra-human' level, to the level, say, of insects like bees or ants; and in addition every device is brought into play for 'organiz-ing' them so that they may become no more different among them-selves than are the individuals of those same species of animals, and perhaps even less so.

As it is not the purpose of this book to enter into the details of certain 'anticipations', which would be only too easy to formulate and too quickly overtaken by events, this subject will now be left. It must suffice to have indicated summarily both the state at which things have now arrived and the tendency they must inevitably con-tinue to follow, at least for a certain time yet. The hatred of secrecy is basically nothing but one of the forms of the hatred for anything that surpasses the level of the 'average', as well as for everything that holds aloof from the uniformity which it is sought to impose on everyone. Nevertheless, there is, within the modern world itself, a secret that is better kept than any other: it is that of the formidable enterprise of suggestion that has produced and that maintains the

existing mentality, that has constituted it and as it were 'manufactured' it in such a way that it can only deny the existence and even
the possibility of any such enterprise; and this is doubtless the best
conceivable means, and a means of truly 'diabolical' cleverness, for
ensuring that the secret shall never be discovered.

13

THE POSTULATES
OF RATIONALISM

IT HAS JUST BEEN SAID that the moderns claim to exclude all 'mystery' from the world as they see it, in the name of a science and a philosophy characterized as 'rational', and it might well be said in addition that the more narrowly limited a conception becomes the more it is looked upon as strictly 'rational'; moreover it is well enough known that, since the time of encyclopaedists of the eighteenth century, the most fanatical deniers of all supra-sensible reality have been particularly fond of invoking 'reason' on all occasions, and of proclaiming themselves to be 'rationalists'. Whatever difference there may be between this popular 'rationalism' and a real philosophic 'rationalism', it is at any rate only a difference of degree, both the one and the other corresponding fully to the same tendencies, which have become more and more exaggerated and at the same time more 'popular' throughout the course of modern times. 'Rationalism' has so frequently been spoken of in the author's earlier works, and its main characteristics have been so fully defined, that it might well suffice to refer the reader to those works;[1] nevertheless, it is so closely bound up with the very conception of a quantitative science that a few more words here and now cannot well be dispensed with.

Let it be recalled, then, that rationalism properly so called goes back to the time of Descartes, and it is worthy of note that it can thus be seen to be directly associated right from its beginnings with the idea of a 'mechanistic' physics; Protestantism had prepared the

1. In particular to *East and West* and to *The Crisis of the Modern World.*

way for this, by introducing into religion, together with 'free enquiry', a sort of rationalism, although the word itself was not then in existence, but was only invented when the same tendency asserted itself more explicitly in the domain of philosophy. Rationalism in all its forms is essentially defined by a belief in the supremacy of reason, proclaimed as a veritable 'dogma', and implying the denial of everything that is of a supra-individual order, notably of pure intellectual intuition, and this carries with it logically the exclusion of all true metaphysical knowledge. This same denial has also as a consequence, in another field, the rejection of all spiritual authority, which is necessarily derived from a 'supra-human' source; rationalism and individualism are thus so closely linked together that they are usually confused, except in the case of certain recent philosophical theories which though not rationalistic are nonetheless exclusively individualistic. It may be noted at this point how well rationalism fits in with the modern tendency to simplification: the latter naturally always operates by the reduction of things to their most inferior elements, and so asserts itself chiefly by the suppression of the entire supra-individual domain, in anticipation of being able later on to bring everything that is left, that is to say everything in the individual order, down to the sensible or corporeal modality alone, and finally that modality itself to a mere aggregation of quantitative determinations. It is easy to see how rigorously these steps are linked together, so as to constitute as it were so many necessary stages in a continuous 'degradation' of the conceptions that man forms of himself and of the world.

There is yet another kind of simplification inherent in Cartesian rationalism, and it is manifested in the first place by the reduction of the whole nature of the spirit to 'thought' and that of the body to 'extension'; this reduction of bodies to extension is, as pointed out earlier, the very foundation of 'mechanistic' physics, and it can be regarded as the starting-point of a fully quantitative science.[2] But

2. As for Descartes' own conception of science, it should be noted that he claims that it is possible to reach the stage of having 'clear and distinct' ideas about everything, that is, ideas like those of mathematics, thus obtaining the sort of 'evidence' that can actually be obtained in mathematics alone.

this is not all: in relation to 'thought' another mischievous simplifi-cation arises from the way in which Descartes actually conceives of reason, which he also calls 'good sense' (and if one thinks of the meaning currently assigned to that expression, it suggests some-thing situated at a singularly mediocre level); he declares too that reason is 'the most widely shared thing in the world,' which at once suggests some sort of 'egalitarian' idea, besides being quite obviously wrong; in all this he is only confusing completely reason 'in act' with 'rationality', insofar as the latter is in itself a character specific to the human being as such.[3] Human nature is of course present in its entirety in every individual, but it is manifested there in very diverse ways, according to the inherent qualities belonging to each individ-ual; in each the inherent qualities are united with the specific nature so as to constitute the integrality of their essence; to think otherwise would be to think that human individuals are all alike and scarcely differ among themselves otherwise than *solo numero*. Yet from thinking of that kind all those notions about the 'unity of the human spirit' are directly derived: they are continually invoked to explain all sorts of things, some of which in no way belong to the 'psychological' order, as for example the fact that the same tradi-tional symbols are met with at all times and in all places. Apart from the fact that these notions do not really concern the 'spirit' but sim-ply the 'mind', the alleged unity must be false, for true unity cannot belong to the individual domain, which alone is within the purview of people who talk in this way, as it is also, and more generally, of those who think it legitimate to speak of the 'human spirit', as if the spirit could be modified by any specific character. In any case, the community of nature of the individuals within the species can only

---

3. In the classical definition of the human being as a 'reasonable animal', 'ratio-nality' represents the 'specific difference' by which man is distinguished from all other species in the animal kingdom; it is not applicable outside that kingdom, or in other words, is properly speaking only what the scholastics called a *differentia ani-malis*; 'rationality' cannot therefore be spoken of in relation to beings belonging to other states of existence, in particular to supra-individual states, those of the angels, for example; and this is quite in agreement with the fact that reason is a faculty of an exclusively individual order, and one that can in no way overstep the boundaries of the human domain.

produce manifestations of a very generalized kind, and is quite inadequate to account for concordances in matters that are, on the contrary, of a very detailed precision; but how could these moderns be brought to understand that the fundamental unity of all the traditions is explained solely by the fact that there is in them something 'supra-human'? On the other hand, to return to things that actually are purely human, Locke, the founder of modern psychology, was evidently inspired by the Cartesian conception when he thought fit to announce that, in order to know what the Greeks and Romans thought in days gone by (for his horizon did not extend beyond Western 'classical' antiquity) it is enough to find out what Englishmen and Frenchmen are thinking today, for 'man is everywhere and always the same.' Nothing could possibly be more false, yet the psychologists have never got beyond that point, for, while they imagine that they are talking of man in general, the greater part of what they say really only applies to the modern European; does it not look as if they believe that the uniformity that is being imposed gradually on all human individuals has already been realized? It is true that, by reason of the efforts that are being made to that end, differences are becoming fewer and fewer, and therefore that the psychological hypothesis is less completely false today than it was in the time of Locke (always on condition that any attempt to apply it, as he did, to past times is carefully guarded against); but nonetheless the limit can never be reached, as was explained earlier, and for as long as the world endures there will always be irreducible differences. Finally, to crown all this, how can a true knowledge of human nature possibly be gained by taking as typical of it an 'ideal' that in all strictness can only be described as 'infra-human'?

That much being established, it still remains to explain why rationalism is linked to the idea of an exclusively quantitative science, or more accurately, why the latter proceeds from the former; and in this connection it must be recognized that there is a considerable element of truth in the analysis which Bergson applies to what he wrongly calls 'intelligence', though it is really only reason, or more correctly a particular way of using reason based on the Cartesian conception, there being no doubt that all the forms of modern rationalism arose out of that conception. It may be remarked incidentally that the contentions of philosophers are often much more justifiable when they are arguing against other philosophers than when they pass on to expound their own views, and as each one generally sees fairly clearly the defects of the others, they more or less destroy one another mutually. Thus it is that Bergson, if one takes the trouble to rectify his mistakes in terminology, gives a good demonstration of the faults of rationalism (which, so far from being one with 'intellectualism', is on the contrary its negation) and of the insufficiencies of reason, but he is no less wrong in his own turn when, to fill the gap thus created, he probes the 'infra-rational' instead of lifting his gaze toward the 'supra-rational' (and this is why his philosophy is just as individualistic and ignores the supra-individual order just as completely as that of his rivals). And so, when he reproaches reason, to which it is only necessary here to restore its rightful name, for 'artificially clipping reality', there is no need to adopt his special notion of 'reality', even purely hypothetically and provisionally, in order fully to understand his meaning: he is evidently thinking in terms of the reduction of all things to elements supposed to be homogenous or identical one with another, which amounts to nothing but a reduction to the quantitative, for elements of that kind can only be conceived from a quantitative point of view; and the idea of 'clipping' itself suggests fairly clearly the efforts that are made to introduce a discontinuity rightly belonging only to pure or numerical quantity, or broadly speaking to the tendency referred to earlier, namely, that of refusing to recognize as 'scientific' anything that cannot be 'put into figures'.[4] In the same way, when he says that reason is not at ease except when it applies itself to something 'solid', wherein it finds its own true domain, he seems to be aware of the inevitable tendency of reason, when reduced to itself alone, to 'materialize' everything in the ordinary sense of the word, that is, to consider in all things only their grossest modalities, because quality is then at a minimum in relation to quantity; only he seems to be considering the end-point of

---

4. It can be said in this connection that of all the meanings that were comprised in the Latin word *ratio* one alone has been retained, that of 'calculation', in the use to which reason is now put in the realm of 'science'.

this tendency rather than its starting-point, which renders him liable to the accusation of exaggeration, for there are evidently degrees of 'materialization'. Nevertheless, if one looks at the existing state of scientific conceptions (or rather, as will be seen later, at a state already on the way to being past) it is quite certain that they represent as nearly as is possible the last or lowest degree of materialization, the degree in which 'solidity' understood in its material sense has reached its maximum, and that in itself is a particularly characteristic mark of the period at which we have arrived. There is evidently no need to suppose that Bergson himself understood these matters in as clear a light as is shed by the above 'translation' of his language, indeed it seems very unlikely that he did, considering the multiple confusions he is constantly perpetrating; but it is nonetheless true that these views were in fact suggested to him by his estimation of what present-day science is, and on that account the testimony of a man who is incontestably a representative of the modern spirit cannot be regarded as negligible. As for what his own theories amount to exactly, their significance will be found in another part of this study, and all that can be said about them for the moment is that they correspond to a different aspect and to some extent to a different stage of the deviation which, taken as a whole, itself constitutes the modern world.

To summarize the foregoing, this much can be said: rationalism, being the denial of every principle superior to reason, brings with it as a 'practical' consequence the exclusive use of reason, but of reason blinded, so to speak, by the very fact that it has been isolated from the pure and transcendent intellect, of which, normally and legitimately, it can only reflect the light in the individual domain. As soon as it has lost all effective communication with the supra-individual intellect, reason cannot but tend more and more toward the lowest level, toward the inferior pole of existence, plunging ever more deeply into 'materiality'; as this tendency grows, it gradually loses hold of the very idea of truth, and arrives at the point of seeking no goal other than that of making things as easy as possible for its own limited comprehension, and in this it finds an immediate satisfaction in the very fact that its own downward tendency leads it in the direction of the simplification and uniformization of all things; it submits all the more readily and speedily to this tendency because the results of this submission conform to its desires, and its ever more rapid descent cannot fail to lead at last to what has been called the 'reign of quantity'.

14

MECHANISM
AND MATERIALISM

THE EARLIEST PRODUCT OF RATIONALISM in the so-called 'scientific' field was Cartesian mechanism; materialism was not due to appear until later, for as explained elsewhere, the word and the thing itself are not actually met with earlier than the eighteenth century; besides, whatever may have been the intentions of Descartes himself (and it is in fact possible, by pursuing to the end the logical consequences of his ideas, to extract from them theories that are mutually very contradictory), there is nonetheless a direct filiation between mechanism and materialism. In this connection it is useful to recall that, although the ancient atomistic conceptions such as those of Democritus and especially of Epicurus can be qualified as mechanistic, these two being the only 'precursors' from the ancient world whom the moderns can with any justification claim as their own in this field, their conceptions are often wrongly looked upon as the earliest form of materialism: for materialism implies above all the modern physicist's notion of 'matter', and at that time this notion was still a long way from having come to birth. The truth is that materialism merely represents one of the two halves of Cartesian dualism, the half to which its author had applied the mechanistic conception; it was sufficient thereafter to ignore or to deny the remaining half, or what comes to the same thing, to claim to bring the whole of reality into the first half, in order to arrive quite naturally at materialism.

Leibnitz, in opposition to Descartes and his disciples, was very successful in demonstrating the insufficiency of a mechanistic physics, which cannot, owing to its very nature, take account of anything but the outward appearance of things and is incapable of affording the smallest explanation of their true essence; thus mechanism can be said to have a value that is purely 'representative' and in no way explanatory; and is not the whole of modern science really in exactly the same position? This is seen to be the case even when an example as simple as that of movement is taken, though movement is ordinarily thought of as being more completely explicable than anything else in purely mechanical terms; but any such explanation, says Leibnitz, is only valid so long as movement is not regarded as involving anything other than a change of situation. From this limited point of view it is a matter of indifference, when the relative positions of two bodies change, whether the first is regarded as moving in relation to the second, or the second in relation to the first, for there is a complete reciprocity between the two; but it is quite another matter when the reason for the movement is taken into account, for if the reason is found to be in one of the two bodies, that one alone must be regarded as moving, while the other plays a purely passive part in the change that has taken place; but any idea of this kind completely eludes conceptions of a mechanistic or quantitative order. Mechanism is limited to giving a simple description of movement, such as it is in its outward appearance, but is powerless to grasp the reason for it and so to express its essential or qualitative aspect, which alone can afford a real explanation. These considerations apply with even greater force in the case of things that may be more complex in character than movement, and where quality may be more predominant over quantity, and that is why a science constituted mechanistically cannot actually be of any value in terms of effective knowledge, even within the confines of the relative and limited domain that encloses it.

The conception which Descartes tried to apply to all the phenomena of the corporeal world is however no less conspicuously insufficient, in that he reduced the whole nature of bodies to extension, and in addition he considered extension only from a purely quantitative point of view; and even at that time, just like the most recent mechanists and the materialists, he made no difference in this connection between so-called 'inorganic' bodies and living beings. Living beings are specified, and not organized bodies only, because the being itself is in effect reduced by him to the body alone, in accordance with the all too famous Cartesian theory of 'animal-machines', and this is really one of the most astonishing absurdities ever engendered by the systematic spirit. Not until he comes to consider human beings does Descartes feel obliged to point out in his physics that what he has in view is only 'man's body'; but what is this concession really worth, seeing that everything that takes place in this body would, by hypothesis, be exactly the same if the 'spirit' were absent? And so, as an inescapable result of dualism, the human being is as it were cut into two parts that do not become reunited and cannot form a real composite whole, since they cannot enter into mutual communication by any means, being supposed to be absolutely heterogeneous, so much so that any effective action by one on the other would be rendered impossible. To complete the picture, an attempt was made to explain mechanically all the phenomena that take place in animals, including those manifestations that are most obviously psychic in character; it is reasonable to ask why the same explanations should not apply to man, and whether it may not be permissible to ignore the other side of dualism as contributing nothing to the explanation of things. From this stage to the stage of looking at that other side as a useless complication and in practice treating it as non-existent, and thence to the point of denying it purely and simply, is no long step, especially for men whose attention is constantly turned toward the domain of perception, as is the case with modern Westerners: thus it is that Descartes' mechanistic physics could not but pave the way for materialism.

The reduction to the quantitative had already taken place theoretically in Descartes' time as far as everything that properly belongs to the corporeal order was concerned, in the sense that the actual constitution of Cartesian physics implied the possibility of such a reduction; it remained to extend the same conception to cover the whole of reality as it was then conceived, but reality had by that time become restricted to the domain of individual existence alone, in accordance with the postulates of rationalism. Taking dualism as point of departure, the reduction in question could not fail to appear as a reduction from 'spirit' to 'matter', taking the form of a relegation into the latter category alone of everything that Descartes had included in either, so as to be able to bring all things indifferently down to quantity. And so, after having previously relegated the essential aspect of things to a position 'above the clouds' as it were, this last step served to suppress it completely, so that thereafter nothing needed to be taken into account but the substantial aspect of things, for 'spirit' and 'matter' respectively correspond to these two aspects, though they only suggest a much diminished and distorted picture of them. Descartes had brought half the world as he conceived it into the quantitative domain, and it was doubtless in his eyes the more important half, for in his secret thoughts, whatever may appear on the surface, he wanted above all to be a physicist; materialism in its turn claimed to bring the whole world into its own domain; there was then nothing more to do but to strive to bring the reduction to quantity into effect by means of theories progressively better adapted to that end, and that was the task to which modern science was destined to apply itself, even when it made no open declaration of materialism.

Besides avowed and formal materialism, there is also what may be called a factual materialism, the influence of which extends much further afield, for many people who regard themselves as being by no means materialists nonetheless behave as such in practice in all circumstances. There is in fact a relationship between these two materialisms rather like that referred to earlier between philosophical rationalism and popular rationalism, except that the merely factual materialist does not generally parade that quality and would often protest if it were attributed to him, whereas the popular rationalist, even when he is philosophically the most ignorant of men, is all the more anxious to proclaim himself a rationalist, while at the same time he proudly adorns himself with the title of 'free-thinker', all unconscious of irony, for all the time he is but the slave of all the current prejudices of his period. However that may be, just as popular rationalism is a product of the diffusion of philosophic rationalism among the 'public at large', with all the inevitable consequences of its being put 'within the reach of all', so materialism properly so called is the starting-point of factual materialism, in the sense that the former has made a diffusion of its characteristic state of mind generally possible and has effectively contributed to its formation;

but it must not be forgotten that all these separate happenings can always be fully explained by the development of the same tendencies, the tendencies that constitute the very foundation of the modern spirit. It is obvious that a scientist, in the modern sense of the word, even if he does not profess materialism, will be influenced by it to the extent that all his special training is oriented in that direction; and even if, as sometimes happens, this scientist believes himself to be not without the 'religious spirit', he will find the means to separate his religion from his scientific activity so completely that his work will in no way be distinguishable from that of the most overt materialist, and so he will play just as important a part as the latter in the 'progressive' building up of a science as exclusively quantitative and as grossly materialistic as it is possible to imagine. In this sort of way does anti-traditional action succeed in using to its own profit even those who ought to be its adversaries, and who might be so if the deviation of the modern mentality had not so shaped beings that they are full of contradictions yet incapable even of becoming aware of the fact. Here again the tendency to uniformity finds its realization, since in practice all men end by thinking and acting in the same way, and the things in respect of which they nevertheless still differ have no more than a minimum of influence, and are not translated into any reality in the outer world. Thus, in such a world, and with the rarest exceptions, a man who professes himself a Christian does not fail to behave in practice as if there were no reality whatever outside corporeal existence alone, and a priest who does 'a little science' does not differ perceptibly from a university materialist; when things have reached this stage, have they much further to go before the lowest point of the 'descent' is reached at last?

15

THE ILLUSION
OF 'ORDINARY LIFE'

THE MATERIALISTIC ATTITUDE, whether it be a question of explicit and formal materialism or of a simple 'practical' materialism, necessarily imposes on the whole 'psycho-physiological' constitution of the human being a real and very important modification. This is easily understood, and in fact it is only necessary to look round in order to conclude that modern man has become quite impermeable to any influences other than such as impinge on his senses; not only have his faculties of comprehension become more and more limited, but also the field of his perception has become correspondingly restricted. The result is a sort of reinforcement of the profane point of view, for this point of view was first born of a defect of comprehension, and thus of a limitation, and this limitation as it becomes accentuated and extends to all domains, itself seems to justify the point of view, at least in the eyes of those who are affected by it. Indeed, what reason can they have thereafter for admitting the existence of something that they can neither perceive nor conceive, that is to say of everything that could show them the insufficiency and the falsity of the profane point of view itself?

Thus arises the idea of what is commonly called 'ordinary life' or 'everyday life'; this is in fact understood to mean above all a life in which nothing that is not purely human can intervene in any way, owing to the elimination from it of any sacred, ritual, or symbolical character (it matters little whether this character be thought of as specifically religious or as conforming to some other traditional modality, because the relevant point in all cases is the effective action of 'spiritual influences'), the very words 'ordinary' or 'every-day' moreover implying that everything that surpasses conceptions of that order is, even when it has not yet been expressly denied, at least relegated to an 'extra-ordinary' domain, regarded as exceptional, strange, and unaccustomed. This is strictly speaking a reversal of the normal order as represented by integrally traditional civilizations, in which the profane point of view does not exist in any way, and the reversal can only logically end in an ignorance or a complete denial of the 'supra-human'. Moreover some people go so far as to make a similar use, with the same meaning, of the expression 'real life', and this usage has a profoundly and singularly ironical character, for the truth is that the thing so named is on the contrary nothing but the worst of illusions; this does not mean that everything it contains is actually devoid of all reality, although such reality as it has, which is broadly speaking that of the sensible order, is at the lowest level of all, there being below it only such things as are definitely beneath the level of all manifested existence. It is however the way in which things are conceived that is so wholly false, because it separates them from every superior principle, and so denies them precisely that which makes all their reality; that is why, in all strictness, no such thing as a profane domain really exists, but only a profane point of view, which becomes more and more invasive until in the end it comprehends human existence in its entirety.

This makes it understandable how, in the conception of 'ordinary life', one stage succeeds another almost insensibly, degeneration becoming progressively more marked all the time. At first it is allowed that some things are not accessible to any traditional influence, then those things themselves come to be looked on as normal; from that point it is all too easy to arrive at considering them as the only 'real' things, which amounts to setting aside as 'unreal' all that is 'supra-human'; and later on, when the human domain comes to be conceived in a more and more narrowly limited way, until it is finally reduced to the corporeal modality alone, everything that belongs to the supra-sensible order is set aside as unreal. It is enough to notice how our contemporaries constantly make use of the word 'real' as a synonym of 'sensible' without even thinking about it, in order at once to become aware that they have indeed fully reached the final stage, and that this way of looking at things has become so completely incorporated into their very nature as to have become so to speak almost instinctive with them. Modern philosophy, which is more than anything else merely a 'systematized' expression of the common mentality, subsequently reacts on the latter to a certain extent, and the two have pursued parallel courses; that of philosophy began with the Cartesian eulogy of 'good sense' alluded to earlier, and which is very revealing in this connection, for 'ordinary life' surely is first and foremost the domain of this so-called 'good sense', also called 'common sense', and is no less limited than it and in the same way; next, through rationalism, which is fundamentally only a more specially philosophical aspect of 'humanism', that is to say, of the reduction of everything to an exclusively human point of view, materialism or positivism are gradually attained: whether one chooses, as in materialism, expressly to deny everything that is beyond the sensible world, or whether one is content, as in positivism (which for that reason likes also to call itself 'agnosticism', making an honourable title for itself out of what is really only the avowal of an incurable ignorance), to refuse to be concerned with anything of the kind and to declare it 'inaccessible' or 'unknowable', the result is exactly the same in either case, and it is precisely the result of which a description has just been given.

It may be repeated here that in most cases there is naturally in question only something that can be called a 'practical' materialism or positivism, not dependent on any philosophical theory, for philosophical theory is now and always will be quite foreign to the majority; but this makes matters all the more serious, not only because the materialistic state of mind thereby obtains an incomparably wider diffusion, but also because it is all the more irremediable the less it is deliberate and clearly conscious, for when it becomes so it has then really penetrated and as it were impregnated the whole nature of the individual. This is sufficiently shown by what has already been said about factual materialism and about the way in which people who nevertheless fancy themselves 'religious' accommodate themselves thereto; the same example also shows that philosophy properly so called has not the conclusive importance that some people would like to assign to it, or at least that its chief importance is as 'representative' of a certain mentality rather than as acting effectively and directly upon it: in any case, how could a particular philosophical conception meet with the smallest success if it did not fit in with some of the predominant tendencies of the period in which it is formulated? This does not mean that philosophers do not play their part just like anyone else in the modern deviation, for that would certainly be an overstatement; it only means that their part is in fact more restricted than one would be tempted to suppose at first sight, and is rather different from what it may seem to be outwardly. In quite a general way moreover whatever is most apparent is always, in accordance with the laws which control all manifestation, a consequence rather than a cause, an end-point rather than a starting-point,[1] and in any case it is no use searching in the apparent for whatever may be the really effective agent in an order more profound, whether the action in question be exercised in a normal and legitimate direction, or in a directly contrary direction, as in the case now under consideration.

Mechanism and materialism themselves have only been able to acquire a widespread influence by extending from the philosophical into the scientific domain: anything related to the latter, or anything that gives the impression, rightly or wrongly, of being endowed with a 'scientific' character, doubtless exercises, for various reasons, much more influence than do philosophical theories on the common mentality, in which there is always at least an implicit belief in the truth of science, for the hypothetical character of science passes quite unperceived, whereas everything classed as 'philosophy' leaves it more or less indifferent; the existence of practical and utilitarian applications in the one case and their absence in the other is no doubt not entirely unconnected with this. This recalls once more the idea of 'ordinary life', in which an effective part is played by a

---

1. It could also legitimately be said to be a 'fruit' rather than a 'seed'; the fact that the fruit itself contains new seeds indicates that the consequence can in its turn play the part of cause at another level, in conformity with the cyclical character of manifestation; but for that to happen it must again pass in one way or another from the 'apparent' to the 'hidden'.

fairly strong dose of 'pragmatism'; and that statement is of course made quite independently of the fact that some of our contemporaries have tried to build up 'pragmatism' into a philosophical system: this only became possible by reason of the utilitarian twist that is inherent in the modern and profane mentality in general, and because, at the present stage of intellectual decadence, the very notion of truth has come to be completely lost to sight, so much so that the notion of utility or of convenience has ended by replacing it entirely. However that may be, as soon as it is agreed that 'reality' consists exclusively in what presents itself to the senses, it is quite natural that the value attributed to any particular thing should to some extent be measured by its capacity to produce effects in the sensible order; it is evident moreover that 'science', considered in the modern fashion as being essentially grouped with industry, if not more or less completely one with it, must for that reason occupy the first rank, science thus finding itself mingled as closely as possible with ordinary life, in which it becomes one of the principal factors; and in return, the hypotheses on which it claims to be founded, however gratuitous and unjustified they may be, must themselves benefit by this privileged situation in the eyes of the people. It goes without saying that the practical applications really depend in no way on the truth of the hypotheses, and it may be wondered what would become of a science of this sort—seeing that as knowledge in the true sense it is nothing—if it were divorced from the applications to which it gives rise; but it is a fact that science such as it is 'succeeds', and for the instinctively utilitarian spirit of the modern public 'results' or 'success' become a sort of 'criterion of truth', if indeed the word 'truth' can be used in this connection and still retain some sort of meaning.

Besides, whatever point of view is being considered, whether philosophical, scientific, or simply 'practical', it is evident that in the end all such points of view only represent so many different aspects of one and the same tendency, and also that this tendency, like all those that have an equal right to be regarded as constituting the modern spirit, can certainly not have developed spontaneously. Advantage has already been taken of many other opportunities to explain this last point, but since this is a matter that cannot be too strongly insisted on, it will be necessary to return later on to a more precise exposition of the place occupied by materialism in the broad 'plan' whereby the modern deviation is brought about. Clearly the materialists themselves are more incapable than anyone else of becoming aware of these things or even of conceiving them as possible, blinded as they are by their preconceived ideas, which close for them every outlet from the narrow domain in which they are accustomed to move; doubtless they would be as astonished to hear of them as they would be to know that men have existed and still exist for whom what they call 'ordinary life' would be quite the most extraordinary thing imaginable, because it corresponds to nothing that occurs at all in their existence. Nevertheless such is the case, and furthermore, these are the men who must be regarded as truly 'normal', while the materialists, with all their boasted 'good sense' and all the 'progress' of which they proudly consider themselves to be the most finished products and the most 'advanced' representatives, are really only beings in whom certain faculties have become atrophied to the extent of being completely abolished. It is incidentally only under such conditions that the sensible world can appear to them as a 'closed system', in the interior of which they feel themselves to be in perfect security: it remains to be shown how this illusion can, in a certain sense and in a certain measure, be 'realized' through the existence of materialism itself; but it will also appear later that this nevertheless represents as it were an eminently unstable state of equilibrium, and that the world has even now reached a point where the security of 'ordinary life', on which the whole outward organization of the modern world has rested up till now, runs serious risks of being troubled by unanticipated 'interferences'.

16

THE DEGENERATION
OF COINAGE

THIS EXPOSITION has now arrived at a point at which it may be useful to branch off from the theme to some extent, at least apparently, in order to give, perhaps rather summarily, a few indications on a question that may seem to be related only to a very specialized field. Nonetheless, it will afford a striking example of the results of the conception of 'ordinary life' and at the same time an excellent 'illustration' of how that conception is bound up with the exclusively quantitative point of view, so that, particularly in this last connection, it is really very directly relevant to our main theme. The question is that of money, and if the merely 'economic' point of view as it is understood today is not departed from, it certainly seems that money is something that appertains as completely as possible to the 'reign of quantity'. This indeed is the reason why it plays so predominant a part in modern society, as is only too obvious, a point on which it would clearly be superfluous to insist; but the truth is that the 'economic' point of view itself, and the exclusively quantitative conception of money that is inherent in it, are but the products of a degeneration which is on the whole fairly recent, and that money possessed at its origin, and retained for a long time, quite a different character and a truly qualitative value, remarkable as this may appear to the majority of our contemporaries.

It may easily be observed, provided only that one has 'eyes to see', that the ancient coins are literally covered with traditional symbols, often chosen from among those that carry some particularly profound meaning; thus for instance it has been observed that among the Celts the symbols figured on the coins can only be explained if they are related to the doctrinal knowledge that belonged to the

Druids alone, which implies a direct intervention of the Druids in the monetary domain. There is not the least doubt that the truth in this matter is the same for the other peoples of antiquity as for the Celts, of course after taking account of the modalities peculiar to their respective traditional organizations. This is fully in agreement with the fact of the inexistence of the profane point of view in strictly traditional civilizations: money itself, where it existed at all, could not be the profane thing it came to be later; and if it had been so, how could the intervention of a spiritual authority, which would then obviously have no concern with money, be explained, and how would it be possible to understand that many traditions speak of coinage as of something really charged with a 'spiritual influence', the action of which could not become effective except by means of the symbols that constituted its normal 'support'? It may be added that right up to very recent times it was still possible to find a last vestige of this notion in devices of a religious character, which certainly retained no real symbolical value, but were at least something like a recollection of the traditional idea, more or less uncomprehended thenceforth; but after having been relegated in certain countries to a place round the rim of coins, in the end these devices disappeared completely; indeed there was no longer any reason for them as soon as the coinage represented nothing more than a 'material' and quantitative token.

The control of money by the spiritual authority, in whatever form it may have been exercised, is by no means exclusively confined to antiquity, for without going outside the Western world, there is much to indicate that it must have been perpetuated until toward the end of the Middle Ages, that is, for as long as the Western world had a traditional civilization. It is impossible to explain in any other way the fact that certain sovereigns were accused at this time of having 'debased the coinage'; since their contemporaries regarded this as a crime on their part, it must be concluded that the sovereigns had not the free disposal of the standard of the coinage, and that, in changing it on their own initiative, they overstepped the recognized rights of the temporal power.[1] If that were not the case,

1. See *Spiritual Authority and Temporal Power*, where the case of Philip the Fair is specially referred to, and where it was suggested that there may be a fairly close connection between the destruction of the Order of Templars and the alteration of

such an accusation would have been quite without meaning; the standard of the coinage would only then have had an importance based on convention, and it would not have mattered, broadly speaking, if it had been made of any sort of metal, or of various sorts, or even been replaced by mere paper as it is for the most part today, for this would have been no hindrance to the continuance of exactly the same 'material' employment of it. An element of another order must therefore have been involved, and it must have been of a superior order, for unless that had been the case the alteration could not have assumed a character so exceptionally serious as to end in compromising the very stability of the royal power; but the royal power by acting in this way usurped the prerogatives of the spiritual authority, which is without any doubt the one authentic source of all legitimacy. In this way the facts, which profane historians seem scarcely to understand, conspire once more to indicate very clearly that the question of money had in the Middle Ages as well as in antiquity aspects quite unknown to the moderns.

What has happened in this case is but an example of a much more general movement, affecting all activities in every department of human existence; all have been gradually divested of any 'sacred' or traditional character, and thereby that existence itself in its entirety has become completely profane and is now at last reduced to the third-rate mediocrity of 'ordinary life' as it is found today. At the same time, the example of money clearly shows that this 'profanization'—if any such neologism be allowable—comes about chiefly by the reduction of things to their quantitative aspect alone; indeed, nobody is able any longer to conceive that money can represent anything other than a simple quantity; but, although the case of money is particularly apt in this connection because it has been as it were carried to the extreme of exaggeration, it is very far from being the only case in which a reduction to the quantitative can be seen as contributing to the confining of existence within the limited

---

the coinage, something easily understood if it is recognized as at least very plausible that this Order then had the function, among others, of exercising spiritual control in this field; the matter need not be pursued further here, but it may be recalled that the beginning of the modern deviation properly so called has been assigned precisely to this moment.

horizon of the profane point of view. This is sufficiently understandable after what has been said of the peculiarly quantitative character of modern industry: by continuously surrounding man with the products of that industry, and so to speak never letting him see anything else (except, as in museums for example, in the guise of mere 'curiosities' having no relation with the 'real' circumstances of his life and consequently no effective influence on it), he is really compelled to shut himself up inside the narrow circle of 'ordinary life', as in a prison without escape. In a traditional civilization, on the contrary, each object was at the same time as perfectly fitted as possible to the use for which it was immediately destined and also made so that it could at any moment, and owing to the very fact that real use was being made of it (instead of its being treated more or less as a dead thing as the moderns do with everything that they consider to be a 'work of art'), serve as a 'support' for meditation, linking the individual with something other than the mere corporeal modality, thus helping everyone to elevate himself to a superior state according to the measure of his capacities:[2] what an abyss there is between these two conceptions of human existence!

The qualitative degeneration of all things is closely linked to that of money, as is shown by the fact that nowadays the 'worth' of an object is ordinarily 'estimated' only in terms of its price, considered simply as a 'figure', a 'sum', or a numerical quantity of money; in fact, with most of our contemporaries, every judgment brought to bear on an object is nearly always based exclusively on what it costs. The word 'estimate' has been emphasized because it has in itself a double meaning, qualitative and quantitative; today the first meaning has been lost to sight, or what amounts to the same thing, means have been found to equate it to the second, and thus it comes about that not only is the 'worth' of an object 'estimated' according to its price, but the 'worth' of a man is 'estimated' according to his wealth.[3] The same thing has naturally happened to the word 'value',

2. Numerous studies by A.K. Coomaraswamy may be consulted on this subject, which he has developed profusely and 'illustrated' in all its aspects with all necessary explanations.

3. The Americans have gone so far in this direction that they commonly say that a man is 'worth' so much, intending to convey in that way the figure to which his

and it may be noticed in passing that on this is based a curious abuse of the word by certain recent philosophers, who have even gone so far as to invent as a description of their theories the expression 'philosophy of values'; underlying their thoughts is the idea that everything, to whatever order it may belong, is capable of being conceived quantitatively and expressed numerically; and 'moralism', which is their other predominant preoccupation, thus comes to be closely associated with the quantitative point of view.[4] These examples show too that there has been a real degeneration of language, inevitably accompanying or following that of everything else; indeed, in a world in which every attempt is made to reduce all things to quantity it is evidently necessary to use a language that itself evokes nothing but purely quantitative ideas.

To return more particularly to the question of money, one more point remains to be dealt with, for a phenomenon has appeared in this field which is well worthy of note, and it is this: since money lost all guarantee of a superior order, it has seen its own actual quantitative value, or what is called in the jargon of the economists its 'purchasing power', becoming ceaselessly less and less, so that it can be imagined that, when it arrives at a limit that is getting ever nearer, it will have lost every justification for its existence, even all merely 'practical' or 'material' justification, and that it will disappear of itself, so to speak, from human existence. It will be agreed that here affairs turn back on themselves in a curious way, but the preceding explanations will make the idea quite easy to understand: for since pure quantity is by its nature beneath all existence, when the trend toward it is pressed to its extreme limit, as in the case of money (more striking than any other because the limit has nearly been reached), the end can only be a real dissolution. The case of money alone already shows clearly enough that, as was said above, the security of 'ordinary life' is in reality a highly precarious thing, and it will be shown later that it is precarious in many other respects as well;

fortune has risen; they say too, not that a man has succeeded in his affairs, but that he 'is a success', and this is as much as to identify the individual completely with his material gains.

4. This association, by the way, is not an entirely new thing, for it actually goes back to the 'moral arithmetic' of Bentham, which dates from the end of the eighteenth century.

but the positive conclusion that will emerge will be always the same, namely, that the real goal of the tendency that is dragging men and things toward pure quantity can only be the final dissolution of the present world.

17

THE SOLIDIFICATION
OF THE WORLD

LET US NOW RETURN to the explanation of how a world conforming as far as is possible to the materialistic conception has been effectively realized in the modern period. If this is to be understood, it must be remembered above all that, as has been often pointed out, the human order and the cosmic order are not in reality separated, as they are nowadays all too readily imagined to be; they are on the contrary closely bound together, in such a way that each continuously reacts on the other, so that there is always correspondence between their respective states. This correspondence is essentially implied in the whole doctrine of cycles; without it the traditional data with which the said doctrine is concerned would be almost entirely unintelligible; the relationship existing between certain critical phases of human history and certain cataclysms that occur according to a known astronomical periodicity affords perhaps the most striking example, but it is obvious that this is only an extreme case of correspondences of this kind, which in fact subsist continuously, for there is never any break in the correspondence, though this fact is no doubt less apparent when modifications are taking place only gradually and so almost insensibly.

That being the case, it is quite natural that in the course of cyclical development both the cosmic manifestation as a whole and also human mentality, which is of course necessarily included therein, together follow the same descending course, the nature of which has already been specified as consisting in a gradual movement away from the principle, and thus away from the primal spirituality inherent in the essential pole of manifestation. This course can be described in terms of current terminology (thus incidentally bringing out clearly the correlation under consideration), as a sort of progressive 'materialization' of the cosmic environment itself, and it is only when this 'materialization' has reached a certain stage, by now already very marked, that the materialistic conception can appear in man as its correlative, together with the general attitude that corresponds with it in practice and fits in, as explained, with the picture of 'ordinary life'; moreover, in the absence of this factual 'materialization' there would not be the least semblance of justification for the corresponding theoretical conception, for the surrounding reality would too obviously give the lie to it all the time. The very idea of matter, as understood by the moderns, could certainly not come to birth except in such conditions; what that idea expresses more or less confusedly is in any case no more than a limit, unattainable while the descent of manifestation is still going on, firstly, because matter is regarded as being in itself something purely quantitative, and secondly because it is supposed to be 'inert', and a world in which there was anything really 'inert' would for that reason forthwith cease to exist; the idea of 'matter' is therefore as illusory as it could possibly be, since it corresponds to no reality of any kind, however lowly its position in the hierarchy of manifested existence. In other words it could be said that 'materialization' exists as a tendency, but that 'materiality', which would be the complete fulfillment of that tendency, is an unrealizable condition. One consequence of this, among others, is that the mechanical laws theoretically formulated by modern science are never susceptible of an exact and rigorous application to the conditions of experience, wherein there always remain elements that are entirely beyond their grasp, even in the phase in which the part played by such elements is in a sense reduced to a minimum. So it is always a case of approximation, and during this phase, leaving out of account cases that will in such times be exceptional, approximation may suffice for immediate practical needs; but a very crude simplification is nevertheless implied, and it deprives the mechanical laws not only of all claim to 'exactitude', but even of all value as 'science' in the true meaning of the word; it is moreover only through an approximation of the same kind that the sensible world can take on the appearance of a 'closed system', either in the eyes of the physicists or in the sequence of the events that constitute 'ordinary life'.

Instead of speaking as heretofore of 'materialization', it would be possible to use the word 'solidification' in a sense that is fundamentally the same, and in a manner perhaps more precise and perhaps even more 'realistic', for solid bodies, owing to their density and their impenetrability, do in fact give the illusion of 'materiality' more strongly than does anything else. At the same time, this recalls how Bergson, as pointed out earlier, speaks of the 'solid' as constituting in some way the true domain of reason, and in this he is evidently referring, whether consciously or otherwise (and doubtless not very consciously, for not only is he speaking generally and without making any reservation, but he even thinks it right to speak of 'intelligence' in this connection, as he always does when what he is talking about really appertains to reason alone), more particularly to what he sees around him, namely the 'scientific' use to which reason is put. Now the actual occurrence of 'solidification' is precisely the true reason why modern science 'succeeds', certainly not in its theories which remain as false as before, and in any case change all the time, but in its practical applications. In other periods, when 'solidification' was not yet so marked, not only could man never have dreamed of industry as we know it today, but any such industry would actually have been completely impossible in its entirety, as would the 'ordinary life' in which industry plays so great a part. This, incidentally, is enough to cut short all the fancies of those so-called 'clairvoyants' who, imagining the past on the model of the present, attribute to certain 'prehistoric' civilizations of a very remote date something quite similar to the contemporary 'machine civilization'; this is only one of the forms of error that gives rise to the common saying that 'history repeats itself', and it implies a total ignorance of what have been called the qualitative determinations of time.

In order to reach the stage that has been described, man must have lost the use of the faculties which in normal times allowed him to pass beyond the bounds of the sensible world, the loss being due to the existence of 'materialization' or 'solidification', naturally as effective in him as in the rest of the cosmic manifestation of which he is a part, and producing considerable modifications in his 'psy-cho-physiological' constitution. For even if the sensible world is in a very real sense surrounded by barriers that can be said to be thicker than they were in its earlier states, it is nonetheless true that there can never anywhere be an absolute separation between different orders of existence; any such separation would have the effect of cutting off from reality itself the domain thus isolated, so that in any such event the existence of that domain, that of the sensible world in this instance, would instantly vanish. It might however legiti-mately be asked how so complete and so general an atrophy of cer-tain faculties has actually come about. In order that it might take place, man had first of all to be induced to turn all his attention exclusively to sensible things; the work of deviation had necessarily to begin in this way, that work which could be said to consist in the 'manufacturing' of the present world, and it clearly could not 'suc-ceed' in its turn except precisely at this phase of the cycle, and by using, in 'diabolical' mode, the existing conditions of the environ-ment itself. So much for this matter, which need not be further insisted on for the moment; nevertheless, the solemn silliness of certain declamations dear to scientific (or rather 'scientistic') 'popu-larizers' can scarcely be too much admired, when they are pleased to assert on all occasions that modern science ceaselessly pushes back the boundaries of the known world, which is in fact the exact oppo-site of the truth: never have those boundaries been so close as they are in the conceptions admitted by this profane self-styled science, never have either the world or man been so shrunken, to the point of their being reduced to mere corporeal entities, deprived, by hypothesis, of the smallest possibility of communication with any other order of reality!

There is also yet another aspect of the question, both reciprocal and complementary to the aspect considered hitherto: man is not restricted at any stage to the passive role of a mere spectator, who must confine himself to forming an idea more or less true, or more or less false, of what is happening around him; on the contrary, he is himself one of the factors that intervene actively in the modification of the world he lives in; and it must be added that he is even a par-ticularly important factor, by reason of the characteristically 'cen-tral' position he occupies in that world. The mention of this human intervention does not imply that the artificial modifications to which industry subjects the terrestrial environment are alone in view, and in any case they are too obvious to be worth spending time on: they are certainly something to be taken into account, but they are not everything, and the matter now particularly to be considered in relation to the point of view of the present discussion is something quite different, and is not willed by man, at least expressly or consciously, though it nonetheless actually covers a much wider field than do any artificial modifications. The truth is that the materialistic conception, once it has been formed and spread abroad in one way or another, can only serve to further reinforce the very 'solidification' of the world that in the first place made it possible; and all the consequences directly or indirectly derived from that conception, including the current notion of 'ordinary life', tend only toward this same end, for the general reactions of the cosmic environment do actually change according to the attitude adopted by man toward it. It can be said with truth that certain aspects of reality conceal themselves from anyone who looks upon reality from a profane and materialistic point of view, and they become inaccessible to his observation: this is not a more or less 'picturesque' manner of speaking, as some people might be tempted to think, but is the simple and direct statement of a fact, just as it is a fact that animals flee spontaneously and instinctively from the presence of anyone who evinces a hostile attitude toward them. That is why there are some things that can never be grasped by men of learning who are materialists or positivists, and this naturally further confirms their belief in the validity of their conceptions by seeming to afford a sort of negative proof of them, whereas it is really neither more nor less than a direct effect of the conceptions themselves. It is of course by no means the case that the things that elude the materialists have in any sense ceased to exist since the time of, or because of, the birth of materialism and positivism, but they do actually 'cut themselves off' from the domain that is within the reach of profane learning, refraining from penetrating into it in any way that could allow their action or even their existence to be suspected, very much as, in another order not unrelated to the order under consideration, the repository of traditional knowledge veils itself and shuts itself in ever more strictly before the invasion of the modern spirit. This is in a sense the 'counterpart' of the limitation of the faculties of the human being to those that are by their nature related to the corporeal modality alone: because of that limitation man becomes, as has been explained, incapable of getting out of the sensible world; because of what has just been called its 'counterpart' he loses in addition all chance of becoming aware of a manifest intervention of supra-sensible elements in the sensible world itself. So for him that world has become to the greatest possible extent completely 'closed', for it has become ever more 'solid' as it has become more isolated from every other order of reality, even from those orders that are nearest to it and simply constitute separate modalities of one and the same individual domain. From the inside of such a world it may appear that 'ordinary life' has only to roll on henceforward without trouble or unforeseen accidents, just like the movements of a well regulated 'mechanism'; is not modern man, having 'mechanized' the world around him doing his very best to 'mechanize' himself, in all the forms of activity that still remain open to his narrowly limited nature?

Nevertheless, the 'solidification' of the world, to whatever length it may actually be carried, can never be complete, and there are limits beyond which it cannot go, since, as explained earlier, arrival at its extreme end-point would be incompatible with any real existence, even of the lowest degree; and moreover, the further 'solidification' goes the more precarious it becomes, for the lowest reality is also the least stable; the ever-growing rapidity of the changes taking place in the world today provides all too eloquent a testimony to the truth of this. It cannot but be that 'fissures' should develop in this imagined 'closed system', which has moreover, owing to its 'mechanical' character, something 'artificial' about it (this word of course being used in a sense much broader than in its usual application to industrial products alone) that is not such as to inspire confidence in its duration; and there are already at this moment numerous signs indicating most clearly that its unstable equilibrium is on the point of being interrupted. So true is this that what has been said about the materialism and mechanism of the modern period could almost in a certain sense be relegated to the past even now; this of course does not mean that their practical consequences may not continue to develop for a certain time to come, nor that their infl-uence on the general mentality will not persist for a more or less considerable period, if only as a consequence of 'popularization' in its various forms, including education in schools at all levels, where there are always plenty of 'survivals' of that sort hanging on (this point will be expanded shortly); but it is nonetheless true that at the present moment the very notion of 'matter', so painfully worked out through so many different theories, seems to be in course of fading away; nevertheless, there is perhaps no reason to be unduly pleased at the occurrence, because, as will become clearer later on, it can only properly be taken to represent yet one more step toward final dissolution.

18

SCIENTIFIC MYTHOLOGY AND POPULARIZATION

REFERENCE HAS ALREADY BEEN MADE to 'survivals' left behind in the common mentality by theories no longer believed in by the scientists, whereby those theories are enabled to continue as before to exercise their influence over the general outlook of mankind, and it will be useful to give some further attention to the subject, for it is one that can contribute toward the explanation of certain aspects of the present period. In this connection it should first be recalled that when profane science leaves the domain of a mere observation of facts, and tries to get something out of the indefinite accumulation of separate details that is its sole immediate result, it retains as one of its chief characteristics the more or less laborious construction of purely hypothetical theories. These theories can necessarily never be more than hypothetical, since their starting-point is wholly empirical, for facts in themselves are always susceptible of diverse explanations and so never have been and never will be able to guarantee the truth of any theory, and as was said earlier, their greater or lesser multiplicity has no bearing on the question; and besides, such hypotheses are really not inspired by the results of experience to nearly the same extent as by certain preconceived ideas and by some of the predominant tendencies of the modern mentality. The ever-growing rapidity with which such hypotheses are abandoned in these days and replaced by others is well known, and these continual changes are enough to make all too obvious the lack of solidity of the hypotheses and the impossibility of recognizing in them any value so far as real knowledge is concerned; they are also assuming more and more, in the eyes of their authors themselves, a conventional character, and so a quality of unreality, and this again may be noted as a symptom of the approach toward final dissolution. Indeed the scientists, and particularly the physicists, can hardly be completely deceived by constructions of this sort, the fragility of which they know all too well, today more so than ever. Not only are they quickly 'worn-out', but from their beginnings the very people who build them up only believe in them to a certain doubtless rather limited extent, and in a more or less 'provisional' way; very often they even seem to regard them less as real attempts at explanation than as mere 'representations' and as 'manners of speaking'. This indeed is really all they are, and we have seen that Leibnitz had already shown that Cartesian mechanism could be nothing but a 'representation' of outward appearances, denuded of all genuinely explanatory value. Under such conditions the least that can be said is that the whole business is rather pointless, and a conception of science that can lead to a labour of that kind is certainly a strange one; but the danger of these illusory theories lies in the influence they are liable to exercise on the 'public at large' by virtue of the fact that they call themselves 'scientific', for the public takes them quite seriously and blindly accepts them as 'dogmas', and that not merely for as long as they last (that time often being not long enough for them to have even come fully to the knowledge of the public) but more especially when the scientists have already abandoned them, and for a long time afterward as well. This happens because they persist, as was pointed out earlier, in elementary teaching and in works of 'popularization', in which they are always presented in a 'simplified' and resolutely assertive form, and not by any means as mere hypotheses, though that is all they ever were for those who elaborated them. The use of the word 'dogma' a moment ago was deliberate, for it is a question of something that, in accordance with the anti-traditional modern spirit, must oppose and be substituted for religious dogmas; an example like that of the 'evolutionary' theories, among others, can leave no doubt on that score; and it is even more significant that most of the 'popularizers' have the habit of sprinkling their writings with more or less violent declamations against all traditional ideas, which shows only too clearly the part they are charged with playing, albeit unconsciously in many cases, in the intellectual subversion of our times.

Thus it comes about that there has grown up in the scientistic 'mentality'—which is, for the largely utilitarian reasons already indicated, more or less the mentality of a great majority of our contemporaries—a real 'mythology': most certainly not in the original and transcendent meaning applicable to the traditional 'myths', but merely in the 'pejorative' meaning that the word has acquired in current speech. Endless examples could be cited: one of the most striking and most 'immediate', so to speak, being the 'imagery' of atoms and the many particles of various kinds into which they have lately become dissociated in the most recent physical theories (the result of this of course being that they are no longer in any sense atoms, which literally means 'indivisibles', though they go on being called by that name in the face of all logic). 'Imagery' is the right word, because it is no more than imagery in the minds of the physicists; but the 'public at large' believes firmly that real 'entities' are in question, such as could be seen and touched by anyone whose senses were sufficiently developed or who had at his disposal sufficiently powerful instruments of observation; is not that a 'mythology' of a most ingenuous kind? This does not prevent the same public from pouring scorn on the conceptions of the ancients at every opportunity, though of course they do not understand a single word about them; even admitting that there may have been 'popular' deformations at all times ('popular' being another word that people are very fond of using wrongly and ineptly, doubtless because of the growing importance accorded to the 'masses'), it is permissible to doubt whether those deformations have ever been so grossly materialistic and at the same time so widely diffused as they are at present, thanks to the tendencies inherent in the mentality of today and at the same time to the much vaunted spread of a 'compulsory education' at once profane and rudimentary!

Too much time must not be spent on this subject, for it would lend itself to an almost indefinite development, since it leads too far afield from the main point at issue; it would for instance be easy to show that, by reason of the 'survival' of hypotheses, elements that really belong to different theories get superimposed and intermingled in such a way in popular notions that they sometimes form the most incongruous combinations; and in any case the contemporary mentality is made up in such a way that it readily accepts the strangest contradictions. But it will be more profitable to stress again a particular aspect of this subject, though admittedly this will involve some anticipation of considerations that will find their place later on, for it concerns things more properly belonging to a phase other than that which has been in view up till now, though these phases cannot be kept quite separate, for that would give much too 'schematic' an impression of our period. At the same time a glimpse can be given of the way in which the tendencies toward 'solidification' and toward dissolution, while they are apparently opposed in some respects, are nevertheless associated from the very fact that they act simultaneously in such a way as to come to an inevitable end in the final catastrophe. The aspect of affairs to which attention will now be directed is the quite particularly extravagant character assumed by the notions in question when they are carried over into a domain other than that to which they were originally intended to be applied; from such misapplications are derived most of the phantasmagoria of what has been called 'neo-spiritualism' in its various forms, and it is just such borrowings from conceptions belonging essentially to the sensible order which explain the sort of 'materialization' of the supra-sensible that is one of its most common characteristics.[1] Without seeking for the moment to determine more precisely the nature and quality of the supra-sensible, insofar as it is actually involved in this matter, it will be useful to observe how far the very people who still admit it and think that they are aware of its action are in reality permeated by materialistic influence: for even if they do not deny all extra-corporeal reality, like the majority of their contemporaries, it is only because they have formed for themselves an idea of it that enables them in some way to assimilate it to the likeness of sensible things, and to do that is certainly scarcely better than to deny it. There is no reason to be surprised at this, considering the

1. This sort of thing is particularly apparent in spiritualism, and in the crudest possible forms; a number of examples were given in *The Spiritist Fallacy*.

extent to which all the occultist, Theosophist, and other schools of that sort are fond of searching assiduously for points of approach to modern scientific theories, from which indeed they draw their inspiration more directly than they are prepared to admit, and the result is what might logically be expected under such conditions. It may even be observed that, in accordance with the continuous changes in scientific theories, the resemblance between the conceptions of a particular school and a particular scientific theory may make it possible to 'date' the school, in default of any more precise information about its history and its origins.

This state of affairs had its beginning at the time when the study and the control of certain psychic influences descended, if it may be so expressed, into the profane domain, and this in a certain sense marks the beginning of the phase of 'dissolution' properly so called in the modern deviation. This time can broadly speaking be placed as far back as the eighteenth century, so that it is seen to be exactly contemporary with materialism itself, showing clearly that these two things, contraries in appearance only, had in fact to appear together; it does not seem that anything of the kind was in evidence at any earlier date, no doubt because the deviation had not then attained the stage of development that could make such a thing possible. The chief characteristic of the scientific 'mythology' of that period was the conception of 'fluids' of different kinds, all physical forces being imagined to exist in some such form; it is precisely this conception that was carried over from the corporeal order into the subtle order in the theory of 'animal magnetism'. If this is related back to the idea of the 'solidification' of the world, it might perhaps be thought that a 'fluid' is by definition the opposite of a 'solid'; but it is nonetheless true that in this case both play exactly the same part, because the conception of 'fluids' has the effect of 'embodying' things that really belong to subtle manifestation. The magnetizers were in a sense the direct precursors of 'neo-spiritualism', if indeed they were not really its first representatives; their theories and their practices influenced to a greater or lesser extent all the schools that came into being later, whether they were openly profane, like spiritualism, or whether they had pseudo-initiatic pretensions, like the many varieties of occultism. This persistent influence is all the more strange in that it seems quite disproportionate to the importance of the psychic phenomena, very elementary as they were, which constituted the field of experiment in magnetism; but perhaps even more astonishing is the part played by this same magnetism, right from the time of its first appearance, in turning aside from all serious work initiatic organizations that had still retained up to that time, if not a very far-reaching effective knowledge, at least an awareness of what they had lost in this respect and the will to do their best to recover it. It is permissible to suppose that this is not the least of the reasons for which magnetism was 'launched' at the appointed time, even though, as almost always happens in similar cases, its apparent promoters were acting only as more or less unconscious instruments.

The 'fluidic' conception survived in the common mentality, though not in the theories of physicists, at least up to about the middle of the nineteenth century (though expressions such as 'electric fluid' continued to be used for even longer, but more in a mechanical way and without a precise imagery any longer being attached to them); spiritualism, which came to birth at that period, inherited the conception all the more naturally through being predisposed to it by an original connection with magnetism; and this connection is much closer than might be at first supposed, for it is highly probable that spiritualism could never have reached any very considerable development but for the divagations of the somnambulists, and also that it was the existence of magnetic 'subjects' which prepared for and made possible the existence of spiritualist 'mediums'. Even today most magnetizers and spiritualists continue to talk of 'fluids', and what is more, to believe seriously in them; this 'anachronism' is all the more strange in that these people are in general fanatical partisans of 'progress'; such an attitude fits in badly with a conception that has for a long time been excluded from the scientific domain and so ought in their eyes to appear very 'backward'. In the present-day mythology, 'fluids' have been replaced by 'waves' and 'radiations', these last in their turn of course effectively playing the part of 'fluids' in the theories most recently invented to try to explain the action of certain subtle influences; it should suffice to mention 'radiaesthesia' which is as 'typical' as possible in this respect. Needless to say, if it were only a question in all these affairs of mere images, of comparisons based on some analogy (and not on identity) with phenomena in the sensible order, the matter would not have very serious consequences, and might even be justified up to a point; but such is not the case, for the 'radiaesthesists' believe very literally that the psychic influences with which they are concerned are 'waves' or 'radiations' propagated in space in the most 'corporeal' manner that it is possible to imagine; moreover, thought itself does not escape from representation in this fashion. Here we find another case of the same 'materialization' continuing to assert itself in a new form, perhaps more insidious than that of 'fluids' because it may appear to be less crude; nonetheless the whole affair belongs fundamentally to exactly the same order and does no more than express the very limitations that are inherent in the modern mentality and consist in an incapacity to conceive of anything whatsoever outside the domain of the formation of mental images of sensible things.[2]

It is scarcely necessary to add that the 'clairvoyants', according to the schools to which they belong, go so far as to see 'fluids' or 'radiations', just as there are some, particularly among the Theosophists, who see atoms and electrons; here, as in many other matters, what they in fact see are their own mental images, which naturally always fit well with the particular theories they believe in. There are some who see the 'fourth dimension', and even other supplementary dimensions of space as well; and this leads to a few words in conclusion on another case that also appertains to 'scientific mythology', and might well be called the 'delirium of the fourth dimension'. It must be agreed that 'hypergeometry' seems to have been devised in order to strike the imagination of people who have not enough mathematical knowledge to be aware of the true character of an algebraic construction expressed in geometrical terms, for that is really what 'hypergeometry' is; and it may be noted in passing that this is another example of the dangers of 'popularization'. Moreover,

---

2. It is as a result of this same incapacity and of the confusion to which it gives rise that Kant, in the philosophic field, did not hesitate to declare to be 'inconceivable' everything that is merely 'unimaginable'; moreover, speaking more generally, it is the very same limitations that really gave birth to all the varieties of 'agnosticism'.

well before the physicists had thought of bringing the 'fourth dimension' into their hypotheses (which had already become much more mathematical than really physical, because their character had become both increasingly quantitative and at the same time increasingly 'conventional') the 'psychists' (they were not yet called 'meta-psychists' in those days) were already making use of it to explain phenomena in which one solid body appears to pass through another; and here again it was not for them a case of a mere picture 'illustrating' in some way what may be called 'interferences' between different domains or states, which would have been unobjectionable, but, according to their ideas, the body in question had quite genuinely passed through the 'fourth dimension'. That was in any case only a beginning, and in recent years, under the influence of the new physics, occultist schools have been observed to go so far as to build up the greater part of their theories on this same conception of a 'fourth dimension'; it may be noted also in this connection that occultism and modern science tend more and more to join up with one another as the 'disintegration' proceeds step by step, because both are traveling toward it by their different paths. The 'fourth dimension' will be spoken of again later from a different point of view; but enough has been said about that sort of thing for the present, and the time has come to turn to other considerations more directly related to the question of the 'solidification' of the world.

19

THE LIMITS
OF HISTORY
AND GEOGRAPHY

It has already been indicated that, because of the qualitative differences between different periods of time, for example between the various phases of a cycle such as our own *Manvantara* (it being obvious that outside the limits of the duration of the present humanity conditions must be still more different), changes come about in the cosmic environment generally, and more especially in the terrestrial environment that concerns us most directly; and also that profane science, with its horizon bounded by the modern world in which alone it had its birth, can form no sort of idea of these changes. The result is that, whatever epoch science may have in view, it pictures to itself a world in which conditions are assumed to be similar to those of today. We have seen that the psychologists imagine in the same way that man has always in the past had a mentality similar to that of today; and what is true in this respect of the psychologists is no less true of the historians, who assess the actions of the men of antiquity or of the Middle Ages exactly as they would assess those of their own contemporaries, attributing to each the same motives and the same intentions. Thus, whether man or his environment be in view, it is evident that those simplified and 'uniformizing' conceptions that correspond so well with present-day tendencies are being brought into play: as for knowing how this 'uniformization' of the past can be reconciled with the 'progressivist' and 'evolutionist' theories that are simultaneously adhered to by the same individuals, that is a problem the solution of which will certainly not be attempted here; it is no doubt only one more example of the endless contradictions of the modern mentality.

In speaking of changes in the environment, the intention is not to allude only to the more or less extensive cataclysms that in one way or another mark the 'critical points' of the cycle; these are abrupt changes corresponding to real ruptures of equilibrium, and even in cases where for example it is only a question of the disappearance of a single continent (and such events have in fact occurred in the course of the history of our present humanity), it is easy to see that the terrestrial environment in its entirety must nevertheless be affected by the repercussions of any such event, and that the 'face of the world', so to speak, must thereby be markedly changed. But there are in addition continuous and imperceptible modifications which, within a period free from any cataclysm, produce bit by bit results that in the end are scarcely less impressive; these are not of course only simple 'geological' modifications as understood by profane science, and it is incidentally an error to consider the cataclysms from this narrow point of view alone, since it is always restricted to whatever is most exterior; what is in view here is something much more profound, bearing on the conditions of the environment themselves in such a way that, even if no account were taken of geological phenomena as being no more than details of secondary importance, beings and things would nonetheless be really changed. As for the artificial modifications produced by man's intervention, they are after all only consequential, because, as previously explained, nothing but the special conditions of this or that period could make them possible; if man can indeed act on his surroundings in some more profound way, it is rather psychically than corporally that he can do so, as may be well enough understood from what has been said about the effects of the materialistic attitude.

The explanations given hitherto make it easy now to understand the general direction in which such changes take place: this direction has been designated as that of the 'solidification' of the world, conferring on all things an aspect corresponding ever more closely (though never really corresponding exactly) to the way in which things appear according to quantitative, mechanistic, or materialistic conceptions; and this is why modern science succeeds in its practical applications, as indicated above, and also why the surrounding reality does not seem to give the lie to it too strikingly. Such could not have been the case in earlier periods, when the world was not so 'solid' as it has become today, and when the corporeal and subtle modalities of the individual domain were not as completely separated (although, as we shall see later, certain reservations must even in the present state of affairs be made with respect to that separation). It was not only that man, whose faculties were then much less narrowly limited, did not see the world with eyes that were the same as those of today, and perceived many things which since then have escaped him entirely; but also, and correlatively, the world itself, as a cosmic entity, was indeed qualitatively different, because possibilities of another order were reflected in the corporeal domain and in a sense 'transfigured' it; thus, for example, when certain 'legends' say that there was a time when precious stones were as common as the most ordinary pebbles are now, the statement need not perhaps be taken only in a purely symbolical sense. The symbolical sense is of course always there in such a case, but this does not imply that it is the only valid sense, for everything manifested is itself necessarily a symbol in relation to some superior reality; it seems unnecessary to insist on this point, which has been adequately explained elsewhere, both in a general way, and as it concerns particular cases such as the symbolic value of the facts of history and geography.

Before going any further, an objection that may arise in connection with the qualitative changes in the 'face of the world' must be met. It may perhaps be argued that, if things were so, the vestiges of bygone periods which are all the time being discovered ought to provide evidence of the fact, whereas, leaving 'geological' epochs out of consideration and keeping to matters that affect human history, archaeologists and even 'prehistorians' never find anything of the kind, however far their researches may be carried into the past. The answer is really very simple: first of all, these vestiges, in the state in which they are found today and inasmuch as they are consequently part of the existing environment, have inevitably participated, like everything else, in the 'solidification' of the world; if they had not done so their existence would no longer be compatible with the pre-vailing conditions and they would have completely disappeared, and this no doubt is what has happened to many things which have not left the smallest trace. Next, the archaeologists examine these vestiges with modern eyes, which only perceive the coarsest modal-ity of manifestation, so that even if, in spite of all, something more subtle has remained attached to the vestiges, the archaeologists are certainly quite incapable of becoming aware of it; in short, they treat these things as the mechanical physicists treat the things they have to deal with, because their mentality is the same and their faculties are equally limited. It is said that when a treasure is sought for by a person for whom, for one reason or another, it is not destined, the gold and precious stones are changed for him into coal and com-mon pebbles; modern lovers of excavations might well turn this particular 'legend' to their profit!

However that may be, it is very sure that historians, simply because they undertake all their researches from a modern and pro-fane point of view, come up against certain 'barriers' in time that prove more or less completely impassable; and, as was pointed out elsewhere, the first of these 'barriers' is met with toward the sixth century before the Christian era, at which point, according to mod-ern conceptions, history properly so called begins; so that all things considered antiquity as understood in this history is a very relative antiquity indeed. It will no doubt be said that recent researches have made it possible to go back much further, by bringing to light the remains of a much more remote antiquity, and that is true up to a point; it is nevertheless rather remarkable that in such cases there is no longer any clearly established chronology, so much so that diver-gences in the estimation of the dates of objects and of events amount to centuries and sometimes even to whole millennia; and in addition, it seems impossible to arrive at even a moderately pre-cise conception of the civilizations of these more distant periods, because terms of comparison with what exists today can no longer be found, although they can be found when it is only a question of 'classical' antiquity. This, however, does not imply that 'classical' antiquity as represented to us by modern historians is not greatly disfigured, the same being true of the Middle Ages though they are even nearer to us in time. Moreover, the truth is that the most ancient things so far made known to us by archaeological research do not belong to a period more remote than about the beginning of the *Kali-Yuga*, where naturally there is situated a second 'barrier'; and if some means could be found for crossing this one, there would be yet a third, corresponding to the time of the last great terrestrial cataclysm, the cataclysm traditionally referred to as the disappearance of Atlantis; it would evidently be quite useless to try to go back further still, for before the historians had been able to reach that point the modern world would have had plenty of time to disappear in its turn!

These few indications are enough to make it clear how vain are all the discussions to which the profane (the word is used here to include all who are affected by the modern spirit) may wish to devote their time on matters connected with the earlier periods of the *Manvantara*, with the 'golden age' or the 'primordial tradition', or even with much less remote events such as the biblical 'deluge', taking this last only in its more immediately literal meaning, in which it relates to the cataclysm of Atlantis; these matters are among those that are wholly beyond their reach and will always be so. That of course is why they deny them, as they deny indifferently everything that goes beyond them in any way, for all their studies and all their researches, being undertaken from a point of view both false and restricted, can most certainly result in nothing but the denial of everything that is not comprehended in that point of view. And on top of all this, these people are so far persuaded of their own 'superiority' that they are unable to admit the existence or even the possibility of anything whatever that eludes their investigations; blind men would surely have equally sound reasons for denying the existence of light and then using that as a pretext for boasting of their superiority over normal men!

What has been said about the limits of history, as conceived according to the profane conception, can also be applied to the limits of geography, wherein there are also many things that have passed completely beyond the horizon of the moderns; anyone who compares the descriptions of ancient geographers with those of modern geographers must often be led to wonder whether it is really possible that both are speaking of the same countries. Nevertheless the ancient geographers are only ancient in a very relative sense, and it is not necessary to go back further than the Middle Ages in order to come across contrasts of that kind; in the interval that separates them from us there has certainly been no notable cataclysm; is it possible that the world has been able in spite of this to change its appearance to such an extent and so quickly? It is of course accepted that the moderns will say that the ancients did not see clearly, or that they did not record clearly what they saw; but any such explanation, which amounts to no more than supposing that all men before our time were troubled with sensorial and mental afflictions, really is a great deal too 'simplistic' and negative; and if the question is examined with true impartiality, why should it not be the moderns who do not see clearly, and who even fail to see some things at all? They triumphantly proclaim that 'the world has now been discovered in its entirety,' though this may perhaps not be as true as they think, and they couple this with the supposition that the greater part of the world was unknown to the ancients; in that connection it may well be wondered what particular ancients they are talking about, and whether they think that there were no men before their own time other than the Westerners of the 'classical' period, and that the inhabited world did not then extend beyond a small fraction of Europe and Asia Minor; and they say too that 'this unknown, because it was unknown, could not be otherwise than mysterious'; but where have they found out that the ancients characterized any of these things as 'mysterious', and is it not they themselves who proclaim them to be so because they no longer understand them? Again, they say that in the beginning 'marvels' were met with, and that later there were only 'singularities' or 'curiosities' and that finally 'it was seen that these singularities conformed to general laws, which men of learning sought to establish'; but is not what they here describe with very fair accuracy precisely the successive stages of the limitation of human faculties, stages of which the last corresponds to what may justly be called the mania for rational explanations, with all the gross insufficiency that is theirs? In fact, this last way of looking at things, from which proceeds modern geography, really only dates from the seventeenth and eighteenth centuries, that is, from the very period that saw the birth and diffusion of the specifically rationalist mentality, and this confirms the explanations given; from that time the faculties of conception and perception that allowed man to reach out to something other than the coarsest and most inferior mode of reality were totally atrophied, while the world itself was at the same time irremediably 'solidified'.

If things are looked at in this way, the following conclusion emerges: either, on the one hand, things could formerly be seen that are no longer visible, because considerable changes have taken place in the terrestrial environment or in human faculties, or rather in both together, such changes moreover becoming more rapid as the present period is approached; or, on the other hand, what is called 'geography' had in the old days a significance quite other than that which it has today. Actually, the two terms of this alternative are not mutually exclusive, and each of them expresses one side of the truth, for the conception formed of a science naturally depends both on the point of view from which its object is considered and on the extent to which the realities implicit in it can be effectively grasped: in relation to both these sides of the truth, a traditional science and a profane science, even if they have identical names (and this generally indicates that the latter is as it were a 'residue' of the former) are so profoundly different that they are in truth separated by an abyss. Now there is really and truly a 'sacred' or traditional geography, as completely unknown to the moderns as is all other knowledge of the same kind; there is a geographical symbolism as well as a historical symbolism, and it is the symbolical value of things that gives them their profound significance, because through it is established their correspondence with realities of a higher order; but it is not possible for this correspondence to be effectively determined unless there is the ability to perceive, in one way or another, the reflection of the said realities in the things themselves. Thus it is that there are places particularly suited to serve as 'support' for the action of 'spiritual influences', and on this fact has always been based the establishment of certain traditional 'centers', whether principal or secondary, the oracles of antiquity and the places of pilgrimage furnishing the most outwardly apparent examples of such 'centers'. There are also other places no less specially favorable to the manifestation of 'influences' quite opposite in character, and belonging to the lowest regions of the subtle domain; but what difference does it make to a modern Westerner whether there be for instance in one place a 'gate of heaven' and in another a 'mouth of hell', since the 'density' of his 'psycho-physiological' constitution is such that he experiences nothing in particular in either the one or the other? Such things therefore are literally non-existent for him, but this of course by no means implies that they have actually ceased to exist; it is moreover true that, communications between the corporeal and the subtle domains having been more or less reduced to a minimum, in order to become aware of such things, a greater development than in the past of certain faculties is needed, and these are just the faculties which, so far from being developed, have on the contrary for the most part become continuously weaker and have ended by disappearing from the 'average' human individual, so that the difficulty and the rarity of perceptions of that order have been doubly accentuated, and this is what allows the moderns to hold the accounts of the ancients in derision.

In this connection, there is one more thing to be said, concerning the descriptions of strange beings met with in such accounts: since these descriptions naturally date at the earliest from 'classical' antiquity, a time at which an undeniable degeneration had already taken place from a traditional point of view, it is quite possible that confusions of more than one kind may have crept in. For instance, one part of these descriptions may really be derived from 'survivals' of a symbolism no longer fully understood,[1] whereas another part may be related to the appearances assumed by the manifestation of certain 'entities' or 'influences' belonging to the subtle domain, and yet another, though doubtless not the most important, may really be a description of beings that had a corporeal existence in more or less remote times, but belonged to species since then extinct or having survived only in exceptional conditions and as great rarities, such as

---

1. Pliny's *Natural History* in particular seems to be an almost inexhaustible source of examples of things of this kind; it is moreover a source on which all those who came after him have drawn most abundantly.

are still sometimes met with today, whatever may be the opinion of people who imagine that there is nothing left in the world that they do not know about. It can be seen that in order to discern what lies at the bottom of all this, a fairly long and difficult piece of work would have to be undertaken, all the more so because the 'sources' available are far from providing uncontaminated traditional data; it is obviously much simpler and more convenient to discard the whole lot *en bloc* as the moderns do; they would anyhow not understand the truly traditional data themselves any better than those that are contaminated and would still see in them only indecipherable enigmas, and they will naturally adhere to this negative attitude until some new changes in the 'face of the world' come to destroy once and for all their deceptive security.

20

FROM SPHERE
TO CUBE

Now that a few 'illustrations' have been given of what has been called the 'solidification' of the world, there remains the question of its representation in geometrical symbolism, wherein it can be figured as a gradual transition from sphere to cube. Indeed, to begin with, the sphere is intrinsically the primordial form, because it is the least 'specified' of all, similar to itself in every direction, in such a way that in any rotatory movement about its center, all its successive positions are strictly superimposable one on another.[1] The sphere, then, can be said to be the most universal form of all, containing in a certain sense all other forms, which will emerge from it by means of differentiations taking place in certain particular directions; and that is why the spherical form is, in all traditions, that of the 'Egg of the World', in other words, the form of that which represents the 'global' integrality, in their first and 'embryonic' state, of all the possibilities that will be developed in the course of a cycle of manifestation.[2] It is as well to note in addition that this first state, so far as our world is concerned, belongs properly to the domain of subtle manifestation, inasmuch as the latter necessarily precedes gross manifestation and is its immediate principle. This is why the

1. See *The Symbolism of the Cross*, chaps. 6 and 20.
2. This same form reappears at the beginning of the embryonic existence of every individual comprised in that cyclical development, the individual embryo (*pinda*) being the microcosmic analogy of what the 'Egg of the World' (*Brahmānda*) is in the macrocosmic order.

form of the perfect sphere, or that of the circle corresponding to it in plane geometry (as a section of the sphere by a given directional plane) is in fact never realized in the corporeal world.[3]

On the other hand, the cube is opposed to the sphere as being the most 'arrested' form of all, if it can be so expressed; this means that it corresponds to a maximum of 'specification'. The cube is also the form that is related to the earth as one of the elements, inasmuch as the earth is the 'terminating and final element' of manifestation in the corporeal state;[4] and consequently it corresponds also to the end of the cycle of manifestation, or to what has been called the 'stopping-point' of the cyclical movement. This form is thus in a sense above all that of the 'solid',[5] and it symbolizes 'stability' insofar as this implies the stoppage of all movement; and it is evident that the equilibrium of a cube resting on one of its faces is in fact more stable than that of any other body. It is important to note that this stability, coming at the end of the descending movement, is not and cannot be anything but an unqualified immobility, of which the nearest representation in the corporeal world is afforded by the minerals; and this immobility, if it could be entirely realized, would really be the inverted reflection at the lowest point of the principial immutability of the highest point. Immobility or stability thus understood, and represented by the cube, is therefore related to the substantial pole of manifestation, just as immutability, in which all

3. The movement of the celestial bodies can be given as an example. It is not exactly circular, but elliptical; the ellipse constitutes as it were a first 'specification' of the circle, by the splitting of the center into two poles or 'foci' in the direction of one of the diameters, which thereafter plays a special 'axial' part, while at the same time all the other diameters are differentiated one from another in respect of their lengths. It may be added incidentally in this connection that, since the planets describe ellipses of which the sun occupies one of the foci, the question arises as to what the other focus corresponds to; as there is nothing corporeal actually there, there must be something belonging only to the subtle order; but that question cannot be further examined here, as it would be quite outside our subject.

4. See Fabre d'Olivet, *The Hebraic Tongue Restored and The True Meaning of the Hebrew Words Re-established and Proved by their Radical Analysis*, (York Beach, ME: Samuel Weiser, 1981).

5. The point is not that earth as an element is assimilated simply and solely to the solid state, as some people wrongly think, but that it is rather the very principle of solidity.

possibilities are comprehended in the 'global' state represented by the sphere, is related to the essential pole;[6] and this is why the cube also symbolizes the idea of 'base' or 'foundation' which again corresponds to the substantial pole.[7] Attention must also be drawn to the fact that the faces of a cube can be considered as being oriented in opposite pairs corresponding to the three dimensions of space, in other words as parallel to the three planes determined by the axes forming the system of coordinates to which that space is related and which allows of its being 'measured', that is, of its being effectively realized in its integrality. It has been explained elsewhere that the three axes forming the three-dimensional cross must be looked upon as being traced through the center of a sphere that fills the whole of space by its indefinite expansion (the three planes determined by these axes also necessarily passing through the same center, which is the 'origin' of the whole system of coordinates), and this establishes the relation that exists between the two extreme forms, sphere and cube, a relation in which what was interior and central in the sphere is so to speak 'turned inside out' to become the surface or the exteriority of the cube.[8]

The cube also represents the earth in all the traditional meanings of that word, that is, not only the earth as a corporeal element in the

6. This is why the spherical form is attributed in the Islamic tradition to the 'Spirit' (ar-Rūḥ) or to the primordial Light.

7. In the Hebrew Kabbalah the cubic form corresponds to Iesod, one of the Sephiroth, and Iesod is in fact the 'foundation' (and if it be objected in this connection that Iesod is nevertheless not the last Sephirah, the answer must be that the only one that follows it is Malkuth, which is actually the final 'synthesization' in which all things are brought back to a state corresponding, at another level, to the principial unity of Kether); in the subtle constitution of the human individuality, according to the Hindu tradition, the same form is related to the 'basic' chakra or mūlādhāra; and this is also connected with the mysteries of the Ka'bah in the Islamic tradition; also, in architectural symbolism, the cube is properly the form of the 'first stone' of a building, otherwise of the 'foundation-stone', laid at the lowest level, to serve as support for the whole structure of the building, thus assuring its stability.

8. In plane geometry a similar relation is obviously found when the sides of the square are considered as being parallel to two rectangular diameters of the circle, and the symbolism of this relation is directly connected with what the Hermetic tradition calls the 'quadrature of the circle', about which a few words will be said later on.

sense in which it was mentioned above, but also as a principle of a much more universal order, the principle designated in the Far-Eastern tradition as Earth (*Ti*) in correlation with Heaven (*T'ien*). Spherical or circular forms are related to Heaven, cubic or square forms to Earth; since these two complementary terms are the equivalents of *Purusha* and *Prakriti* in the Hindu doctrine, which means that they are simply another expression for essence and substance taken in their universal meaning, exactly the same conclusion as before is arrived at in this instance. It is also evident that, like the conceptions of essence and substance, the same symbolism is always susceptible of application at different levels, that is to say either to the principles of a particular state of existence, or to the integrality of universal manifestation. Not only are these two geometrical forms related to Heaven and to Earth, but so also are the instruments used to draw them, namely, the compass and the square, and this is so in the symbolism of the Far-Eastern tradition as well as in that of Western initiatic traditions;[9] and the different correspondences of these two forms give rise in different circumstances to multiple symbolical and ritual applications.[10]

Another case in which the relation of these same geometrical forms is in evidence is that of the symbolism of the 'Terrestrial Paradise' and of the 'Heavenly Jerusalem', to which reference has already been made elsewhere;[11] and this case is specially important from the point of view adopted in this book, since the symbolism in question is in fact concerned with the two extremities of the present cycle.

9. In certain symbolical representations the compass and the square respectively are placed in the hands of Fu Hsi and his sister Niu-koua, just as, in the alchemical figures of Basil Valentine, they are placed in the hands of the two halves, masculine and feminine, of the *Rebis* or Hermetic Androgyne; this shows that Fu Hsi and Niu-koua are in a sense analogically assimilated, as regards their respective functions, to the essential or masculine principle and to the substantial or feminine principle of manifestation.

10. Thus, for example, the ritual garments of the ancient sovereigns in China had to be round in shape at the top and square at the bottom; the sovereign then represented the type of man himself (*Jen*) in his cosmic function, as the third term of the 'Great Triad', exercising that function as intermediary between Heaven and Earth, and uniting in himself the powers of both.

11. See *The King of the World*, also *The Symbolism of the Cross*, chap. 9.

Now the form of the 'Terrestrial Paradise', corresponding to the beginning of the cycle, is circular, whereas that of the 'Heavenly Jerusalem', corresponding to its end, is square;[12] and the circular boundary of the 'Terrestrial Paradise' is none other than the horizontal section of the 'Egg of the World', that is of the universal and primordial spherical form.[13] It could be said that this circle itself is finally changed into a square, since the two extremities must join, or rather (the cycle never being really closed, for that would imply an impossible repetition) they must correspond exactly; the presence of the same 'Tree of Life' in the center in each case shows clearly that it is only actually a question of two states of one and the same thing, the square here representing the accomplishment of the possibilities of the cycle, which were in a germinal condition in the circular 'organic girdle' of the beginning, and are subsequently fixed and stabilized in a state of definition so to speak, at least in relation to the particular cycle concerned. This final result can also be represented as a 'crystallization', again showing affinity with the cubic form (or the square in the plane section): it becomes a 'city' with a mineral symbolism, whereas at the beginning there was a 'garden' with a vegetable symbolism, vegetation representing the elaboration of the germs in the sphere of vital assimilation.[14] Reference was made above to the immobility of minerals as being an image of the final state toward which the 'solidification' of the world is tending: but it

12. If this is compared with the correspondences previously pointed out, it might appear that there had been an inversion in the use of the two words 'Heavenly' and 'Terrestrial' and there is in fact a discrepancy, except in the following particular connection: at the beginning of the cycle, this world was not such as it is now, and the 'Terrestrial Paradise' constituted the direct projection, at that time visibly manifested, of the specifically celestial and principial form (it was besides situated in a sense at the confines of heaven and earth, since it is said that it touched the 'sphere of the Moon', that is, the 'first heaven'); at the end of the cycle, the 'Heavenly Jerusalem' descends from heaven to earth, and it is only at the end of that descent that it appears in the form of a square, because then the cyclic movement has come to a stop.

13. It is worth noting that this circle is divided up by the cross formed by the four rivers which rise at its center, thus giving exactly the figure alluded to when the relation of the circle and the square was being dealt with.

14. See *The Esoterism of Dante*.

is as well to add that in considering the 'Heavenly Jerusalem' the mineral has been regarded as already being in a 'transformed' or 'sublimated' state, for it figures as precious stones in the description of that City; that is why the fixation is only final with respect to the present cycle, and beyond the 'stopping-point' the same 'Heavenly Jerusalem' must, by virtue of the causal linkage that admits of no actual discontinuity, become the 'Terrestrial Paradise' of the future cycle, the end of the one and the beginning of the other being actually one and the same moment viewed from two opposite sides.[15]

It is nonetheless true that, if consideration is confined to the present cycle, a moment finally arrives at which 'the wheel stops turning', and here, as always, the symbolism is perfectly coherent: for a wheel is circular in shape, and if it were to get out of shape in such a way as to end by being square, it is obvious that it could not do otherwise than stop. This is why the moment in question appears as an 'end of time'; it is then, according to the Hindu tradition, that the 'twelve suns' will shine simultaneously, for time is in fact measured by the passage of the sun through the twelve signs of the zodiac, making the annual cycle, and when the rotation is stopped, the twelve corresponding aspects will so to speak be merged into one, thus returning into the essential and primordial unity of their common nature, since they do not differ except in their relation to universal manifestation, which will then be at an end.[16] Moreover, the changing of the circle into an equivalent square[17] is also what is known as the 'squaring of the circle'; those who declare that this is

15. This moment is also represented as that of the 'reversal of the poles' or as the day when 'the stars will rise in the West and set in the East', for a rotational movement appears to take place in two opposite directions according as it is looked at from one side or the other, though it is really always the same continuous movement, but seen from another point of view, corresponding to the course of a new cycle.

16. See *The King of the World*. The twelve signs of the zodiac, instead of being arranged in a circle, become the twelve gates of the 'Heavenly Jerusalem', three being placed on each side of the square, and the 'twelve suns' appear in the center of the 'city' as the twelve fruits of the 'Tree of Life'.

17. That is, a square of the same surface area, if a quantitative point of view is adopted; but this is merely a wholly exteriorized expression of what is really in question.

an insoluble problem, though they be wholly unaware of its symbolical significance, are thus right in fact, since the 'squaring' understood in its true sense cannot be realized until the end of the cycle.[18]

A consequence of all this is that the solidification of the world appears to some extent to have a double meaning: considered in itself and from within the cycle as being a consequence of a movement leading down toward quantity and 'materiality', it evidently has an 'unfavorable' significance, even a 'sinister' one, opposed to spirituality; but, in another aspect, it is nonetheless necessary in order to prepare, though it be in a manner that could be called 'negative', the ultimate fixation of the results of the cycle in the form of the 'Heavenly Jerusalem', where these results will at once become the germs of the possibilities of the future cycle. Nevertheless, it goes without saying that in the final fixation itself, and in order that it may indeed become a restoration of the 'primordial state', the immediate intervention of a transcendent principle is necessary, otherwise nothing could be saved and the 'cosmos' would simply evaporate into 'chaos'. It is this intervention that produces the final 'reversal' already prefigured by the 'transmutation' of minerals in the 'Heavenly Jerusalem', and bringing about the reappearance of the 'Terrestrial Paradise' in the visible world, where there will thereafter be 'a new heaven and a new earth', since it will be the beginning of another *Manvantara* and of the existence of another humanity.

---

18. The corresponding numerical formula is that of the Pythagorean *Tetraktys*: $1 + 2 + 3 + 4 = 10$; if the numbers are taken in the reverse order: $4 + 3 + 2 + 1$, this gives the proportions of the four *Yugas*, the sum of which is the denary, that is to say the complete and finished cycle.

21

CAIN
AND ABEL

THE 'SOLIDIFICATION' OF THE WORLD has yet other consequences not mentioned hitherto in the human and social order, for it engenders therein a state of affairs in which everything is counted, recorded, and regulated, and this is really only another kind of 'mechanization'; it is only too easy nowadays to find typical instances anywhere, such as for example the mania for census-taking (which is of course directly connected with the importance attributed to statistics),[1] and more generally, the endless multiplication of administrative interventions in all the circumstances of life. These interventions must naturally have the effect of ensuring the most complete uniformity possible between individuals, all the more so because it is almost a 'principle' of all modern administration to treat individuals as mere numerical units all exactly alike, that is, to act as if, by hypothesis, the 'ideal' of uniformity had already been realized, thus constraining all men to adjust themselves, so to speak, to the same 'average' level. In another respect,

1. Much could be said about the prohibitions formulated in certain traditions against the taking of censuses otherwise than in exceptional cases, if it were to be stated that such operations, like all those of the 'civil state' as it is called, have among other inconveniences that of contributing to the cutting down of the length of human life (and this is anyhow in conformity with the progress of the cycle, especially in its later periods), but the statement would simply not be believed; nevertheless, in some countries the most ignorant peasants know very well, as a fact of ordinary experience, that if animals are counted too often far more of them die than if they are not counted; but in the eyes of moderns who call themselves 'enlightened' such things cannot be anything but 'superstitions'.

this ever more inordinate regulation has a highly paradoxical consequence, and it is this: the growing rapidity and ease of communication between the most distant countries, thanks to the inventions of
modern industry, are matters of pride, yet at the same time every
possible obstacle is put in the way of the freedom of these communications, to the extent that it is often practically impossible to get
from one country to another, and in any case it has become much
more difficult now than it was when no mechanical means of trans-
port existed. This is another special aspect of 'solidification': in such
a world there is no longer any room for nomadic peoples such as
formerly survived in various circumstances, for these peoples gradually come to a point at which they no longer find in front of them
any free space; and in addition to this, all possible means are used to
cause them to adopt a sedentary life,[2] so that in this connection also
the time seems not to be far distant when the 'wheel will stop turning'; while in addition, within the sedentary life, the towns, representing something like the final degree of 'fixation', take on an
overwhelming importance and tend more and more to absorb
everything else;[3] this is how it comes about that, toward the end of
the cycle, Cain really and finally slays Abel.

Cain is represented in Biblical symbolism as being primarily a
farmer and Abel as a stockmaster, thus they are the types of the two
sorts of peoples who have existed since the origins of the present
humanity, or at least since the earliest differentiation took place,
namely that between the sedentary peoples, devoted to the cultiva-
tion of the soil, and the nomads, devoted to the raising of flocks and
herds.[4] It must be emphasized that these two occupations are essential and primordial in the two human types; anything else is only

2. Two particularly significant examples may be cited here: the 'Zionist' projects
as they affect the Jews, and the attempts recently made to fix the Bohemians in certain countries of Eastern Europe.

3. It must be recalled in this connection that the 'Heavenly Jerusalem' itself is
symbolically a town, which shows that in this case also there is reason to take
account of a double meaning in 'solidification'.

4. It may be added that, as Cain is said to be the elder, agriculture therefore
appears to have some kind of anteriority, indeed Adam himself is represented as having had the function of 'cultivating the garden' in the period before the fall. This is

accidental, derived, or superadded, and to speak of people as hunt-ers or fishers for example, as modern ethnologists so often do, is either to mistake the accidental for the essential, or it is to restrict attention to more or less late cases of anomaly or degeneration, such as can be met with in certain savages (but the mainly commercial or industrial peoples of the modern West are by no means less abnor-mal, though in another way).[5] Each of these two categories naturally had its own traditional law, different from that of the other, and adapted to its way of life and the nature of its occupations; this difference was particularly apparent in the sacrificial rites, hence the special mention made of the vegetable offerings of Cain and the ani-mal offerings of Abel in the account given in Genesis.[6] As Biblical symbolism in particular is now being considered, it is as well to note at once in that connection that the Hebrew *Torah* belongs properly to the type of law appropriate to nomadic peoples. Hence the way in which the story of Cain and Abel is presented, for it would appear in a different light in the eyes of a sedentary people and would be sus-ceptible of a different interpretation, although the aspects corre-sponding to the two points of view are of course both included in the profound meaning of the story; this is nothing more than an

---

also related more particularly to the vegetable symbolism in the representation of the beginning of the cycle (hence there was a symbolical and even an initiatic 'agri-culture', the very same as that which Saturn was said by the Latins to have taught to the men of the 'Golden Age'); but however that may be, all we have to consider here is the state of affairs symbolized by the opposition (which is at the same time a complementarism) between Cain and Abel, arising when the distinction between agricultural and pastoral peoples was already an established fact.

5. The names *Iran* and *Turan* have frequently been treated as if they were the names of races, but they really represented the sedentary and the nomadic peoples respectively; *Iran* or *Airyana* comes from the word *arya* (whence *ārya* by exten-sion), meaning 'laborer' (derived from the root *ar*, found again in the Latin *arare*, *arator* and also *arvum*, 'field'); and the use of the word *arya* as a title of honor (for the superior castes) is consequently characteristic of the tradition of agricultural peoples.

6. On the very special importance of the sacrifice and of the rites connected with it in the different traditional forms, see Frithjof Schuon, 'On Sacrifice', in *The Eye of the Heart* (Bloomington, IN: World Wisdom Books, 1997), and A. K. Cooma-raswamy, '*Ātmayajña*: Self-Sacrifice', in *The Door in the Sky: Coomaraswamy on Myth and Meaning* (Princeton: Princeton University Press, 1997), chap. 4.

application of the double meaning of symbols, to which some allusion was made in connection with 'solidification', since this question, as will perhaps appear more clearly from what follows, is closely bound up with the symbolism of the murder of Abel by Cain. The special character of the Hebrew tradition is also responsible for the disapproval that is brought to bear on certain arts and certain trades specially appropriate to sedentary peoples, notably on everything connected with the construction of fixed dwellings; at any rate that was the state of affairs until the time when Israel actually ceased, at least for several centuries, to be nomadic, that is, up to the time of David and Solomon, and we know that it was even then necessary to resort to foreign workers for the building of the Temple in Jerusalem.[7]

The agricultural peoples, just because they are sedentary, are naturally those who arrive sooner or later at the building of towns; indeed, it is said that the first town was founded by Cain himself; moreover its foundation did not take place till well after the time during which he is said to have been occupied in agriculture, which shows clearly that there are as it were two successive phases in 'sedentarism', the second representing a relatively more pronounced degree of fixity and spatial 'constriction' than the first. It could be said in a general way that the works of sedentary peoples are works of time: these peoples are fixed in space within a strictly limited domain, and develop their activities in a temporal continuity that appears to them to be indefinite. On the other hand, nomadic and pastoral peoples build nothing durable, and do not work for a future that escapes them; but they have space before them, not facing them with any limitation, but on the contrary always offering them new possibilities. In this way is revealed the correspondence of the cosmic principles to which, in another order, the symbolism of Cain and Abel is related: the principle of compression, represented by time, and the principle of expansion, represented by space.[8] In

---

7. The fixation of the Hebrew people was essentially dependent on the existence of the Temple in Jerusalem; as soon as the Temple was destroyed nomadism reappeared in the special form of the 'dispersion'.

8. Fabre d'Olivet's works may be consulted on this cosmological interpretation.

actual fact, both these two principles are manifested simultaneously in time and in space, as in everything else; it is necessary to point this out in order to avoid unduly 'simplified' identifications or assimilations, as well as to resolve occasional apparent oppositions; but it is no less certain that the action of the principle of compression predominates in the temporal condition, and of expansion in the spatial condition. Moreover, time uses up space, if it may be put so; and correspondingly in the course of the ages the sedentary peoples gradually absorb the nomads; this gives, as indicated above, a social and historical significance to the murder of Abel by Cain.

Nomads direct their activities particularly to the animal kingdom, mobile like themselves; sedentary peoples on the other hand direct them in the first place to the two non-mobile kingdoms, the vegetable and the mineral.[9] Furthermore, it is in the nature of things that sedentary peoples should tend to the making of visual symbols, images made up of various substances, and these images can always be related back, in their essential significance, more or less directly to the geometrical viewpoint, the origin and foundation of all spatial conception. Nomads, on the other hand, to whom images are forbidden, like everything else that might tend to attach them to some definite place, make sonorous symbols, the only symbols compatible with their state of continual migration.[10] It is, however, remarkable that, among the sensible faculties, sight is directly related to space, and hearing to time: the elements of the visual symbol occur simultaneously, and those of the sonorous symbol in succession; so that there is in this respect a kind of reversal of the

9. The use of the mineral elements includes more especially building and metallurgy; the latter will be further considered later; Biblical symbolism attributes its origin to Tubalcain, that is, to a direct descendant of Cain, and Cain's very name reappears as a constituent in the formation of his descendant's name, indicating that there is a very close connection between the two.

10. The distinction between these two fundamental categories of symbols is, in the Hindu tradition, that between the *yantra*, a figured symbol, and the *mantra*, a sonorous symbol; it naturally carries with it a corresponding distinction in the rites in which these symbolical elements are respectively used, though there is not always such a clear separation as can be conceived theoretically; in fact, every combination of the two in different proportions is possible.

relations previously considered: but this reversal is in fact necessary so that some equilibrium may be established between the two contrary principles mentioned above, and so that their respective actions may be kept within limits compatible with normal human existence. Thus the sedentary peoples create the plastic arts (architecture, sculpture, painting), the arts consisting of forms developed in space; the nomads create the phonetic arts (music, poetry), the arts consisting of forms unfolded in time; for, let us say it again, all art is in its origin essentially symbolical and ritual, and only through a late degeneration, indeed a very recent degeneration, has it lost its sacred character so as to become at last the purely profane 'recreation' to which it has been reduced among our contemporaries.[11]

Thus the complementarism of the conditions of existence is manifested in the following way: those who work for time are stabilized in space; those who wander in space are ceaselessly modified within time. And the antinomy of the 'inverse sense' appears as follows: those who live according to time, the changing and destroying element, fix and conserve themselves; those who live according to space, the fixed and permanent element, disperse themselves and change unceasingly. This must be so in order that the existence of each may remain possible, for in this way at least a relative equilibrium is established between the terms representing the two contrary tendencies; if only one or the other of the compressive and expansive tendencies were in action the end would come soon, either by 'crystallization' or by 'volatilization', if it be allowable to use symbolical expressions in this connection such as must recall the 'coagulation' and 'solution' of the alchemists; moreover these expressions do actually correspond to two phases in the present world of which the exact significance will be explained later.[12] Here indeed we find

11. It is scarcely necessary to observe that, in all the considerations now under examination, the correlative and in a way symmetrical character of the spatial and the temporal conditions, seen under their qualitative aspect, becomes clearly apparent.

12. This is why nomadism, in its 'malefic' and deviated aspect, easily comes to exercise a 'dissolving' action on everything with which it comes into contact; sedentarism on its side, and under the same aspect, must inevitably lead only toward the grossest forms of an aimless materialism.

ourselves in a domain where all the consequences of the cosmic dualities show themselves with special clarity, those dualities being more or less distant images or reflections of the primary duality, that of essence and substance, of Heaven and Earth, or *Purusha* and *Prakriti*, which generates and rules all manifestation.

To return to Biblical symbolism, the animal sacrifice is fatal to Abel,[13] and the vegetable offering of Cain was not accepted;[14] he who is blessed dies, he who lives is accursed. Equilibrium is thus broken on both sides; how can it be re-established except by exchanges such that each has its part in the productions of the other? Thus it is that movement brings together time and space, being in a way a resultant of their combination, and reconciles in them the two opposed tendencies just mentioned;[15] movement itself is moreover only a series of disequilibria, but the sum of these constitutes a relative equilibrium compatible with the law of manifestation or of 'becoming', that is to say with contingent existence itself. Every exchange between beings subject to spatial and temporal conditions is in effect a movement, or rather a combination of two inverse and reciprocal movements, which harmonize and compensate one another; in this case equilibrium is realized directly by

13. As Abel shed the blood of animals, his blood was shed by Cain; this is as it were an expression of a 'law of compensation' by virtue of which the partial disequilibria, in which the whole of manifestation consists fundamentally, are integrated in the total equilibrium.

14. It is important to note that the Hebrew Bible nevertheless admits the validity of the bloodless sacrifice considered in itself: as in the case of the sacrifice of Melchizedek, consisting in the essentially vegetable offering of bread and wine; but this is really connected with the rite of the Vedic *Soma* and the direct perpetuation of the Hebraic and 'Abrahamic' tradition and even much further back, to a period before the laws of the sedentary and nomadic peoples were distinguished; this again recalls the association of a vegetable symbolism with the 'Terrestrial Paradise', that is, with the 'primordial state' of our humanity. The acceptance of the sacrifice of Abel and the rejection of that of Cain are sometimes pictured in rather a curious symbolical way: the smoke of the former rises vertically toward the sky, whereas the smoke of the latter spreads horizontally over the surface of the earth; thus they trace respectively the altitude and the base of a triangle representing the domain of human manifestation.

15. These two tendencies are again manifested in movement itself, in the form of centripetal and centrifugal movement respectively.

virtue of the fact that this compensation exists.[16] The alternating movement of the exchanges may impinge on the three domains, spiritual (or pure intellectual), psychic, and corporeal, corresponding to the 'three worlds': the exchange of principles, of symbols, and of offerings—such is the triple foundation, in the true traditional history of terrestrial humanity, on which rests the mystery of pacts, alliances, and benedictions, basically equivalent to the sharing out of the 'spiritual influences' at work in our world; but these last considerations cannot be dwelt on, for they obviously belong to a normal state of affairs from which we are now very far removed in all respects, a state of which the modern world as such is in truth no more than the simple and direct negation.[17]

16. Equilibrium, harmony, and justice are really but three forms or aspects of one and the same thing; they could even in a certain sense be brought respectively into correspondence with the three domains shortly to be referred to, on condition of course that justice be taken in its most immediate meaning, of which in the modern world mere 'honesty' in commercial transactions represents an expression, diminished and degraded by the reduction of all things to the profane point of view and the narrow banality of 'ordinary life'.

17. The intervention of the spiritual authority in the matter of money in traditional civilizations is directly connected with what has just been said: indeed money itself is in a certain sense the very embodiment of exchange, hence a much more exact idea can be formed of the real purpose of the symbols that it bore and that therefore circulated with it, for they gave to exchange a significance quite other than is contained in its mere 'materiality', though this last is all that it retains under the profane conditions that govern the relations of peoples, no less than those of individuals, in the modern world.

22

THE SIGNIFICANCE
OF METALLURGY

WE HAVE SEEN THAT THE ARTS OR CRAFTS that involve a direction of activity toward the mineral kingdom belong properly to the sedentary peoples, and that such activities were forbidden by the traditional laws of the nomadic peoples, of which the Hebrew law is the most generally known example; it is indeed evident that these arts tend toward 'solidification', and in the corporeal world as we know it 'solidification' in fact reaches its most pronounced form in minerals as such. Moreover, minerals, in their commonest form, that of stone, are principally used in the construction of stable buildings;[1] a town, considered as the collectivity of the buildings of which it is made up, appears in particular as something like an artificial agglomeration of minerals; and it must be reiterated that life in towns represents a more complete sedentarism than does agricultural life, just as the mineral is more fixed and more 'solid' than the vegetable. But there is something more: the arts applied to minerals include metallurgy in all its forms; now the evident fact that metal tends increasingly in these days to be substituted for stone in building, just as stone was formerly substituted for wood, leads to a supposition that this change must be a symptom of a more 'advanced' phase in the downward movement of the cycle; and this supposition is confirmed by the fact that in a general way metal

---

1. It is true that among many peoples the buildings of most ancient date were of wood, but such buildings were obviously not so durable, and consequently not so fixed, as stone buildings; the use of minerals in building thus always implies a greater degree of 'solidity' in every sense of the word.

plays an ever-growing part in the 'industrialized' and 'mechanized' civilization of today, and that from a destructive point of view, if it may be so expressed, no less than from a constructive point of view, for the consumption of metal brought about by modern wars is truly prodigious.

This observation moreover is in accord with a peculiarity met with in the Hebrew tradition: from the beginning of the time when the use of stone was allowed in special cases, such as in the building of an altar, it was nevertheless specified that these stones must be 'whole', for 'you shall lift up no iron tool upon them';[2] according to the precise terms of this passage, insistence is directed not so much to the stone being unworked as to no metal being used on it: the prohibition of the use of metal was thus more especially strict in the case of anything intended to be put to a specifically ritual use.[3] Traces of this prohibition still persisted even when Israel had ceased to be nomadic and had built, or caused to be built, stable edifices: when the Temple of Jerusalem was built the stone was 'prepared at the quarry; so that neither hammer nor ax nor any tool of iron was heard in the temple, while it was being built.'[4] There is nothing at all exceptional in this, and a mass of concordant indications of the same kind could be found: for instance, in many countries a sort of partial exclusion from the community, or at least a 'holding aloof', was practiced and even still is practiced so far as metal-workers are concerned, and more particularly blacksmiths, whose craft is often associated with the practice of an inferior and dangerous kind of magic, which has eventually degenerated in most cases into mere sorcery. Nevertheless, on the other side, metallurgy has been specially revered in some traditional forms, and has even served as the

2. Deut. 27:5–6.
3. Hence the continuing employment of stone knives for the rite of circumcision as well.
4. 1 Kings 6:7. Nevertheless the Temple of Jerusalem held a large quantity of metallic objects, but their employment is connected with the other aspect of the symbolism of metals, which is twofold, as we shall see presently: it seems moreover that the prohibition ended by being to some extent 'localized', mainly against the use of iron, and iron is the very metal of all others that plays the predominant part in modern times.

basis of very important initiatic organizations; it must suffice to quote in this connection the instance of the Kabiric Mysteries, without dwelling longer at this point on a very complex subject that would lead much too far afield; all that need be said for the moment is that metallurgy has both a 'sacred' aspect and an 'execrated' aspect, and that in their origin these two aspects proceed from a twofold symbolism inherent in the metals themselves.

If this is to be understood, it must be remembered in the first place that the metals, by reason of their astral correspondences, are in a certain sense the 'planets of the lower world'; naturally therefore they must have, like the planets themselves, of which they can be said to receive and to condense the influences in the terrestrial environment, a 'benefic' aspect and a 'malefic' aspect.[5] Furthermore, since an inferior reflection is in question, corresponding to the actual situation of the metallic mines in the interior of the earth, the 'malefic' aspect must readily become predominant; and it must not be forgotten that from the traditional point of view metals and metallurgy are in direct relation with the 'subterranean fire', the idea of which is associated in many respects with that of the 'infernal regions'.[6] Nonetheless, if the metallic influences are taken in their 'benefic' aspect by making use of them in a manner truly 'ritual', in the most complete sense of the word, they are susceptible of 'transmutation' and 'sublimation', and are then all the more capable of becoming a spiritual 'support', since whatever is at the lowest level corresponds, by inverse analogy, to what is at the highest level; the

5. In the Zoroastrian tradition it seems that the planets were envisaged almost exclusively as 'malefic'; this may be the result of a point of view peculiar to that tradition, but in any case all that is known about what still remains of Zoroastrianism consists only of fragments so mutilated that it is not possible to form any exact judgment on such questions.

6. As concerns the relationship to the 'subterranean fire', the obvious resemblance of the name of Vulcan to that of the Biblical name Tubalcain is particularly significant: moreover they are both said to have been smiths; and while on the subject of smiths it may be added that the association of their craft with the 'infernal regions' sufficiently explains what was said above about its 'sinister' aspect. The Kabires, on the other hand, while they too were smiths, had a dual aspect both celestial and terrestrial, bringing them into relationship both with the metals and the corresponding planets.

whole mineral symbolism of alchemy is based on this very fact, and so is the symbolism of the ancient Kabiric initiations.[7] On the other hand, when nothing is in question but the profane utilization of metals, in view of the fact that the profane point of view as such necessarily brings with it the cutting off of all communication with superior principles, nothing is then left that is capable of effective action save the 'malefic' side of the metallic influences, and this will develop all the more strongly because it will inevitably be isolated from everything that could restrain it or counterbalance it; this particular instance of an exclusively profane utilization is clearly one that is realized in all its fullness in the modern world.[8]

The point of view adopted so far has been mainly concerned with the 'solidification' of the world, having as its end-point nothing other than the 'reign of quantity', of which the use of metals is only an aspect, this being the point of view that has actually been most obviously manifested in all fields up to the phase at which the world has arrived today. But things can go further yet, and the metals, by virtue of the subtle influences attached to them, can also play a part in a later phase leading more directly to the final dissolution. During the course of the period that may be called 'materialistic', these subtle influences have undoubtedly passed more or less into a latent state, like everything else that is outside the limits of the purely corporeal order; but this does not mean that they have ceased to exist, nor even that they have entirely ceased to act, though in a hidden manner, of which the 'satanic' side of 'mechanistic' theory and practice, especially (but not solely) in its destructive applications, is after all but a manifestation, though naturally the materialists can have

7. It should be stated that alchemy properly so called did not go beyond the 'intermediary world' and held to a point of view that may be called 'cosmological', but its symbolism was nonetheless capable of being transposed so as to give it a truly spiritual and initiatic value.

8. The case of money, as it stands today, can also serve as a typical example: deprived of everything that was able, in traditional civilizations, to make it as it were a vehicle of 'spiritual influences', not only is it now reduced to being in itself no more than a mere 'material' and quantitative emblem, but also it can no longer play a part that is otherwise than truly nefarious and 'satanic', and it is all too easy to see that such indeed is the part it plays in our time.

no suspicion of the fact. These same influences then need only wait for a favorable opportunity to assert their activity more openly, of course always in the same 'malefic' direction, because so far as 'benefic' influences are concerned the world has so to speak been closed to them by the profane attitude of modernity: moreover their opportunity may no longer be very far distant, for the instability that nowadays continues to increase in every domain shows clearly that the point corresponding to the greatest effective predominance of 'solidity' and 'materiality' has already been passed.

It may facilitate the understanding of what has just been said if it is pointed out that, according to traditional symbolism, the metals are in relation not only with the 'subterranean fire' as already indicated, but also with the 'hidden treasure', all these matters being rather closely interwoven, for reasons that cannot possibly be developed here, but that can go some way toward explaining how it is that human interventions are capable of provoking, or more exactly of 'releasing', certain natural cataclysms. However that may be, all the 'legends' (using the language of today) about these 'treasures' show clearly that their 'guardians', who are none other than the subtle influences attached to them, are psychic 'entities' that it is extremely dangerous for anyone to approach who has not got the required 'qualifications' and does not take the necessary precautions; but what precautions could the moderns, completely ignorant of such matters, in fact be expected to take in this matter? They are all too obviously lacking in any 'qualification', as well as in any means of action in the domain in question, for it eludes them in consequence of the attitude they adopt toward anything and everything. True enough, they constantly boast about 'conquering the forces of nature', but they are certainly far from suspecting that behind these same forces, which they look upon as being exclusively corporeal, there is something of another order, of which the apparent forces are really but the vehicles and as it were the outward likenesses; it is this other thing that might well one day revolt and finally turn against those who have failed to recognize it.

It will be as well to add here incidentally a further note on something that may perhaps seem to be only a singularity or a curiosity, but will furnish the occasion for some further remarks later: the 'guardians of the hidden treasure', who are at the same time the smiths working in the 'subterranean fire', are represented in the different 'legends' sometimes as giants and sometimes as dwarfs. Something of the kind is also found in the case of the Kabires, and this shows that this category of symbolism is, like others, capable of being applied so as to relate it to a superior order; but owing to the conditions of our own period, it is necessary to adhere to a point of view from which only what may be called its 'infernal' aspect can be seen; in other words, the said conditions are no more than an expression of influences belonging to the inferior and 'tenebrous' side of what may be called the 'cosmic psychism'; and, as will appear more clearly as this study proceeds, influences of this sort, in their multitudinous forms, are today actively threatening the 'solidity' of the world.

To complete this short summary, one more point related to the 'malefic' aspect of the influence of metals must be mentioned, and that is the frequent prohibition of the carrying of metallic objects while certain rites are being accomplished, both in the case of exoteric rites,[9] and in the case of initiatic rites properly so called.[10] The character of all rules of this kind is no doubt principally symbolical, and from that character they derive their profound significance; but it is important not to lose sight of the fact that the truly traditional symbolism (which must on no account be confused with the false

9. This prohibition is in force, at least in principle, notably in the Islamic rites of pilgrimage, though in fact it is no longer strictly observed today; furthermore, anyone who has accomplished these rites in their entirety, including that part of them that constitutes their most 'interior' aspect, must thenceforth abstain from all work involving the use of fire, and this includes more particularly the work of blacksmiths and metallurgists.

10. In Western initiations this takes the form, in the ritual preparation of the recipient, of what is designated as the 'stripping of metals'. It could be said that in a case of this kind the metals, apart from their real power to affect adversely the transmission of 'spiritual influences', are taken as representing more or less what the Hebrew Kabbalah calls the 'rinds' or the 'shells' (*qlippoth*), meaning all that is most inferior in the subtle domain, thus constituting, if the expression be allowable, the infra-corporeal 'pit' of our world.

interpretations and counterfeits to which the moderns sometimes wrongly apply these words)[11] always has an effective meaning, and that its ritual applications in particular have perfectly real effects, although the narrowly limited faculties of modern man can rarely perceive them. This is not a question of vaguely 'idealistic' notions, but on the contrary concerns things of which the reality is sometimes manifested in a more or less 'tangible' way; if that were not the case, what would be the explanation of the fact that there are people who, when they are in a particular spiritual state, cannot endure the least contact, even indirect, with metals, and that this is so even if the contact has been brought about without their knowledge and in conditions such that it is impossible that they should be aware of it through their bodily senses, thereby necessarily excluding the psychological and over-simplified explanation of 'auto-suggestion'?[12] It can further be stated that a contact of this kind can in comparable cases go so far as to produce outwardly the physiological effects of a real burn, and it must be admitted that such facts ought to provide material for reflection, if the moderns were still capable of anything of the kind; but the profane and materialistic attitude and the prejudices arising out of it have plunged them into an incurable blindness.

11. Thus, those who in the first half of the nineteenth century wrote 'histories of religion' invented something to which they applied the word 'symbolical', which was a system of interpretation having only a very remote connection with true symbolism; as for merely literary misuses of the word 'symbolism', they are evidently not worth the trouble of mentioning.

12. The case of Shri Ramakrishna can be cited as a known example.

23

TIME CHANGED
INTO SPACE

IN AN EARLIER CHAPTER it was stated that in a certain sense time consumes space, and that it does so in consequence of the power of contraction contained in it, which tends continuously to reduce the spatial expansion to which it is opposed: but time, in its active opposition to the antagonistic principle, unfolds itself with ever-growing speed, for it is far from being homogenous, as people who consider it solely from a quantitative point of view imagine, but on the contrary it is 'qualified' at every moment in a different way by the cyclical conditions of the manifestation to which it belongs. The acceleration of time is becoming more apparent than ever in our day, because it becomes exaggerated in the final periods of a cycle, but it nevertheless actually goes on constantly from the beginning of the cycle to the end: it can therefore be said not only that time compresses space, but also that time is itself subject to a progressive contraction, appearing in the proportionate shortening of the four *Yugas*, with all that this implies, not excepting the corresponding diminution in the length of human life. It is sometimes said, doubt-less without any understanding of the real reason, that today men live faster than in the past, and this is literally true; the haste with which the moderns characteristically approach everything they do being ultimately only a consequence of the confused impressions they experience.

If carried to its extreme limit the contraction of time would in the end reduce it to a single instant, and then duration would really have ceased to exist, for it is evident that there can no longer be any succession within the instant. Thus it is that 'time the devourer ends by devouring itself', in such a way that, at the 'end of the world', that is to say at the extreme limit of cyclical manifestation, 'there will be no more time'; this is also why it is said that 'death is the last being to die', for wherever there is no succession of any kind death is no longer possible.[1] As soon as succession has come to an end, or, in symbolical terms, 'the wheel has ceased to turn', all that exists cannot but be in perfect simultaneity; succession is thus as it were transformed into simultaneity, and this can also be expressed by saying that 'time has been changed into space'.[2] Thus a 'reversal' takes place at the last, to the disadvantage of time and to the advantage of space: at the very moment when time seemed on the point of finally devouring space, space in its turn absorbs time; and this, in terms of the cosmological meaning of the Biblical symbolism, can be said to be the final revenge of Abel on Cain.

There is a sort of 'prefiguration' of the absorption of time by space, of which its authors are no doubt quite unconscious, in the recent physico-mathematical theories that treat the 'space-time' complex as a single and indivisible whole, these theories incidentally usually being interpreted inaccurately, when they are regarded as treating time as if it were a 'fourth dimension' of space. It would be more correct to say that time is treated as being comparable to a 'fourth dimension' only in the sense that in equations of movement it plays the part of a fourth coordinate added to the three representing the three dimensions of space; and it is important to note that this implies the geometrical representation of time in a rectilinear

1. Nevertheless, since Yama is designated in Hindu tradition as the 'first death", and is assimilated to 'Death' itself (*Mṛtyu*), or, if the language of the Islamic tradition is preferred, to the 'Angel of Death', it will be seen that in this as in so many other cases the 'first' and the 'last' meet and become more or less identified through the correspondence between the two extremities of the cycle.

2. Wagner wrote in *Parsifal*: 'Here, time is changed into space,' the place referred to being Montsalvat, which represents the 'center of the world' (this point will be returned to shortly); there is however little likelihood that he really understood the profound meaning of the words, for he scarcely seems to deserve the reputation of being an 'esoterist' attributed to him by some people; everything really esoteric found in his works properly belongs to the 'legends' used by him, the meaning of which he all too often merely diminished.

form, the insufficiency of which has previously been pointed out, though it could not be otherwise in theories so purely quantitative in character as those in question. But this last statement, while it corrects up to a certain point the 'popular' explanation, is nevertheless still inexact. In reality, that which plays the part of a fourth coordinate is not time, but something that the mathematicians call 'imaginal time';[3] and this expression, itself no more than a singularity of language arising from the use of an entirely 'conventional' notation, here takes on a rather unexpected significance. Indeed, to say that time must become 'imaginal' in order to become assimilable to a fourth dimension of space, is really and truly as much as to say that what must happen is that time should actually cease to exist as such, or in other words that the transmutation of time into space is in fact only realizable at the 'end of the world'.[4]

The conclusion may be drawn that it is quite useless to look for anything that might be a 'fourth dimension' of space under the conditions of the present world, and this has at least the advantage that it cuts short all the 'neo-spiritualist' divagations briefly referred to earlier; but is it necessary also to conclude that the absorption of time by space must necessarily take the form of the addition of a supplementary dimension to space, or is that too only a 'figure of speech'? All that it is possible to say about this is that when the expansive tendency of space is no longer opposed and restrained by the compressive tendency of time, then space must naturally, in one way or another, undergo a dilatation such as will raise its indefinity to a higher power;[5] but it should scarcely be necessary to add that this occurrence cannot be represented by any image borrowed from the corporeal domain. Indeed, since time is one of the determining conditions of corporeal existence, it is evident that its suppression is

3. In other words, if the three coordinates of space are x, y, and z, the fourth coordinate is not t, which designates time, but the expression $t\sqrt{-1}$.

4. It is of interest to note that, although the 'end of the world' is commonly spoken of as the 'end of time', it is never spoken of as the 'end of space'; this observation might seem insignificant to those who only see things superficially, nonetheless it is actually very significant.

5. On the successive powers of the indefinite, see *The Symbolism of the Cross*, chap. 12.

by itself sufficient to cause everything to be taken right out of the
world; the being is then in what has been called elsewhere an extra-
corporeal 'prolongation' of the same individual state of existence as
that of which the corporeal world represents but a mere modality:
this also serves to indicate that the end of the corporeal world is by
no means the end of the said state of existence considered in its integrality. Furthermore, the end of a cycle such as that of the present
humanity is really only the end of the corporeal world itself in quite
a relative sense, and only in relation to the possibilities that have
been included in the cycle and so have completed their development
in corporeal mode; but in reality the corporeal world is not annihilated, but 'transmuted', and it immediately receives a new existence,
because, beyond the 'stopping-point' corresponding to the unique
instant at which time is no more, 'the wheel begins to turn again for
the accomplishment of another cycle'.

Another important consequence arising from these considerations is that the end of the cycle as well as its beginning is 'intem-
poral', and this is necessarily so because of the strict analogical
correspondence existing between the two extreme points; thus it
comes about that the end is in fact the restoration of the 'primordial
state for the humanity of the cycle in question', and this also makes
clear the symbolical relation of the 'Heavenly Jerusalem' to the 'Terrestrial Paradise'. It is also a return to the 'center of the world', the
exterior manifestation of the center taking the forms, at either end
of the cycle, of the 'Terrestrial Paradise' and the 'Heavenly Jerusalem' respectively, with the 'axial' tree growing in the middle of both
the one and the other. During the whole interval between the two,
that is, during the course of the cycle, the center is however hidden,
becoming indeed more and more so, because humanity has moved
gradually away from it, and this is fundamentally the real meaning
of the 'fall'. The conception of a movement away from the center is
only another way of representing the descending course of the cycle,
for the center of a state such as ours, being the point of direct communication with superior states, is at the same time the essential
pole of existence for that state; a movement from essence toward
substance is thus a movement from the center toward the circum-
ference, from the interior toward the exterior, and also, as is clearly

shown in this case by the geometrical representation, from unity toward multiplicity.[6]

The *Pardes*, inasmuch as it is the 'center of the world', is, according to the primary meaning of its Sanskrit equivalent *paradesha*, the 'supreme region', but it is also, according to a secondary meaning of the same word, the 'distant region', ever since it has become, in the course of cyclical development, actually inaccessible to ordinary humanity. It is in fact, at least apparently, the most distant of all things, being situated at the 'end of the world' both in the spatial sense (the summit of the mountain of the 'Terrestrial Paradise' touching the lunar sphere) and in the temporal sense (the 'Heavenly Jerusalem' descending to the earth at the end of the cycle); nevertheless, it is always in reality the nearest of all things, since it has never ceased to be at the center of all things,[7] and this brings out the inversion of relationship between the 'exterior' and 'interior' points of view. Only, in order that this proximity may be actually realized, the temporal condition must necessarily be suppressed, because it is the unfolding of time in conformity with the laws of manifestation that has brought about the apparent separation from the center, and also because time, according to the very definition of succession, cannot turn back on its course; release from the temporal condition is always possible for certain beings in particular, but as far as humanity (or more exactly a humanity) taken in its entirety is concerned, a release from time obviously implies that the said humanity has passed completely through the cycle of its corporeal manifestation: only then can it, together with the whole of the terrestrial environment that depends on it and participates in the same cyclic movement, be really reintegrated into the 'primordial state', or, what is the same thing, into the 'center of the world'. This center is where

6. Another significance of the 'inversion of the poles' can be deduced from this, since the course of the manifested world toward its substantial pole ends at last in a 'reversal', which brings it back, by an instantaneous transmutation, to its essential pole; and it may be added that, in view of this instantaneity, and contrary to certain erroneous conceptions of the cyclical movement, there can be no 'reascent' of an exterior order following the 'descent', the course of manifestation as such being always descending from the beginning to the end.

7. This is the *Regnum Dei intra vos est* of the Gospel.

'time is changed into space', because it is where the direct reflection in our state of existence of the principial eternity is found, and thereby all succession is excluded: moreover death cannot attain thereto, so that it is also the very 'seat of immortality';[8] all things appear therein in perfect simultaneity in a changeless present, through the power of the 'third eye' with which man has recovered the 'sense of eternity'.[9]

8. On the 'seat of immortality' and what corresponds to it in the human being, see *The King of the World*.

9. On the symbolism of the 'third eye', see *Man and His Becoming according to the Vedānta* and *The King of the World*.

24

TOWARD
DISSOLUTION

HAVING GIVEN SOME ATTENTION to the end of the cycle, it is now necessary as it were to turn back again, in order to examine more fully the causes that can, under the conditions of the present period, play an effective part in leading humanity and the world toward that end. Two contributing tendencies may be distinguished, and their description involves the use of terms suggesting an apparent antinomy: on one side is the tendency toward what has been called the 'solidification' of the world, and it is this that has been mainly considered so far, and on the other side is the tendency toward the dissolution of the world, and it remains to examine in detail the action of the latter, for it must not be forgotten that every such end necessarily takes one form and one only, that of a dissolution of the manifested as such. Let it be said at once that the second of the two tendencies now seems to be beginning to predominate; for, in the first place, materialism properly so called, corresponding as it clearly does to 'solidification' in its grossest form (the word 'petrifaction' could almost be used, by analogy with what minerals represent in this connection), has already lost much ground, at least in the domain of scientific and philosophical theory, if not yet in that of the common mentality; and this is so far true that, as pointed out earlier, the very notion of 'matter' as it existed in these theories has begun to fade away and to dissolve. In the second place, and correlatively to this change, the illusion of security that held sway at the time when materialism had attained its greatest influence, and that was then more or less inseparable from the prevailing idea of 'ordinary life', has in the main been dissipated by the events that have taken place and the speed of their succession, so much so that the dominant impression today is very different, for it has become an impression of instability extending to all domains. Since 'solidity' necessarily implies stability, this again shows clearly that the point of greatest effective 'solidity' within the possibilities of our world has not only been reached, but has also already been passed, and consequently that dissolution is the goal toward which the world will be traveling henceforth.

The acceleration of time itself, as it becomes ever more pronounced and causes changes to be ever more rapid, seems to lead of its own accord toward dissolution, but it cannot for that reason be said that the general direction of events has been modified, for the cyclical movement inevitably continues to follow the same descending course. Moreover, the physical theories just referred to, while they too change with growing rapidity like everything else, continue nonetheless to take on a more and more exclusively quantitative character, to such a point that their character has now become assimilated to that of purely mathematical theories, and this change, as previously indicated, takes them yet further away from the sensible reality that they claim to explain, and leads them into a domain that is necessarily situated on a lower plane than that of sensible reality, as was explained earlier when pure quantity was under consideration. In any case, the 'solid', even at its greatest conceivable density and impenetrability, by no means corresponds to pure quantity, having always at least a minimum of qualitative elements; it is moreover corporeal by definition, and is even in a sense the most corporeal thing possible; now 'corporeality' is by definition such that space, however 'compressed' it may be under the conditions appertaining to a 'solid', is necessarily inherent in its constitution, and space, let it be recalled again, can in no way be assimilated to pure quantity. Even if the point of view of modern science were to be adopted momentarily, so that on the one hand 'corporeality' could be reduced to extension in accordance with Descartes' ideas, and on the other hand space could be regarded as nothing but a mere mode of quantity, the difficulty still remaining would be that everything would be still be in the domain of continuous quantity;

a change to the domain of discontinuous quantity, that is, of number, which alone can be looked upon as representing pure quantity, must then obviously imply, by reason of the said discontinuity alone, that neither the 'solid', nor anything else that is corporeal, can subsequently be taken into account.

A point is therefore reached in the gradual reduction of everything to the quantitative at which this reduction no longer leads toward 'solidification', and at this point there arises a desire to assimilate continuous quantity to discontinuous quantity. Bodies can then no longer persist as such, but are dissolved into a sort of 'atomic' dust without cohesion; it would therefore be possible to speak of a real 'pulverization' of the world, and such is evidently one of the possible forms of cyclic dissolution.[1] Nevertheless, although dissolution can be envisaged in this way from a certain point of view, it also appears from another point of view, and in accordance with a mode of expression made use of earlier, as a 'volatilization'. 'Pulverization', however complete it may be imagined to be, always leaves 'residues', even though they may be really impalpable; but as against this, the end of the cycle, if it is to be fully accomplished, implies that everything that is comprised in the cycle disappears completely insofar as it was manifested; these two different conceptions however each represent a part of the truth. Indeed, the positive results of cyclical manifestation are 'crystallized' in order that they may then be 'transmuted' into the germs of the possibilities of the future cycle, and this constitutes the end-point of 'solidification' under its 'benefic' aspect (implying essentially the 'sublimation' that coincides with the final 'reversal'), whereas whatever cannot be used in this way, that is to say, broadly speaking, whatever constitutes the purely negative results of the particular manifestation, is 'precipitated' in the form of a *caput mortuum* in the alchemist's sense of the word, into the most inferior 'prolongations' of our state of existence,

---

1. *Solvet saeclum in favilla* are the exact words of the Catholic liturgy, which incidentally calls upon both the testimony of David and that of the Sibyl in this matter, and this in itself is one of the ways in which the unanimous agreement of the different traditions is confirmed.

or into that part of the subtle domain that can properly be qualified as 'infra-corporeal';[2] but in either case a passage has taken place into extra-corporeal modalities, respectively superior and inferior, in such a way that it can be said that corporeal manifestation itself, so far as the particular cycle is concerned, has really disappeared completely or has been 'volatilized'. It can be seen that it is always necessary at all stages up to the very last to bear in mind the two terms corresponding to what are called in Hermetism 'coagulation' and 'solution', and to do so from two sides at once: thus on the 'benefic' side are 'crystallization' and 'sublimation', and on the 'malefic' side are 'precipitation' and the final return to the indistinction of 'chaos'.[3]

At this point, the following question must be put: in order that dissolution may be fully realized, is it sufficient that the movement by which the 'reign of quantity' asserts itself with ever-growing intensity should be more or less left to itself, and be allowed to pursue its own course right up to its final goal? The truth is that such a possibility, which has indeed already been suggested in what has been said about the contemporary conceptions of the physicists and the implications they carry as it were unconsciously (for it is obvious that modern 'scientists' have no idea where they are going), belongs rather to a theoretical outlook on the situation, a 'unilateral' outlook affording only a very partial view of what must really happen. Actually, in order to undo the 'knots' resulting from the 'solidification' that has been going on up till now (and the word 'knots' is used intentionally, as it suggests the effects of a certain kind of 'coagulation' particularly connected with the realm of magic) the intervention of something more directly effective for the purpose in view is required, and this something must no longer belong to the domain, the very restricted domain, to which the 'reign of quantity' itself properly belongs. It is easy to perceive, from the occasional

2. This is what the Hebrew Kabbalah, as was pointed out earlier, calls the 'world of rinds' (*ōlam qlippoth*); into this the 'ancient kings of Edom' fall, inasmuch as they represent the unusable residues of past *Manvantaras*.

3. It should be evident that the two sides here referred to as 'benefic' and 'malefic' correspond exactly to the 'right' and 'left' sides on which the 'elect' and the damned respectively are drawn up in the 'Last Judgment', which is nothing other than the final 'discrimination' of the results of cyclical manifestation.

indications already given, that the action of influences of the subtle order is involved; such action really began long ago to operate in the modern world, although at first it did so in no very apparent manner, and it has actually always co-existed with materialism from the very moment at which the latter was first constituted in a clearly defined form, as was indicated earlier when dealing with magnetism and spiritualism, and the borrowings they have made from the scientific 'mythology' of the period in which they came to birth. As has also been pointed out before, though it be true that the hold of materialism is slackening, there is no occasion to rejoice at the fact, for cyclical manifestation is not yet complete, and the 'fissures' then alluded to, the nature of which will shortly receive further consideration, can only be produced from below; in other words, that which 'interferes' with the sensible world through those 'fissures' can be nothing but an inferior 'cosmic psychism' in its most destructive and disorganizing forms, and it is moreover clear that influences of this kind are the only ones that are really suited for action having dissolution as its objective. It is not difficult to see that thenceforth everything that tends to favor and to extend these 'interferences' merely corresponds, whether consciously or otherwise, to a fresh phase of the deviation of which materialism in reality represented a less 'advanced' stage, even though the outward appearances of things may not seem to support this view, appearances often being highly deceptive.

While on this subject it seems desirable to point out that ill-informed 'traditionalists'[4] thoughtlessly rejoice at seeing modern science in its various branches escaping to some extent from the narrow limits within which its conceptions have been enclosed up till now, and taking an attitude less grossly materialistic than that maintained in the last century; they are even ready to suppose that in some way or another profane science will in the end be reunited with traditional science (of which their knowledge is minimal in extent and singularly inaccurate, being chiefly based on modern

---

4. The word 'traditionalism' denotes only a tendency that may be more or less vague and often wrongly applied, because it does not imply any effective knowledge of traditional truths; this matter will again be referred to later.

deformations and 'counterfeits'), but this, for reasons of principle that have often been insisted on, is quite impossible. These same 'traditionalists' also rejoice, perhaps even more unreservedly, at seeing certain manifestations of subtle influences coming more and more into the open, but it does not occur to them to wonder what in the end may prove to be the true 'quality' of these influences (perhaps they do not even suspect that there is any occasion to ask such a question); and they base great hopes on what today is called 'metapsychics' as the key to the cure of the ills of the modern world, which they are usually content to attribute exclusively to materialism as such, this again being a rather unfortunate delusion. What they do not see (and in this they are much more influenced than they think by the modern spirit with all the insufficiencies inherent in it) is that they are really faced with a fresh stage in the development, perfectly logical but of a logic truly 'diabolical', of the 'plan' according to which the progressive deviation of the modern world is brought about. In this 'plan' materialism has of course played its part, and undeniably a highly important part, but the mere negation that it represents has now become inadequate. It has given efficient service in denying to man access to possibilities of a superior order, but it has not the power to unchain the inferior forces that alone can bring to finality the work of disorder and dissolution.

The materialistic attitude, because of its inherent limitations, involves risks that are similarly limited; its 'thickness', figuratively speaking, protects anyone who persists in holding to it from all subtle influences without distinction, and confers on him a sort of immunity more or less like that of a mollusc living firmly enclosed in its shell, the materialist deriving from this immunity the impression of security previously referred to. The shell may be taken to represent the aggregate of conventionally recognized scientific conceptions and of the corresponding mental habits, together with the 'hardening' of the 'psycho-physiological' constitution of the individual which they produce,[5] and if an opening is made in this shell from below, as described earlier, the destructive subtle influences

5. It is of interest to note that the expression 'hardened materialist' is freely used in current speech, doubtless without any suspicion that it is no mere figure of speech, but actually corresponds to something very real.

will at once make their way in, and they will do so all the more easily because, thanks to the negative work accomplished in the preceding phase, no element of a superior order will be able to intervene in such a way as to counteract them. It could also be said that the period of materialism constitutes no more than a sort of preparation, predominantly theoretical, whereas the period of inferior psychism introduces a 'pseudo-realization' leading in exactly the opposite direction to that of true spiritual realization, but a fuller explanation of this last point must await a later chapter. The paltry security of 'ordinary life', which was the inseparable accompaniment of materialism, is indeed from now onward seriously threatened, and it will no doubt soon be seen more and more clearly, and by more and more people, as having been a mere delusion; but what advantage can this perception bring, if its sole result is an immediate fall into another delusion, worse and more dangerous from every point of view, because it involves consequences much more extensive and more profound? This other delusion is that of an 'inverted spirituality', and the various 'neo-spiritualist' movements that have arisen and reached a certain development in our times, not excepting those which already show a more definitely 'subversive' character, still represent no more than a weak and tentative prelude to it.

25

THE FISSURES
IN THE GREAT WALL

HOWEVER FAR THE 'SOLIDIFICATION' of the sensible world may have gone, it can never be carried so far as to turn the world into a 'closed system' such as is imagined by the materialists. The very nature of things sets limits to 'solidification', and the more nearly those limits are approached the more unstable is the corresponding state of affairs; in actual fact, as we have seen, the point corresponding to a maximum of 'solidification' has already been passed, and the impression that the world is a 'closed system' can only from now onward become more and more illusory and inadequate to the reality. 'Fissures' have been mentioned previously as being the paths whereby certain destructive forces are already entering, and must continue to enter ever more freely; according to traditional symbolism these 'fissures' occur in the 'Great Wall' that surrounds the world and protects it from the intrusion of malefic influences coming from the inferior subtle domain.[1] In order that this symbolism may be fully understood in all its aspects, it is important to note that a wall acts both as a protection and as a limitation: in a sense therefore it can be said to have both advantages and inconveniences;

---

1. In the symbolism of the Hindu tradition the 'Great Wall' is the circular mountain *Lokāloka*, which divides the 'cosmos' (*loka*) from the 'outer darkness' (*aloka*); and this symbolism is of course susceptible of analogical application either to more extensive or to less extensive domains within the totality of cosmic manifestation, hence the special application now being made with respect to the corporeal world alone.

but insofar as its principal purpose is to ensure an adequate defence against attacks coming from below, the advantages are incomparably the more important, for it is on the whole more useful to anyone who happens to be enclosed within its perimeter to be kept out of reach of what is below, than it is to be continuously exposed to the ravages of the enemy, or worse still to a more or less complete destruction. In any case, a walled space as such is not closed in at the top, so that communication with superior domains is not prevented, and this state of affairs is the normal one; but in the modern period the 'shell' with no outlet built by materialism has cut off that communication. Moreover, as already explained, because the 'descent' has not yet come to an end, the 'shell' must necessarily remain intact overhead, that is, in the direction of that from which humanity need not be protected since on the contrary only beneficient influences can come that way; the 'fissures' occur only at the base, and therefore in the actual protective wall itself, and the inferior forces that make their way in through them meet with a much reduced resistance because under such conditions no power of a superior order can intervene in order to oppose them effectively. Thus the world is exposed defenceless to all the attacks of its enemies, the more so because, the present-day mentality being what it is, the dangers that threaten it are wholly unperceived.

In the Islamic tradition these 'fissures' are those by which, at the end of the cycle, the devastating hordes of Gog and Magog will force their way in,[2] for they are unremitting in their efforts to invade this world; these 'entities' represent the inferior influences in question. They are considered as maintaining an underground existence, and are described both as giants and as dwarfs; they may thus be identified, in accordance with what was said earlier on the subject, and at least in certain connections, with the 'guardians of the hidden treasure' and with the smiths of the 'subterranean fire', who have, it may be recalled, an exceedingly malefic aspect; in all such symbolisms the same kind of 'infra-corporeal' subtle influences are really always

---

2. In the Hindu tradition they are the demons *Koka* and *Vikoka*, whose names are obviously similar.

involved.[3] If the truth be told, the attempts of these 'entities' to insinuate themselves into the corporeal and human world are no new thing, for they go back at least to somewhere near the beginning of the *Kali-Yuga*, a period far more remote than that of 'classical' antiquity, by which the horizon of profane historians is bounded. In this connection, the Chinese tradition relates in symbolical terms that 'Niu-koua [sister and wife of Fu Hsi, who is said to have reigned jointly with him] melted stones of five colors[4] in order to repair a tear in the sky made by a giant' (apparently, though it is not made quite clear, the tear was situated on the terrestrial horizon);[5] and this took place at a period not more than a few centuries after the beginning of the *Kali-Yuga*.

Nevertheless, although the *Kali-Yuga* as a whole is intrinsically a period of obscuration, so that 'fissures' have been possible ever since it began, the degree of obscuration pervading its later phases is far from having been attained at once, and that is why 'fissures' could be repaired relatively easily in earlier times; it was nonetheless necessary to maintain a constant vigilance against them, and this task was naturally among those assigned to the spiritual centers of the various traditions. Later on there came a period when, as a consequence of the extreme 'solidification' of the world, these same 'fissures' were much less to be feared, at least temporarily; this period corresponds to the first part of modern times, the part that can be defined as

---

3. The symbolism of the 'subterranean world' is twofold, and, as in other cases, it also has a superior meaning, a point more particularly explained in some of the considerations set out in *The King of the World*; but naturally only the inferior meaning is here in question, a meaning which could be said to be literally 'infernal'.

4. These five colors are white, black, blue, red, and yellow, corresponding in the Far-Eastern tradition to the five elements, as well as to the four cardinal points and the center.

5. It is also stated that 'Niu-Koua cut off the four feet of the tortoise to put the four extremities of the world in their place,' so as to stabilize the earth; reference to what was said earlier about the analogical correspondences between Fu Hsi and Niu-koua will make it clear that the function of ensuring the stability and 'solidity' of the world belongs, according to this symbolism, to the substantial side of manifestation, and this agrees exactly with all the explanations given in this book on that subject. [Guénon provides no references in his French text for these citations regarding Niu-koua, but see *Symbols of Sacred Science*, chap. 20. ED.]

being characteristically mechanistic and materialistic, in which the 'closed system' alluded to was most nearly realized, at least to the extent that any such thing is actually possible. Nowadays, that is to say in the period which can be called the second part of modern times and which has already begun, conditions are certainly very different from the conditions obtaining in all earlier periods: not only can 'fissures' occur more and more extensively, and be much more serious in character, because a greater proportion of the descending course of manifestation has been accomplished, but also the possibilities of repairing them are not the same as they used to be; the action of the spiritual centers has indeed become ever more enclosed, because the superior influences that they normally transmit to our world can no longer be manifested externally, since they are held back by the 'shell' alluded to above; and when the whole of the human and cosmic order is in such a condition, where could a means of defence possibly be found such as might be effective in any way against the 'hordes of Gog and Magog'?

But that is not all: what has been said so far covers so to speak only the negative side of the growing difficulties encountered by all attempts to oppose the intrusion of malefic influences, among these difficulties being a sort of inertia resulting from the general ignorance of such matters, and from 'survivals' of the materialistic mentality and of the outlook it engenders; this inertia may endure longer than it otherwise would because the outlook in question has become more or less instinctive in the moderns and is now incorporated in their very nature. Of course a majority of 'spiritualists' and even of 'traditionalists', or of people who call themselves such, are in fact quite as materialistic as other people when matters of this kind are in question, so that the situation is made even more irremediable by the fact that those who most sincerely want to combat the modern spirit are almost all unwittingly affected by it, and all their efforts are therefore condemned to remain without any appreciable result; for these are matters in which goodwill is far from being sufficient; effective knowledge being needed as well, indeed, more needed than anything else. But effective knowledge is the very thing that is made impossible by the influence of the modern spirit with all its limitations, even in the case of those who might have some intellectual capabilities of the required kind if conditions were less abnormal.

But apart from all these negative elements, the difficulties now under review have an aspect that can be called positive, and this may be taken to include everything in our world as we know it that is actively favorable to the intervention of subtle influences of an inferior kind, whether its work be done consciously or unconsciously. The logical sequence here would be to consider in the first place the more or less 'determining' part played by the actual agents of the whole modern deviation, since the intervention of inferior influences really represents a new phase in the said deviation, and fits in exactly with the sequence of the 'plan' by which it is brought about; it would clearly be necessary to seek in some such direction for the conscious auxiliaries of the malefic forces, though the extent to which they are individually conscious of what they are doing may actually differ greatly in particular cases. As for the other auxiliaries, those who act in good faith then, because they know nothing of the true nature of the forces involved (thanks to the recently mentioned influence of the modern spirit) are never anything but mere dupes, though this does not prevent their activity from being proportional to their sincerity and to their blindness; these auxiliaries are already virtually numberless, and they can be placed in many categories, ranging from the ingenuous adherents of all sorts of 'neo-spiritualist' organizations to the 'intuitionist' philosophers, by way of the 'metapsychical' scientists and the psychologists of the more recent schools. This matter need not be pursued any further for the moment, for to do so would be to anticipate what will come later; in the meantime some examples must be given of some of the ways in which 'fissures' can actually be brought about, also of the 'supports' that the inferior order of subtle or psychic influences (for the terms 'subtle' and 'psychic' applied to a domain are for present purposes synonymous) are able to find in the cosmic environment itself, to assist them in bringing their action to bear on the human world and to enable them to propagate themselves therein.

26

SHAMANISM
AND SORCERY

THE PRESENT PERIOD corresponds to the final phases of a cyclical manifestation, and for that reason must exhaust its most inferior possibilities; that is why the period can be said to be using up everything that had been set aside in earlier periods: that and nothing else is truly characteristic of the modern experimental and quantitative sciences in particular, together with their industrial applications. For similar reasons the profane sciences, as has been said, even when considered from a historical point of view as well as from the point of view of their content, are really and truly 'residues' of some of the traditional sciences.[1] There is yet another fact that accords with those just mentioned, though its real significance is scarcely ever grasped, and that is the frenzy with which the moderns have undertaken the exhumation of the vestiges of past periods and vanished civilizations, despite their incapacity really to understand anything about them. This in itself is not a very reassuring symptom, because of the nature of the subtle influences that remain attached to such vestiges and are brought back into the light of day with them, and are so to speak set at liberty by the exhumation as such, without

---

1. But only of some of them, for there were other traditional sciences which have not left in the modern world even the smallest trace, however deformed and deviated. It goes without saying, too, that all the enumerations and classifications of the philosophers apply only to the profane sciences, and that the traditional sciences could in no way be made to fit into their narrow and 'systematic' categories; at this time, more appropriately than ever before, could the Arabic saying be applied to the current period, to the effect that 'there are many sciences, but few scientists' (*al-'ulūm kathīr walakin al-'ulamā' qalīl*).

raising any suspicion in the minds of the investigators. In order to explain this more fully, it will first be necessary to deal briefly with certain things that in themselves are as a matter of fact wholly outside the modern world, but are not for that reason any the less capable of being used so as to exert a particularly 'disorganizing' influence in that world; the rest of this chapter is therefore a digression only in appearance, and it will incidentally provide an opportunity for the elucidation of certain matters about which too little is generally known.

In the first place, yet one more confusion and error of interpretation arising from the modern mentality must be dissipated, and that is the idea that there exist things that are purely 'material'. This conception belongs exclusively to the modern mentality, and when it is disencumbered from all the secondary complications added to it by the special theories of the physicists, it amounts to no more than the idea that there exist beings and things that are solely corporeal, and that their existence and their constitution involve no element that is not corporeal. This idea is directly linked to the profane point of view as expressed, perhaps in its most complete form, in the sciences of today, for these sciences are characterized by the absence of any attachment to principles of a superior order, and thus the things taken as the objects of their study must themselves be thought of as being without any such attachment (whereby the 'residual' character of the said sciences is once again made evident); this kind of outlook can be regarded as indispensable in order to enable science to deal with its object, for if a contrary admission were made, science would at once be compelled to recognize that the real nature of its object eludes it. It may perhaps be superfluous to seek elsewhere the reason for the enthusiasm displayed by scientists in discrediting any other conception, by presenting it as a 'superstition' arising in the imagination of 'primitive' peoples, who, it is suggested, can have been nothing but savages or men of an infantile mentality, as the 'evolutionist' theories make them out to have been; but whether the reason be mere incomprehension on their part or a conscious partisanship, the scientists do succeed in producing a caricature of the situation convincing enough to induce a complete acceptance of their interpretation in everyone who believes implicitly in whatever they say, namely, in a large majority of our contemporaries. This is what has happened in the particular case of the ethnologists' theories about what they have agreed to call 'animism'; strictly speaking this word might well possess an unobjectionable meaning, but only on condition that it were understood quite otherwise than they understand it, and that no meaning which is not justifiable etymologically were admitted.

The truth is that the corporeal world cannot be regarded as being a whole sufficient to itself, nor as being isolated from the totality of universal manifestation: on the contrary, whatever the present state of things may look like as a result of 'solidification', the corporeal world proceeds entirely from the subtle order, in which it can be said to have its immediate principle, and through that order as intermediary it is attached successively to formless manifestation and finally to the non-manifested. If that were not so, its existence could be nothing but a pure illusion, a sort of phantasmagoria behind which there would be nothing at all, which amounts to saying that it would not really exist in any way. That being the case, there cannot be anything in the corporeal world such that its existence does not depend directly on elements belonging to the subtle order, and beyond them, on some principle that can be called 'spiritual', for without the latter no manifestation of any kind is possible, on any level whatsoever. Confining attention to the subtle elements, which must therefore be present in everything and are merely more or less hidden according to circumstances, it can be said that they correspond to that which properly speaking constitutes the 'psychic' order in the human being; it is therefore legitimate in every case, by a natural extension implying no 'anthropomorphism' but only a perfectly valid analogy, also to call them 'psychic' (and that is why a cosmic psychism was spoken of previously), or even 'animic', for these two words, according to their original meanings and their respectively Greek and Latin derivations, are really precisely synonymous. It follows from this that there can in fact be no 'inanimate' objects in existence, and also that 'life' is one of the conditions to which all corporeal existence without exception is subject; and that is why nobody has ever arrived at a satisfactory definition of the difference between the 'living' and the 'non-living', for that question, like so many others in modern philosophy and science, is only insoluble because there is no good reason for posing it, since the 'non-living' has no place in the domain to which the question is related, and the only differences involved are really no more than mere differences of degree.

Such a way of looking at things can be called 'animism' without objection, if that word is held to imply nothing more or other than the affirmation that there are 'animic' elements in all things; it is clear that this kind of animism is directly opposed to mechanism, just as reality itself is opposed to mere outward appearance. It is equally clear that this conception is 'primitive', but it is so quite simply because it is true, which is almost exactly the opposite of what the evolutionists mean when they qualify it in that way. At the same time, and for the same reasons, this conception is necessarily common to all the traditional doctrines; it can therefore be said to be 'normal', whereas the opposite idea, that of 'inanimate' things (of which one of the most extreme expressions is found in the Cartesian theory of 'animal-machines') represents a real anomaly, but then so do all specifically modern and profane ideas. But it must be clearly understood that the traditional conception in no way implies any 'personification' of the natural forces that are studied by the physicists after their own fashion, and still less any 'adoration' of those forces, as is made out to be the case by those for whom 'animism' is something they think they can call 'primitive religion'; in actual fact the only considerations involved are such as belong exclusively to the domain of cosmology, and they can find their applications in various traditional sciences. It should be superfluous to point out that the question of the 'psychic' elements inherent in things, or of forces of that order expressed or manifested through things, has nothing whatever to do with the 'spiritual'; the confusion of these two domains is yet another purely modern phenomenon, and is doubtless not unconnected with the idea of making a 'religion' out of what is really science in the most precise sense of the word; our contemporaries, despite their pretensions to 'clear ideas' (evidently a direct inheritance from the mechanism and 'universal materialism' of Descartes) mix up in a very curious way the most heterogeneous things and those that are the most essentially distinct!

It is important to note at this point, in view of what is to follow, that the ethnologists habitually treat as 'primitive' forms that are only degenerate to a greater or less extent; and these forms are in any case very often not really on as low a level as might be supposed from the accounts that are given of them; however that may be, this explains how 'animism', which is in itself only a particular feature of a doctrine, has come to be taken as characterizing a doctrine in its entirety. Indeed, where there is degeneration, it is naturally the superior part of the doctrine, its metaphysical or spiritual side, that disappears more or less completely, so that something that was originally only secondary, and in particular the cosmological and 'psychic' side—to which 'animism' and its applications properly belong—inevitably assumes a preponderant importance. The remainder, even if it still persists to some extent, may easily elude the observer from outside, all the more so because that observer, being ignorant of the profound significance of rites and symbols, is unable to recognize in them any elements belonging to a superior order (any more than he can recognize them in the vestiges of completely extinct civilizations) and thinks that everything can be explained indifferently in terms of magic, or even sometimes of mere 'sorcery'.

A very clear example of this sort of thing can be found in a case such as that of 'shamanism', which is generally regarded as one of the typical forms of 'animism'; the derivation of the word is rather uncertain, but it is generally used to denote the aggregate of the traditional doctrines and practices of certain Mongol peoples of Siberia, though a few people extend its meaning to cover anything that may present similar features in any country. Many people regard 'shamanism' as almost synonymous with sorcery, but it certainly should not be so, for the two things are quite distinct; the word has undergone a deviation opposite to that of 'fetishism', which really has etymologically the meaning of 'sorcery', but has been applied to things that include nothing of the kind. It may be noted in this connection that the distinction some people have tried to establish between 'shamanism' and 'fetishism', regarded as being two varieties of 'animism', is neither as clear nor as important as they think: whether human beings, as in the first case, or various objects, as in the second, chiefly serve as 'supports' or 'condensers', if that is the right word, for certain subtle influences, the difference is only one of 'technical' modalities involving in themselves no truly essential differences.[2]

If we consider 'shamanism' properly so called, the existence of a highly developed cosmology becomes apparent, of a kind that might suggest concordances with other traditions in many respects, and first with respect to a separation of the 'three worlds', which seems to be its very foundation. 'Shamanism' will also be found to include rites comparable to some that belong to traditions of the highest order: some of them, for example, recall in a striking way the Vedic rites, and particularly those that are most clearly derived from the primordial tradition, such as those in which the symbols of the tree and of the swan predominate. There can therefore be no doubt that 'shamanism' is derived from some form that was, at least originally, a regular and normal traditional form; moreover it has retained up to the present day a certain 'transmission' of the powers necessary for the exercise of the functions of the 'shaman'; but as soon as it becomes clear that the 'shaman' directs his activity particularly toward the most inferior traditional sciences, such as magic and divination, a very real degeneration must be suspected, such as may sometimes amount to a real deviation, as can happen all too easily to such sciences whenever they become over-developed. There are indeed some rather disquieting indications in that direction, one of them being the connection established between the 'shaman' and an animal, a connection restricted to a single individual and so in no way assimilable to the collective connection rightly or wrongly called 'totemism'. It should be added that all this could in itself receive a perfectly legitimate explanation quite unconnected with sorcery; what gives it a suspicious character is the fact that among some peoples, if not among all, the animal is considered as being more or less a form of the 'shaman' himself; and there may be

2. In what follows, a certain amount of information about 'shamanism' is drawn from an exposition called 'Shamanism of the Natives of Siberia' by I.M. Casanowicz (taken from the *Smithsonian Report* for 1924) to which the author's attention was kindly called by A. K. Coomaraswamy.

no great distance between an identification of that kind, and 'lycanthropy' as it exists more particularly among the black races.[3]

But there is something else as well, and something more directly connected with our subject: from among the psychic influences with which they deal, the 'shamans' quite naturally distinguish two kinds, one benefic and the other malefic, and as there is obviously nothing to be feared from the former, they pay attention almost exclusively to the latter: such at any rate appears most often to be the case, though it may be that 'shamanism' includes various forms that might show differences in that respect. But there is never any question of a 'cult' devoted to the malefic influences, which would be a sort of conscious 'satanism', as has often been wrongly imagined; the only objective is, in principle, that of preventing them from doing harm, or of neutralizing or diverting their activity. The same could be said with truth of other supposed 'devil-worshippers' living in various places: in a general way it is scarcely likely that real 'satanism' could be characteristic of an entire people. Nevertheless, it is still true that, whatever may be the original intention, the handling of influences of this sort, when no appeal is made to influences of a superior order (still less to truly spiritual influences), finally leads by force of circumstances to real sorcery, which is a very different thing of course from the sorcery of the common 'rustic magician' of the West, for this last represents no more than the last scraps of a magical knowledge as degenerate and diminished as it could be, and on the point of complete extinction. The magical part of 'shamanism' doubtless has a vitality of quite a different order, and that is why it is something really to be feared in more than one respect; for the practically constant contact with inferior psychic forces is as dangerous as could be, first for the 'shaman' himself, as is to be expected, but also from another point of view of a much less narrowly 'localized' interest. There are indeed people who, by working

---

3. There is evidence worthy of belief to the effect that there exists in a distant part of the Sudan a whole population of at least twenty thousand people who are 'lycanthropic'; there are also, in other African countries, secret organizations, such as that to which the name of 'Society of the Leopard' was given, in which certain forms of lycanthropy play a predominant part.

more consciously and with a more extensive knowledge (and this does not mean knowledge of a higher order) might be able to make use of these same forces for quite different ends, unbeknown to the 'shamans' or those whose work is similar, for they act as nothing more than mere instruments for accumulating the forces in question at pre-determined points. It is known that there are in the world a certain number of 'repositories' of influences, the distribution of which is certainly no matter of chance, serving only too well the designs of the 'powers' responsible for the whole modern deviation; but that demands some further explanations, for it may seem surprising at first sight that the remains of what was once an authentic tradition should lend themselves to a 'subversion' of this kind.

27

PSYCHIC
RESIDUES

THE LAST POINT MENTIONED in connection with 'shamanism' needs to be clarified, for it contains the main reason for the introduction of the subject; for this purpose it must be made clear that the case of the persistent vestiges of a degenerate tradition that has lost its superior or 'spiritual' part is fully comparable to the case of the psychic remains left behind by a human being in passing to another state, for these remains can be used for any purpose once they have been abandoned by the 'spirit'. Whether they be made use of consciously by a magician or a sorcerer, or unconsciously by spiritualists, the more or less malefic effects that can accrue obviously have nothing to do with the inherent character of the being to whom they belonged before; they are no longer anything but a special category of 'wandering influences', to use the terminology of the Far-Eastern tradition, and they have kept at the most a purely illusory likeness to the said being. Comparisons of this kind can only be fully understood if it is remembered that even spiritual influences themselves must necessarily, if they are to come into action in our world, take appropriate 'supports', first of all in the psychic order, then in the corporeal order itself, so that the result is something analogous to the constitution of a human being. If later on the spiritual influences for any reason withdraw themselves, their former corporeal supports, whether places or objects (and when places are in question their situation is naturally connected with the 'sacred geography' mentioned earlier) will nonetheless remain charged with psychic elements that will be all the stronger and more persistent through having previously served as the intermediaries and the instruments of a yet more powerful action. It would be logical to conclude that important traditional and initiatic centers, more or less long since extinct, must in general be the most important potential sources of danger, whether arising from violent reactions provoked in the psychic conglomerates persisting in such places by sheer imprudence, or more especially from the seizure of these elements by 'black magicians', to use the accepted expression, who could then manoeuvre them at will in order to obtain results conforming to a plan.

The existence of the first of these two sources of danger goes a long way toward explaining the harmful character of certain vestiges of extinct civilizations when they come to be exhumed by people who, like the modern archaeologists, know nothing of such matters, and so inevitably fail to act with prudence. That is not to say that there may not sometimes be other factors in the situation: for instance, a particular ancient civilization may have degenerated through an excessive development of magic in its final phases,[1] and its remains will naturally then always bear the imprint of that development in the shape of psychic influences of a very inferior order. It is also possible, even in the absence of any degeneration of that sort, that places or objects may have been specially prepared by way of defensive action against anyone who might touch them improperly, for precautions of this kind are in no way illegitimate as such, although the fact of attaching too great an importance to them is none too favorable an indication, for it affords evidence of preoccupations rather remote from pure spirituality, and even perhaps of a certain lack of knowledge of the power possessed by pure spirituality, which should make it unnecessary to resort to such 'extras'. But apart from all this, persistent psychic influences, when deprived of the 'spirit' that formerly directed them, are reduced to a sort of 'larval' state, and can easily by themselves react to a particular provocation, however involuntary it may be, in a more or less disordered manner, and in any case in a manner quite unrelated to the intentions of those who used them formerly for purposes of quite another order. Just in the same way the gruesome manifestations of

1. Such appears to have been the case with ancient Egypt in particular.

psychic 'corpses' that sometimes occur in spiritualist seances, have absolutely no relation in any circumstances whatever to the possibilities of action or of desire of the individualities whose subtle forms they were, and whose posthumous 'identity' they imitate more or less badly, to the great amazement of the ingenuous who are all too ready to take them for 'spirits'.

So under many conditions the influences in question can be quite pernicious enough, even when they are simply left to themselves; this fact is merely a result of the inherent nature of the forces of the 'intermediary world', about which nobody can do anything, any more than they can prevent 'physical' forces, meaning the forces belonging to the corporeal order studied by the physicists, from acting in certain circumstances so as to cause accidents for which no human will can be held responsible; what is revealed by all this is the true significance of modern antiquarian researches, and the part they actually play in opening up some of the 'fissures' previously referred to. But in addition, these same influences are at the mercy of anyone who knows how to 'capture' them, just as are 'physical' forces; it goes without saying that either can be made to serve the most diverse and even the most contradictory ends, according to the intentions of whoever has taken control of them and can direct them to his chosen purpose; and, when subtle influences are involved, if their controller happens to be a 'black magician', it is obvious that they will be used by him for a purpose quite contrary to that for which they might have been used in earlier times by the qualified representatives of a regular tradition.

All that has been said so far relates to the vestiges left by an entirely extinct tradition; but there is another case to be considered alongside this one: that of an ancient traditional civilization that lives on so to speak for itself alone, in the sense that its degeneration has proceeded to such a point that the 'spirit' has at last withdrawn entirely from it. Certain kinds of knowledge, having nothing of the spiritual in them and belonging only to the order of contingent applications, may still continue to be transmitted, particularly the more inferior among them, but they will naturally thereafter be liable to every kind of deviation, for they themselves represent nothing more than 'residues' of another kind, the pure doctrine on which they ought normally to depend having disappeared. In this sort of case of 'survival' the psychic influences set to work in earlier times by the representatives of the tradition will again be liable to be 'captured', even without the knowledge of their apparent guardians, who will thenceforth be illegitimate and entirely without real authority; those who really make use of the influences through them will thus have the advantage of having at their disposal not only so-called 'inanimate' objects as unconscious instruments of the action they want to exercise, but also living men who serve no less well as 'supports' to the influences, and whose real existence confers on them a much greater vitality. Exactly this sort of thing was in view in quoting an example like that of 'shamanism', but of course with the reservation that it must not be held to apply indiscriminately to all the things that are commonly grouped under that rather conventional heading, for they may not all have arrived at an equal degree of decadence.

A tradition deviated to that extent is really dead as such, just as dead as a tradition that no longer even appears to be in existence; if there were any life left in it, however little, no such subversion could in any event take place, for it consists in nothing but a reversal of what remains of the tradition so as to make it work in a direction by definition anti-traditional. It is however as well to add that before things reach that point, and as soon as traditional organizations are so diminished and enfeebled as no longer to be capable of adequate resistance, the more or less direct agents of the 'adversary'[2] can begin to work their way in with a view to hastening the time when 'subversion' will become possible; they are not always sure to succeed, for whatever still has some life can always recover itself; but if death takes place, the enemy will then be found to be as it were in possession and ready to take advantage of his position and to use the 'corpse' for his own purposes. The representatives of everything in the Western world that still retains an authentically traditional character, in the exoteric as well as in the initiatic domain, might be thought to have the strongest possible interest in paying attention to

---

2. The literal meaning of the Hebrew word *Shayṭān* is 'adversary', and the 'powers' now under consideration are truly 'satanic' in character.

this last observation while there is still time, for all around them the menacing signs indicating 'infiltrations' of this kind are unfortunately by no means indiscernible by anyone who knows how to find them.

Another consideration having its own importance is this: if the 'adversary' (as to whose nature some more exact indications will follow) has something to gain by taking possession of places that were the seat of former spiritual centers, it is not solely because of the psychic influences accumulated in them and more or less free to be made use of, but it is also for the very reason that the places are where they are, for of course they were not chosen arbitrarily for the part they had to play at one time or another, and in connection with one traditional form or another. 'Sacred geography', the knowledge of which determines the choice in question, is susceptible, like every other traditional science of a contingent order, of being diverted from its legitimate purpose and of being applied 'inversely'. If a place is 'privileged' to serve for the emission and direction of psychic influences when they are operating as vehicles of a spiritual action, it will be no less so when these same psychic influences are used in quite another way and for ends opposed to all spirituality. It may be observed in passing that the danger of the misdirection of certain kinds of knowledge, of which this last is a very clear example, accounts for much of the secrecy that is quite natural in a normal civilization; but the moderns show themselves to be entirely incapable of understanding this, for they commonly mistake what is really a measure designed as far as possible to prevent the misuse of knowledge for a desire to monopolize that knowledge. And in truth secrecy only ceases to be effective when the organizations that are the repositories of the knowledge in question allow unqualified individuals to penetrate into their ranks, for these individuals may even be agents of the 'adversary', and if they are so one of their first objects will be to discover the secrets. All this has of course no direct relation to the true initiatic secret, which resides, as explained earlier, exclusively in the 'ineffable' and 'incommunicable', and is therefore obviously protected from all indiscreet research; nevertheless, although none but contingent matters are in question here, it must be recognized that the precautions that may be taken within the contingent order with a view to avoiding all deviation, and thus all harmful action that might arise from it, are far from having in practice only a relatively negligible interest.

In any case, whether it be a question of the places themselves, of the influences remaining attached to them, or again of knowledge of the kind just mentioned, the old adage *corruptio optimi pessima* may be recalled, and may be applied perhaps more accurately here than in any other case; and moreover 'corruption' is just the right word, even in its most literal sense, for the 'residues' here concerned are, as stated at the beginning, comparable to the products of the decomposition of a once living being; and as all corruption is more or less contagious, these products of the dissolution of things past will themselves exercise, wherever they may be 'projected', a particularly dissolving and disaggregating action, especially if they are made use of by a will clearly conscious of its objectives. All this may be likened to a sort of 'necromancy', making use of psychic remains quite other than those of human individuals, and it is by no means the least redoubtable sort, for it has by its nature a field of action far more extensive than that of common witchcraft, indeed no comparison between the two being possible in that respect: matters have reached such a point nowadays that our contemporaries must indeed be blind not to have even the least suspicion of where they stand!

28

THE SUCCESSIVE STAGES IN ANTI-TRADITIONAL ACTION

THE MATERIAL PRESENTED to the reader hitherto and the examples given should make it easier to understand, if only in a general way, the precise character of the stages in the anti-traditional action that has really 'made' the modern world as such; but it is of first importance not to forget that, since all effective action necessarily presupposes agents, anti-traditional action is like all other kinds of action, so that it cannot be a sort of spontaneous or 'fortuitous' production, and, since it is exercised particularly in the human domain, it must of necessity involve the intervention of human agents. The fact that it has conformed to the specific character of the cyclic period in which it has been working explains why it was possible and why it was successful, but is not enough to explain the manner of its realization, nor to indicate the various measures put into operation to arrive at its result. In any case, a little reflection on what follows should suffice to bring conviction, for the spiritual influences themselves act in every traditional organization through human beings as intermediaries and as authorized representatives of the tradition, although the tradition is really 'supra-human' in its essence; there is all the more reason why the same condition should apply when only psychic influences come into the picture, especially such as are of the lowest order, and are the very antithesis of a power transcendent with respect to our world, apart from the fact that the character of 'counterfeit', everywhere manifested in this domain, and to be referred to again later, makes human intermediaries even more rigorously necessary. On the other hand, initiation, in whatever form it may appear, is that which really incarnates the 'spirit' of a tradition, and is also that which allows of the effective realization of 'supra-human' states; obviously therefore initiation is the thing that must be opposed (at least insofar as any such opposition is really conceivable) by anti-traditional action, which tries by every means to drag men toward the 'infra-human'. The term 'counter-initiation' is therefore the best for describing that to which the human agents through whom the anti-traditional action is accomplished belong, both as a whole and in their various degrees (for, like initiation itself, it must necessarily comprise degrees); and this term is not merely a conventional expression used for convenience to designate something that really has no name, for in its form and in its meaning it corresponds as exactly as possible to very precise realities.

It is rather remarkable that in considering the whole assemblage of all the things that really constitute modern civilization, from whatever point of view it is envisaged, one is always driven to the conclusion that everything seems to be increasingly artificial, denatured, and falsified. Many of those who criticize modern civilization today are struck by the fact, even when they do not know how to carry the matter any further and have not the least suspicion of what really lies behind it. A little logic should, it seems, be enough to indicate that if everything has become artificial, the mentality to which this state of things corresponds must be no less artificial than everything else, that it too must be 'manufactured' and not spontaneous; and once this simple reflection has been made, indications pointing in the same direction cannot fail to be seen in almost indefinitely growing multitude everywhere. Nevertheless it seems unfortunately to be very difficult to escape sufficiently far from the 'suggestions' to which the modern world owes both its existence as such and its persistence, for even those who declare themselves most resolutely 'anti-modern' generally see nothing whatever of all this, and that is why their expenditure of effort is so often a dead loss, or at any rate has almost no real significance.

The anti-traditional action necessarily had to aim both at a change in the general mentality and at the destruction of all traditional institutions in the West, since the West is where it began to work first and most directly, while awaiting the proper time for an attempt to extend its operations over the whole world, using the Westerners duly prepared to become its instruments. Moreover, once the mentality had been changed, the institutions could be the more easily destroyed because they would then no longer conform to it; the work that aims at a deviation of mentality therefore appears to be really fundamental, and on that work all else must depend in one way or another; attention will therefore be chiefly directed toward it. It is a work that obviously could not be made effective all at once, although perhaps the most astonishing thing of all is the speed with which it has been possible to induce Westerners to forget everything connected with the existence of a traditional civilization in their countries; if one thinks of the total incomprehension of the Middle Ages and everything connected with them which became apparent in the seventeenth and eighteenth centuries, it becomes easy to understand that so complete and abrupt a change cannot have come about in a natural and spontaneous way. However that may be, the first task was as it were to confine men within the limits of their own individuality, and this was the task of rationalism, as previously explained, for rationalism denies to the being the possession or use of any faculty of a transcendent order; it goes without saying moreover that rationalism began its work before ever it was known by that name, and before it took on its more especially philosophical form, as has been shown in connection with Protestantism; and besides, the 'humanism' of the Renaissance was no more than the direct precursor of rationalism properly so called, for the very word 'humanism' implies a pretension to bring everything down to purely human elements and thus (at least in practice if not yet by virtue of an expressly formulated theory) to exclude everything of a supra-individual order. The next thing to do was to turn the attention of the individual toward external and sensible objects, in order as it were to enclose him, not only within the human domain, but within the much narrower limits of the corporeal world alone; that is the starting-point of the whole of modern science, which was destined to continue to work in the same direction, thus making the limitation more and more effective. The constitution of scientific or, if preferred, of philosophico-scientific theories also had to be embarked upon gradually (and here it is necessary to do no more than to summarize matters already dealt with); mechanism prepared the way directly for materialism, which was to mark the more or less irremediable limitation of the mental horizon to the corporeal domain, thenceforth looked upon as the only 'reality', and itself stripped of everything that could not be regarded as simply 'material'; naturally, the elaboration of the very notion of 'matter' by the physicists had an important part to play at this point. This is the point at which the 'reign of quantity' was really entered upon: profane science, mechanistic ever since Descartes, became more specifically materialistic after the second half of the eighteenth century, and was to become more and more exclusively quantitative in its successive theories, while at the same time materialism insinuated itself into the general mentality and finally succeeded in stabilizing that attitude, without resort to any kind of theoretical formulation; thus it became all the more diffused and passed finally into the state of being the sort of 'instinct' that has been called 'practical materialism'. This attitude was to be yet further reinforced by the industrial applications of quantitative science, which had the effect of attaching men more and more completely to purely material realizations. Man 'mechanized' everything and ended at last by mechanizing himself, falling little by little into the condition of numerical units, parodying unity, yet lost in the uniformity and indistinction of the 'masses', that is, in pure multiplicity and nothing else. Surely that is the most complete triumph of quantity over quality that can be imagined.

Nevertheless, while the work of 'materialization' and 'quantification' was proceeding (and by the way it is not yet finished and never can be, because a complete reduction to pure quantity is not realizable within manifestation), another work, opposed to it only in appearance, had already begun, and it may be remembered that it really began concurrently with materialism properly so called. This second part of anti-traditional action had to lead not to 'solidification' but to 'dissolution'; nevertheless, far from contradicting the tendency characterized as reduction to quantity, it was bound to reinforce it as soon as the greatest possible 'solidification' had been reached, and as soon as the said tendency had passed beyond its first objective and had begun to try to assimilate the continuous to the discontinuous, thus itself becoming a tendency toward dissolution. This is the moment at which the second kind of work, which had at first only been carried out in a more or less hidden manner by way of preparation, and in any case on a restricted scale, had to come into the open and in its turn to cover an increasingly wide field, while at the same time quantitative science became less strictly materialistic in the proper sense of the word, and even in the end ceased to lean on the notion of 'matter', which had been rendered more and more inconsistent and 'evanescent' as a consequence of theoretical elaborations applied to it. This is the condition in which we now are: materialism merely survives for its own sake, and no doubt it may well survive a good deal longer, especially in the form of 'practical materialism', but in any case, it has ceased henceforth to play the principal part in anti-traditional action.

After having enclosed the corporeal world as completely as possible, it was necessary, while guarding against the re-establishment of any communication with superior domains, to open it up again from below, so as to allow the dissolving and destructive forces of the inferior subtle domain to penetrate into it. It is the 'unleashing' of these forces, so to speak, and the setting of them to work to complete the deviation of our world and effectively to bring it toward final dissolution, that constitutes the second part or second phase referred to. It is right to regard the two phases as distinct, though they have in part been simultaneous, for in the total plan of the modern deviation they follow one another logically and only reach their full effectiveness successively; moreover, as soon as materialism had been established, the first phase was in a sense virtually complete and could be left to take its course in the form of a development of everything implied in materialism as such. That is the moment at which the preparation of the second phase began, and none but its first effects have as yet become apparent, but they have become sufficiently apparent to allow their sequel to be foreseen, and to make it possible to say with no exaggeration whatever that the second aspect of anti-traditional action moves from now onwards into first place in the designs of what was at first comprehensively described as the 'adversary' but can now, and with greater exactitude, be named the 'counter-initiation'.

29

DEVIATION
AND SUBVERSION

THE ANTI-TRADITIONAL ACTION by which the modern world has in a sense been 'manufactured' has hitherto been considered as an operation designed primarily to bring about a deviation from the normal state, that is, from the state normal to all traditional civilizations whatever may be their particular forms, something easy to understand and requiring no further comment. On the other hand, there is a distinction to be made between deviation and subversion: deviation can be regarded as comprising an indefinite multiplicity of degrees, so that it can go to work gradually and imperceptibly; this is exemplified by the gradual passage of the modern mentality from 'humanism' and rationalism to mechanism, and thence to materialism, and again in the process whereby profane science has elaborated successive theories each more purely quantitative in character than the last. This makes it possible to say that all such deviation, from its earliest beginnings, has steadily and progressively tended toward the establishment of the 'reign of quantity'. But when deviation reaches its limit, it ends by being a real 'contradiction', that is to say a state diametrically opposed to the normal order, and only then can 'subversion' in the etymological sense of the word properly be spoken of; needless to say, 'subversion' in this sense must in no way be confused with the 'reversal' referred to in connection with the final instant of the cycle, it being indeed the exact opposite since the 'reversal' actually happens after the 'subversion' and at the moment when subversion seems complete, and is really a rectification whereby the normal order is re-established, and whereby the 'primordial state', representing perfection in the human domain, is restored.

As against this, it could be said that subversion, thus understood, is but the last stage of deviation and is its goal, or, in other words, that deviation as a whole has no tendency other than to bring about subversion, and that is true enough; in the present state of affairs, though it cannot yet be said that subversion is complete, the signs of it are very evident in everything in which the special characteristic of 'counterfeit' or 'parody' is conspicuous. This characteristic has already been mentioned more than once, and is to be dealt with more fully later. For the moment no more need be said than that this particular characteristic affords by itself a very significant indication of the origin of anything that shows it, and consequently of the origin of the modern deviation itself, the 'satanic' nature of which is thus brought out very clearly. The word 'satanic' can indeed be properly applied to all negation and reversal of order, such as is so incontestably in evidence in everything we now see around us: is the modern world really anything whatever but a direct denial of all traditional truth? At the same time, and more or less of necessity, the spirit of negation is the spirit of lying; it wears every disguise, often the most unexpected, in order to avoid being recognized for what it is, and even in order to pass itself off as the very opposite of what it is; this is where counterfeit comes in; and this is the moment to recall that it is said that 'Satan is the ape of God', and also that he 'transfigures himself into an angel of light'. In the end, this amounts to saying that he imitates in his own way, by altering and falsifying it so as always to make it serve his own ends, the very thing he sets out to oppose: thus, he will so manage matters that disorder takes on the appearance of a false order, he will hide the negation of all principle under the affirmation of false principles, and so on. Naturally, nothing of that kind can ever really be more than dissimulation and even caricature, but it is presented cleverly enough to induce an immense majority of men to allow themselves to be deceived by it; and why should we be astonished at this, when it is so easy to observe both the extent to which trickery, even of the crudest sort, succeeds in imposing itself on the crowd, and also the difficulty of subsequently undeceiving them? *Vulgus vult decipi* was already a saying of the ancients of the 'classical period', and no doubt there have always been people, though never as many as in our days, ready to add: *ergo decipiatur!*

Nevertheless, anyone who speaks of counterfeit thereby suggests the idea of parody, for they are almost synonyms; there is invariably a grotesque element in affairs of this kind, and it may be more apparent or less so, but it ought never to escape the notice of observers, even observers of only a very moderate perspicacity, were it not for the fact that natural perspicacity in that direction is abolished by the 'suggestions' to which they are unconsciously subjected. This is the direction in which falsehood, however clever it may be, cannot do otherwise than betray itself; it is also of course a 'label' of origin, inseparable from counterfeit itself, which should normally make it recognizable as such. If it were necessary to give examples chosen from the various manifestations of the modern spirit, there would be only too many from which to choose, beginning with the 'civic' or 'lay' pseudo-rites that have developed so extensively in the last few years, and are intended to provide the 'masses' with a purely human substitute for real religious rites, down to the extravagance of a self-styled 'naturism', which in spite of its name is no less artificial, not to say 'anti-natural', than are the useless complications of existence against which it lays claim to react by means of a ludicrous comedy having as its real purpose to make people believe that the 'state of nature' is to be confused with animality; meanwhile, something more than the mere comfort of the human being is now threatened with denaturation by the growth of the idea, so contradictory in itself but conforming well to a democratic 'egalitarianism', of an 'organization of leisure'.[1] The things mentioned here are intentionally only such as are known to everyone and they undeniably belong to what may be called the 'public domain' and can be grasped without trouble by anyone; is it not strange that those who feel the absurdity of all this, to say nothing of its danger, are so rare as to be really exceptional? Such things as these ought to be spoken of as 'pseudo-religion', 'pseudo-nature', 'pseudo-comfort', and the same is true of many other things; if one wanted always to speak strictly according to truth, the word 'pseudo' would continually have to be put in front of the name of all

---

1. It is opportune to add that this 'organization of leisure' is an integral part of the efforts referred to earlier, such as are intended to oblige men to live 'in common' as far as possible.

the products of the modern world, including that of profane science itself—for it is only a 'pseudo-science' or imitation of knowledge—in order to give a true indication of what it all amounts to: falsifications and nothing else, and falsifications of which the objective is only too clear to anyone still capable of reflection.

So much for that; and now let us return to considerations of a more general kind. What is it that makes this counterfeit possible, and even increasingly possible and increasingly perfect of its kind, if indeed any such words can be used in such a connection, as the descending course of the cycle proceeds? The profound reason lies in the relation of inverse analogy that exists, as explained, between the highest and the lowest points: it is this that makes possible in particular, and in a degree corresponding to that of the approach to the domain of pure quantity, the realization of those sorts of counterfeits of principial unity as are manifested in the 'uniformity' and 'simplicity' toward which the modern spirit tends, and in which its efforts to bring everything down to the quantitative point of view are most completely expressed. This perhaps shows more clearly than anything else that deviation has, so to speak, only to be developed and allowed to pursue its course to the end in order finally to lead to subversion properly so called, for when that which is most inferior (it being in this case a question of something inferior even to all possible existence) seeks to imitate and make a counterfeit of superior and transcendent principles, then is the time when real subversion can justly be spoken of. Nevertheless it is as well to recall that in the nature of things the tendency to pure quantity can never produce its full effect; therefore, in order that subversion may reach its term the intervention of something else is necessary. At this stage what was said earlier on the subject of dissolution could be repeated, but from a slightly different point of view; obviously that which appertains to the final point of cyclic manifestation is equally concerned in both cases; and that is exactly why the 'rectification' of the ultimate instant must appear precisely as a reversal of all things, when it is seen in relation to the state of subversion existing immediately before that instant.

Bearing in mind this last point, this much more can be said: the first of the two phases that have been distinguished in anti-traditional action represents simply a work of deviation, the particular end of which is a materialism of the crudest and most complete kind; as for the second phase, it could be specially characterized as a work of subversion (for that is the point to which it leads most directly) destined to end in the setting-up of what has been called an inverted spirituality, as will be seen more clearly from what follows. The inferior subtle forces that are called in during this second phase can certainly be described as 'subversive' from every point of view; and it was considered right to apply the word 'subversion' above to the 'inverted' utilization of the remains of ancient traditions abandoned by the 'spirit'; and the two cases are in any case similar, for under such conditions corrupt vestiges themselves necessarily fall into the lower regions of the subtle domain. Another particularly clear example of the work of subversion will be given in the next chapter, in the form of the intentional inversion of the legitimate and normal meaning of traditional symbols; this will afford in addition an opportunity to give a fuller explanation of the double meaning usually contained in symbols themselves; for so many references to double meanings of this kind have already been made in the course of this study that a little more detail on the subject will not be out of place.

30

THE INVERSION
OF SYMBOLS

SURPRISE IS SOMETIMES EXPRESSED at the fact that one and the same symbol can be taken in two senses, which are, at least apparently, directly contrary one to the other. This question is not merely one of the multiplicity of meanings that can, generally speaking, be carried by any symbol according to the point of view or the level from which it is considered, any kind of 'systematization' of symbols being made impossible by this very adaptability, but is a question more particularly of two aspects linked together through a mutual correlation, taking the form of an opposition, in such a way that one is so to speak the reverse or the 'negative' of the other. In order to understand this, duality must in the first place be considered as presupposed by all manifestation, and consequently as conditioning manifestation in all its modes, and it must always be traceable therein in one form or another;[1] it is true that any such duality is in truth a complementarism and not an opposition; but two terms that are really complementary can appear from a relatively exterior or contingent point of view to be opposed.[2] All opposition only exists as such at a certain level, for there can be no such

---

1. As it is one of the linguistic errors that are of common occurrence and are not without serious inconveniences, it may be useful to state clearly here that 'duality' and 'dualism' are two quite different things: dualism (of which the Cartesian conception of 'spirit' and 'matter' is among the best known examples) properly consists in regarding a duality as irreducible and in taking account of nothing beyond it, thereby denying the common principle from which the two terms of the duality really proceed by 'polarization'.

2. See *The Symbolism of the Cross*, chap. 7.

thing as an irreducible opposition; at a higher level it is always resolved into a complementarism, in which its two terms are found to be reconciled and harmonized, until they return at last into the unity of the common principle from which they both proceed. It can therefore be said that the point of view of complementarism is in a certain sense intermediate between that of opposition and that of unification; and each of these points of view has its good reason and its own value in the order to which it applies, although the three are obviously not situated at the same level of reality; what matters therefore is to know how to put each aspect into its proper hierarchical place, and not to try to carry it over into a domain in which it would no longer have any valid significance.

That being so, it is understandable that there is nothing in any way illegitimate in taking account of two contrary aspects in a symbol, and in addition that the consideration of either of these aspects in no way excludes the other, since each of them is equally true in a particular relation, and lastly even that by virtue of their correlation their existence is a single existence. It is therefore a mistake, and incidentally rather a common one, to suppose that the special consideration of one aspect or the other must be peculiar to doctrines or to schools that are themselves in opposition.[3] In such cases everything depends solely on the predominance that may be assigned to one or the other, and sometimes also on the intention with which the symbol is used, for example as an element taking part in particular rites, or again as a means of recognition for the members of particular organizations; but this is a point to which we shall return. The fact that the two aspects may be united in one and the same complex symbolical figuration shows clearly that they are not mutually exclusive and can be considered simultaneously; and in this connection it will be well to note, although there can be no question of developing the subject fully, that a duality, which can be an opposition or a complementarism according to the point of view adopted, can be arranged, so far as the relative situation of its terms

3. Attention has been drawn elsewhere to a mistake of this kind in connection with the representation of the swastika with its arms turned so as to indicate opposite directions of rotation (*The Symbolism of the Cross*, chap. 10).

is concerned, either vertically or horizontally, this being an immediate consequence of the cross-shaped arrangement of the quaternary, which can be resolved into two dualities, one vertical and the other horizontal. The vertical duality can be related to the two extremities of an axis or to the two contrary directions in which that axis may be followed; the horizontal duality is that of two elements situated symmetrically on either side of that same axis. As an example of the first case the two triangles of the seal of Solomon can be cited (as well as all other symbols of analogy disposed according to a similar geometrical arrangement), and as an example of the second the two serpents of the caduceus; and it will be noticed that only in the vertical duality are the two terms clearly distinguished one from the other by their reversed positions, whereas in the horizontal duality they can appear completely similar or equivalent when considered separately, although their significance is not really any less contrary in this case than in the other. It can also be said that in the spatial order the vertical duality is that of up and down, and the horizontal that of right and left; though this observation may perhaps seem rather too obvious, it nonetheless has its importance, because symbolically (and this leads back to the intrinsically qualitative value of the directions of space) these two pairs of terms are themselves susceptible of multiple applications, traces of which could without difficulty be found even in current language, showing that matters of very general application are here in question.

So much being established in principle, certain consequences may easily be deduced in connection with what could be called the practical use of symbols; but here a consideration of a more special kind must first be introduced, namely, that of the case in which the two contrary aspects are taken as 'benefic' and 'malefic' respectively. It must be made clear that these two terms are used for want of any better, as on a previous occasion; they have in fact the disadvantage of leading to a supposition that some more or less 'moral' interpretation is admitted, whereas really there is nothing of the kind, and the words must be understood here in a purely 'technical' sense. Furthermore, it must be clearly understood that the 'benefic' or 'malefic' quality is not attached absolutely to one or the other of the two aspects, because it appertains only to a special application which is such that all opposition, of whatever kind, could not possibly be brought indifferently within its range, and also because this quality would in any case necessarily disappear when the point of view of opposition is replaced by that of complementarism, to which any such consideration is wholly strange. Within these limits and after taking account of these reservations, the point of view of 'beneficence' or 'maleficence' has its normal place among all others; but it is also from this very point of view, or rather from the misuses to which it leads, that the subversion of the interpretation and use of symbolism now to be referred to may arise, a subversion constituting one of the 'marks' characteristic of everything that is derived, consciously or otherwise, from the domain of the 'counter-initiation', or is more or less directly subject to its influence.

This kind of subversion may consist either in attributing to the 'malefic' aspect, while continuing to recognize it as such, the place that normally belongs to the 'benefic' aspect, even to the point of giving it a sort of supremacy over the latter, or alternatively in attributing to symbols a meaning opposite to their legitimate meaning, by treating as 'benefic' the aspect that is really 'malefic', or the other way round. It must also be noted that, in accordance with what was said above, a subversion of this kind may not appear visibly in the representation of the symbols, because there are some in which the two contrary aspects are not marked by any outward difference recognizable at first sight. Thus, in the figurations related to what is commonly but very improperly called 'serpent-worship', it would often be impossible, at least if only the serpent itself were considered, to say *a priori* whether the *Agathodaimón* or the *Kakodaimón* is symbolized; hence many misunderstandings arise, especially on the part of those who are ignorant of the dual significance of the serpent and are tempted to see in it everywhere and always only a 'malefic' symbol, as has been in fact the case for a long time past with the generality of Westerners;[4] and what has been said of the serpent could equally well be applied to many other symbolical animals, for it has become a habit for one reason or another no

---

4. For the same reason the Far-Eastern Dragon itself, really a symbol of the Word, has often been taken by Western ignorance to be a 'diabolical' symbol.

longer to consider more than one of the two opposed aspects in reality borne by these animals. In the case of symbols that can be made to take up two opposite positions, and especially those that are reduced to geometrical forms, it might be thought that the difference ought to be much more clearly apparent; nevertheless it is not always so, because the two positions of the same symbol are each capable of carrying a legitimate meaning, also because their relation is not necessarily that of 'beneficence' and 'maleficence', for, let it be said once more, that relation is only a particular application among all others. What it is important to know in such a case is whether there can be said to be a real intention to 'invert' in such a way as formally to contradict the normal and legitimate value of the symbol; that is why, for example, the use of the inverted triangle is very far from being always a sign of 'black magic' as some people think,[5] although it certainly is so in some cases, namely, whenever it is accompanied by an intention to adopt an attitude opposed to what the triangle represents when its apex is turned upward. Incidentally, it may be remarked that an intentional 'inversion' of this kind can also be applied to words or to formulas, in such a way as to form various sorts of reversed *mantras*, as may be seen in certain of the practices of sorcery, even in the simple 'country witchcraft' such as still exists in the West.

Thus it can be seen that the question of the inversion of symbols is rather complicated, and it might well also be described as rather delicate; for in order to know what the real position is in any particular case it is necessary to examine, not so much the figurations seen in what may be called their 'materiality', as the accompanying interpretations which express the intention that dictated their adoption. And furthermore, the cleverest and most dangerous subversion is not the one that betrays itself by too obvious singularities easily noticed by anyone, but it is the one that deforms the meaning of symbols or reverses their import while making no change in their outward appearance. But the most diabolical trick of all is perhaps that which consists in attributing to the orthodox symbolism itself,

5. Instances can even be found in which the inverted triangles occurring among the alchemical symbols of the elements have been interpreted in that sense.

as it exists in truly traditional organizations and more especially in initiatic organizations (the latter being specially liable to attack in this case), the inverted interpretation that is specifically characteristic of the 'counter-initiation'; and the 'counter-initiation' does not fail to take advantage of this method of promoting confusions and uncertainties when it can derive some profit from them. This is really the whole secret of certain campaigns, very significant in view of the character of the present period, conducted either against esoterism in general or against any one initiatic form in particular, with the unconscious help of people who would be very astonished, and even appalled, if they could become aware of the use that is being made of them; unfortunately however it sometimes so happens that people who imagine that they are fighting the devil, whatever their particular notion of the devil may be, are thus turned, without the least suspicion of the fact on their part, into his best servants!

31

TRADITION
AND TRADITIONALISM

THE FALSIFICATION of everything has been shown to be one of the characteristic features of our period, but falsification is not in itself subversion properly so called, though contributing fairly directly to the preparation for it. Perhaps the clearest indication of this is what may be called the falsification of language, taking the form of the misuse of certain words that have been diverted from their true meaning; misuse of this kind is to some extent imposed by constant suggestion on the part of everyone who exercises any kind of influence over the mentality of the public. It is a case of something more than the mere degeneration alluded to earlier, whereby many words have come to lose their original qualitative meaning, keeping only one that is purely quantitative; it is more a question of a 'diversion', whereby words are applied to things that they do not fit in any way, and sometimes in a sense directly opposed to their normal meaning. This is one of the most obvious symptoms of the intellectual confusion that reigns everywhere in the present world; but it must not be forgotten that this very confusion is willed by that which lies hidden behind the whole modern deviation; this thought obtrudes itself particularly in view of the simultaneous appearance in many different quarters of attempts to make illegitimate use of the very idea of 'tradition' by people who want improperly to assimilate its significance to their own conceptions in one domain or another. Of course there is no question of suspecting the good faith of any particular party, for very often it may be a case of mere incomprehension and nothing more, the ignorance of most of our contemporaries about anything possessing a truly traditional character being so complete that this need cause no surprise. Nevertheless it must also be recognized that such errors of interpretation and involuntary misconceptions serve the purpose of certain 'plans' so well that it is permissible to wonder whether their growing diffusion may not be due to some of the 'suggestions' that dominate the modern mentality, all of which lead ultimately to nothing less than the destruction of all that is tradition in the true sense of the word.

The modern mentality itself, in everything that characterizes it specifically as such (and this must be said once more, for it is something that cannot be too often insisted on), is no more than the product of a vast collective suggestion, which has operated continuously for several centuries and has determined the formation and progressive development of the anti-traditional spirit; and in that spirit the whole of the distinctive features of the modern mentality are comprised. Nevertheless, however powerful and clever the suggestion may be, a moment may always come when the resulting state of disorder and disequilibrium becomes so apparent that some cannot fail to become aware of it, and then there is a risk of a 'reaction' that might compromise the desired result. It certainly seems that matters have today just reached that stage, and it is noticeable that this moment coincides exactly, by a sort of 'immanent logic', with the moment at which the merely negative phase of the modern deviation comes to an end, the phase represented by the complete and unrivaled domination of the materialistic mentality. This is where the falsification of the traditional idea comes in with great effect; it is made possible by the ignorance already mentioned, itself but one of the products of the negative phase; the very idea of tradition has been destroyed to such an extent that those who aspire to recover it no longer know which way to turn, and are only too ready to accept all the false ideas presented to them in its place and under its name. Such people may have become aware, at least up to a point, that they had been deceived by openly anti-traditional suggestions, and that the beliefs imposed on them represented only error and deceit; that is certainly a change in the direction of the 'reaction' alluded to, but no effective result could accrue if nothing further were to happen. This is clear enough from the growing quantity of literature containing the most pertinent criticisms of our present civilization, but contemplating measures for the cure of the evils so rightly denounced that are, as indicated earlier, curiously disproportionate and insignificant, and often more or less infantile: such proposals can be said to be 'scholarly' or 'academic' and nothing more, and there is anyhow nothing in them that gives evidence of the least knowledge of a profound order. This is the stage at which the effort made, however praiseworthy and meritorious it may be, can easily allow itself to be turned aside toward activities that will, in their own way and despite appearances, only contribute in the end to the further growth of the disorder and confusion of the 'civilization', the rectification of which they were intended to bring about.

The people just referred to are such as can properly be described as 'traditionalists', meaning people who only have a sort of tendency or aspiration toward tradition without really knowing anything at all about it; this is the measure of the distance dividing the 'traditionalist' spirit from the truly traditional spirit, for the latter implies a real knowledge, being indeed in a sense the same as that knowledge. In short, the 'traditionalist' is and can be no more than a mere 'seeker', and that is why he is always in danger of going astray, not being in possession of the principles that alone could provide him with infallible guidance; and his danger is all the greater because he will find in his path, like so many ambushes, all the false ideas set on foot by the power of illusion, which has a keen interest in preventing him from reaching the true goal of his search. It is indeed evident that this power can only maintain itself and continue to exercise its action on condition that all restoration of the traditional idea is made impossible, and more than ever so when it is preparing to take a further step in the direction of subversion, subversion being, as explained, the second phase of its action. So it is quite as important for the power in question to divert searchings tending toward traditional knowledge as it is to divert those concerned with the origins or real causes of the modern deviation, and thus liable to reveal something of the true nature of the said power and the means of its influence; these two devices are both necessary and in a sense complementary, and they could fairly be regarded as the positive and negative aspects of a single plan of action having domination as its objective.

All misuses of the word 'tradition' can serve this same purpose in one way or another, beginning with the most popular of all, whereby it is made synonymous with 'custom' or 'usage', thus bringing about a confusion of tradition with things that are on the lower human level and are completely lacking in profound significance. But there are other and more subtle deformations, all the more dangerous because of their subtlety, that share the common characteristic of bringing the idea of tradition down to a purely human level, whereas on the contrary there is nothing and can be nothing truly traditional that does not contain some element of a supra-human order. This indeed is the essential point, containing as it were the very definition of tradition and all that appertains to it; this is also therefore the very point that must on no account be allowed to emerge if the modern mentality is to be maintained in its state of delusion, and still more if it is to have yet other delusions imposed on it, such as will not only suppress any tendency toward a restoration of the supra-human, but will also direct the modern mentality more effectively toward the worst modalities of the infra-human. Moreover, in order to become aware of the importance assigned to the negation of the supra-human by the conscious and unconscious agents of the modern deviation, it is enough to observe how all who lay claim to be 'historians' of religion and of other forms of the tradition (and in any case they usually mix all these forms together under the general title of 'religion') are eager above all to explain everything in terms of exclusively human factors; it matters little whether, according to school of thought, these factors are psychological, social, or anything else, the very multiplicity of the different explanations facilitating the seduction of a greater number; common to all is the well-defined desire to reduce everything to the human level and to retain nothing that surpasses it; and those who believe in the value of this destructive 'criticism' are thenceforth very ready to confuse tradition with anything whatever, since there is nothing in the ideas inculcated into them such as might enable tradition to be distinguished from that which is wholly lacking in traditional character.

Granted that nothing that is of a purely human order can for that very reason legitimately be called 'traditional', there cannot possibly be, for instance, a 'philosophical tradition' or a 'scientific tradition' in the modern and profane sense of the words, any more, of course, than there can be a 'political tradition', at least where all traditional social organization is lacking, as is the case in the modern Western world. Such expressions are nevertheless in common use today, each in its way denaturing the idea of tradition; and it is obvious that if the 'traditionalists' referred to above can be persuaded to allow their activity to be turned aside toward one or another of these domains and to confine their activity to it, their aspirations will be 'neutralized' and rendered perfectly harmless, and may even sometimes be used without their knowledge for a purpose exactly contrary to what they intend. Indeed it sometimes happens that people go so far as to apply the word 'tradition' to things that by their very nature are as directly anti-traditional as possible: thus they talk about a 'humanist tradition', and a 'national tradition', despite the fact that humanism is nothing if not an explicit denial of the supra-human, and the formation of 'nationalities' was the means employed for the destruction of the traditional civilization of the Middle Ages. In the circumstances it would not be surprising if people began one day to talk about a 'protestant tradition' or even a 'lay tradition' or a 'revolutionary tradition' or if the materialists themselves ended by proclaiming themselves the defenders of a 'tradition', if only in their capacity as the representatives of something already belonging in a great measure to the past! Most of our contemporaries have reached such a state of mental confusion that associations of the most manifestly contradictory words bring about no reaction on their part and do not even provide them with food for thought.

This leads at once to another important observation: when a few people have become conscious of the disorder of these days owing to the all too obvious effects of its present stage of development (more particularly since the stage corresponding to a maximum of 'solidification' has been left behind), and when these people try to 'react' in one way or another, the best means for making their desire for 'reaction' ineffective is surely to direct it toward one of the earlier and less 'advanced' stages of the same deviation, some stage in which disorder had not yet become so apparent, and was as it were presented under an outward aspect more acceptable to anyone not yet completely blinded by certain suggestions. Anyone who considers himself a 'traditionalist' must normally declare himself 'anti-modern', but he may not be any the less affected, though he be unaware of the fact, by modern ideas in a more or less attenuated form; they are then less easily detected, but they always correspond in fact to one or another of the stages passed through by these same ideas in the course of their development; no concession, even unconscious or involuntary, is admissible on this point, for from the very beginning up to the present day, and beyond that too, everything holds together and is inexorably interlinked. In that connection, this much more must be said: the work that has as its object to prevent all 'reaction' from aiming at anything further back than a return to a lesser disorder, while at the same time concealing the character of the lesser disorder so that it may pass as 'order', fits in very exactly with the other work carried out with a view to securing the penetration of the modern spirit into the interior of whatever is left of traditional organizations of any kind in the West; the same 'neutralizing' effect on forces of which the opposition might become formidable is obtained in both cases. Moreover, something more than mere 'neutralization' is involved, for a struggle must necessarily take place between the elements thus brought together as it were on the same level and on the same ground, and their reciprocal enmity is therefore no more than an enmity between the various and apparently opposed productions of one and the same modern deviation; thus the final result can only be a fresh increase in disorder and confusion, which simply amounts to one more step toward final dissolution.

As between all the more or less incoherent things that are today in constant agitation and mutual collision, as between all external 'movements' of whatever kind they may be, there is no occasion to 'take sides', to use the common expression, whether from a traditional or from a merely 'traditionalist' point of view, for to do so is to become a dupe. Since the same influences are really operating behind all these things, it is really playing their game to join in the struggles promoted and directed by them; therefore the mere fact of 'taking sides' under such conditions is necessarily to adopt, however unwittingly, a truly anti-traditional attitude. No particular applications need be specified here, but it must at least be made clear in a general way that in all this agitation principles are always and everywhere lacking, despite the fact that 'principles' have surely never been so much talked about as they are today on all sides, the word being commonly applied more or less regardlessly to things that are least worthy of it, and sometimes even to things that imply the negation of all true principle. This particular misuse of a word is again highly significant of the real trend of the falsification of language already well exemplified by the perversion of the word 'tradition'; that example has been specially stressed because it is most closely connected with the subject of this study, insofar as the latter is intended to give a picture of the last phases of the cyclical 'descent'. It is not in fact possible to stop short at the point that represents most nearly the apogee of the 'reign of quantity', for what follows that point is too closely connected with what precedes it to allow of any separation being made otherwise than quite artificially; no 'abstractions' are therefore admitted here, for they only represent a particular form of the 'simplification' so dear to the modern mentality; on the contrary, the object is as far as possible to present reality as it is, without omitting anything that is essential for the understanding of the conditions of the present period.

32

NEO-SPIRITUALISM

IN THE PREVIOUS CHAPTER there was occasion to refer to people who would like to react against the existing disorder, but have not the knowledge necessary to enable them to do so effectively, and so are 'neutralized' in one way or another and directed into blind alleys; but in addition to these people there are also others who are only too easily driven yet further along the road leading to subversion. The pretext put before the latter, as things are at present, is most often that of 'fighting materialism', and no doubt most of them believe sincerely that they are doing so; but people in the first-named category who want to live up to this belief merely end up in the dreariness of a vague 'spiritualist' philosophy that is without any real significance but is at least relatively harmless, whereas those in the second category are moving toward the domain of the worst psychic delusions, and that is far more dangerous. The former are indeed all more or less affected unknowingly by the modern spirit, but not deeply enough to be entirely blinded by it, but it is the latter whom we must now consider, and they are wholly penetrated by it, and moreover they usually glory in their 'modernity'; the only thing that horrifies them among all the various manifestations of the modern spirit is materialism, and they are so fascinated by this one idea that they do not see that many other things, such as the science and the industry they admire, are closely dependent, both in their origin and in their intrinsic nature, on the very materialism that so distresses them. This makes it easy to see why the sort of attitude they display must now be encouraged and spread: such people are the best unconscious auxiliaries it would be possible to find for the second phase of anti-traditional action. Materialism has nearly played its part, and these are the people to spread its successor about the world: they will even be used to assist actively in opening the 'fissures' spoken of earlier, for in this domain it is not merely 'ideas' or theories of one sort or another that count, but also and simultaneously a 'practice' that will bring them into direct relations with subtle forces of the lowest order; and they lend themselves all the more readily to this work owing to their total ignorance of the true nature of such forces, to which they go so far as to attribute a 'spiritual' character.

This is what has in a general way been described as 'neo-spiritualism', to distinguish it from mere philosophical 'spiritualism'; it might be sufficient only to mention it here for the purpose of 'putting it on record', since two earlier studies have been specially devoted to its most widespread forms,[1] but it is too important an element among those that are specially characteristic of the contemporary period to justify the omission of some mention at least of its main features, keeping back for the moment the 'pseudo-initiatic' aspect of the work of most of the schools attached to it (with the exception of the spiritualist schools that are openly profane and must be so owing to the exigencies of their extreme 'popularization'), for that is a matter that will have to be returned to later. First of all it should be noted that there is no question of a homogenous whole, but of something that assumes a multitude of different forms, though they always show enough common characteristics to admit of being legitimately grouped together under one designation; it is therefore all the more strange that all such groups, schools, and 'movements' are constantly in a state of rivalry or even of conflict one with another, to such an extent that it would be difficult to find elsewhere, except perhaps between political 'parties', hatreds more violent than those that exist between their adherents, while all the time, by a curious irony, they all have a mania for preaching 'fraternity' in season and out of season! Here is a truly 'chaotic' phenomenon, which may give the impression even to superficial observers of disorder carried to an extreme: it is indeed an indication that 'neo-spiritualism' already represents a fairly advanced stage on the road to dissolution.

1. *The Spiritist Fallacy* and *Theosophy: History of a Pseudo-Religion.*

On the other hand, in spite of the aversion it evinces toward materialism, 'neo-spiritualism' resembles it in more than one way, so much so that it has been referred to not unjustly as 'transposed materialism', meaning materialism extended beyond the limits of the corporeal world, this being clearly exemplified by the crude representations of the subtle world, wrongly called 'spiritual', already alluded to and consisting almost entirely of images borrowed from the corporeal domain. This same 'neo-spiritualism' is also attached to the earlier stages of the modern deviation, in a more effective way, through what may be called its 'scientistic' side; that too has been previously alluded to when dealing with the influence exerted on the various schools from the moment of their birth by scientific 'mythology'; and it is worthwhile to note more especially the important part played in these conceptions, in quite a general way and without any exception, by 'progressivist' and 'evolutionary' ideas, which are indeed among the most typical features of the modern mentality, and would suffice by themselves to characterize any conceptions as being beyond all doubt the products of that mentality. Moreover, even the schools that affect an appearance of 'archaism' by making use in their own way of fragments of uncomprehended and deformed traditional ideas, or by disguising modern ideas as they think fit under a vocabulary borrowed from some traditional form either Eastern or Western (all of which things, by the way, are in formal contradiction to their belief in 'progress' and 'evolution'), are constantly preoccupied in adapting these ancient ideas, or what are imagined to be such, to the theories of modern science. This work has of course continually to be done afresh as the scientific theories change, though it is true that those who undertake it find their task simplified by their almost universal reliance on material drawn from works of 'popularization'.

Apart from this, 'neo-spiritualism' is also, on the side alluded to above as 'practical', closely in conformity with the 'experimental' tendencies of the modern mentality. In this way it has gradually come to exert an appreciable influence on science itself, into which it has more or less insinuated itself by means of what is called 'metapsychics'. Doubtless the phenomena considered in 'metapsychics' are in themselves just as worthy of study as are those of the corporeal world; but what gives rise to objection is the way in which the study is undertaken, that is, the application to it of the point of view of profane science; physicists (who are so obstinate in sticking to their quantitative methods as to want to try to 'weigh the soul'!) and even psychologists in the 'official' sense of the word, are surely as ill-prepared as possible for a study of this kind, and for that very reason more liable than anyone else to allow themselves to be deluded in every way.[2] And there is something more: in actual fact 'metapsychic' researches are scarcely ever undertaken independently of all support from 'neo-spiritualists', and especially from 'spiritists', and this proves that these people fully intend that the researches shall serve the purposes of their propaganda. Perhaps the most serious thing in this connection is that the experimenters are so placed that they find themselves obliged to have recourse to spirit 'mediums', that is, to individuals whose preconceived ideas markedly modify the phenomena in question, and give them what might be called a special 'coloring', and who moreover have been drilled with particular care (for there are even 'schools for mediums') so as to serve as instruments and passive 'supports' to certain influences belonging to the lowest depths of the subtle world; and they act as 'vehicles' of these influences wherever they go, so that nobody, scientist or otherwise, can fail to be dangerously affected if he comes into contact with them and if he is, through ignorance of what lies behind it all, totally incapable of defending himself. Further insistence on this aspect of affairs is unnecessary, because it has been fully dealt with in other works, to which anyone who would like to have a fuller account of them may now be referred; but it is worthwhile, because it is something entirely peculiar to the present day, to underline the strangeness of the part played by the 'mediums' and of the supposed necessity of their presence for the production of phenomena arising in the subtle world. Why was there nothing of that kind formerly, for forces of that order were in no

---

2. It is a question here, not so much of the more or less important part to be assigned to fraud, conscious or unconscious, but also of delusions as to the nature of the forces that intervene in the actual production of the phenomena called 'metapsychic'.

way prevented by that fact from manifesting themselves spontaneously in certain circumstances, and on a far larger scale than in
spiritist or 'metapsychic' seances (and very often in uninhabited
houses or in desert places, whereby the too convenient hypothesis
of the presence of a medium unconscious of his own powers is
excluded)? It may be wondered whether some change has not come
about, since the appearance of spiritualism, in the very manner in
which the subtle world acts in its 'interferences' with the corporeal
world: such a change would only be a fresh example of modifications in the environment such as has already been considered in
connection with the effects of materialism; but the one thing certain
in any case is that there is something here that fits in perfectly with
the exigencies of a 'control' exerted over inferior psychic influences,
themselves already essentially 'malefic', in order that they may be
used more directly with certain defined ends in view, in conformity
with the pre-established 'plan' of the work of subversion, for which
purpose they are now being 'unchained' in our world.

33

CONTEMPORARY
INTUITIONISM

IN THE DOMAIN OF PHILOSOPHY AND PSYCHOLOGY, the tendencies corresponding to the second phase of anti-traditional action
are naturally marked by the importance assigned to the 'subconscious' in all its forms, in other words to the most inferior psychic
elements of the human being, something particularly apparent so
far as philosophy properly so called is concerned in the theories of
William James as well as in the 'intuitionism' of Bergson. The work
of Bergson has been considered in an earlier chapter, in relation to
the justifiable criticisms of rationalism and its consequences formulated therein, though never very clearly and often in equivocal
terms; but the characteristic feature of what may be called (if the
term be admissible) the 'positive' part of his philosophy is that,
instead of seeking above reason for something that might remedy its
insufficiencies, he takes the opposite course and seeks beneath it;
thus, instead of turning toward true intellectual intuition, of which
he is as completely ignorant as are the rationalists, he appeals to an
imagined 'intuition' of an exclusively sensitive and 'vital' order, and
in the very confused notions that emerge the intuition of the senses
properly so called is mingled with the most obscure forces of
instinct and sentiment. So it is not as a result of a more or less 'fortuitous' encounter that Bergson's 'intuitionism' has manifest affini-
ties, particularly marked in what may be called its 'final state' (and
this applies equally to the philosophy of William James), with 'neo-
spiritualism', but it is as a result of the fact that both are expressions
of the same tendencies: the attitude of the one in relation to rationalism is more or less parallel to that of the other in relation to

materialism, the one leaning toward the 'sub-rational' just as the other leans toward the 'sub-corporeal' (doubtless no less unconsciously), so that the direction followed in both cases is undoubtedly toward the 'infra-human'.

This is not the place for a detailed examination of these theories, but attention must at least be called to certain features closely connected with the subject of this book. The first is their 'evolutionism', which remains unbroken and is carried to an extreme, for all reality is placed exclusively within 'becoming', involving the formal denial of all immutable principle, and consequently of all metaphysics; hence their 'fleeting' and inconsistent quality, which really affords, in contrast with the rationalist and materialist 'solidification', something like a prefiguration of the dissolution of all things in the final chaos. A significant example is found in Bergson's view of religion, which is set out appropriately enough in a work of his exemplifying the 'final state' mentioned above.[1] Not that there is really anything new in that work, for the origins of the thesis maintained are in fact very simple: in this field all modern theories have as a common feature the desire to bring religion down to a purely human level, which amounts to denying it, consciously or otherwise, since it really represents a refusal to take account of what is its very essence; and Bergson's conception does not differ from the others in that respect.

These theories of religion, taken as a whole, can be grouped into two main types: one is 'psychological' and claims to explain religion by the nature of the human individual, and the other is 'sociological' and tries to see in religion a fact of an exclusively social kind, the product of a sort of 'collective consciousness' imagined as dominating individuals and imposing itself on them. Bergson's originality consists only in having tried to combine these two sorts of explanation, and he does so in rather a curious way: instead of considering them as more or less mutually exclusive, as do most of the partisans of one or the other, he accepts both explanations, but relates them to two different things, each called by the same name of 'religion', the 'two sources' of religion postulated by him really amounting to

---

1. *The Two Sources of Morality and Religion.*

that and nothing more.[2] For him therefore there are two sorts of religion, one 'static' and the other 'dynamic', alternatively and somewhat oddly called by him 'closed religion' and 'open religion'; the first is social in its nature and the second psychological; and naturally his preference is for the second, which he regards as the superior form of religion—we say 'naturally' because it is very evident that it could not be otherwise in a 'philosophy of becoming' such as his, since from that point of view whatever does not change does not correspond to anything real, and even prevents man from grasping the real such as it is imagined to be. But someone will say that a philosophy of this kind, since it admits of no 'eternal truths',[3] must logically refuse all value not only to metaphysics but also to religion; and that is exactly what happens, for religion in the true sense of the word is just what Bergson calls 'static religion', in which he chooses to see nothing but a wholly imaginary 'story-telling'; as for his 'dynamic religion', the truth is that it is not religion at all.

His so-called 'dynamic religion' in fact contains none of the characteristic elements that go to make up the definition of religion: there are no dogmas, since they are immutable or, as Bergson says, 'fixed'; no more, of course, are there any rites, for the same reason and because of their social character, dogmas and rites necessarily being left to 'static religion'; and as for morality, Bergson starts by setting it aside as something quite outside religion as he understands it. So there is nothing left, or at least nothing is left but a vague 'religiosity', a sort of confused aspiration toward an 'ideal' of some description, rather near to the aspirations of modernists and liberal Protestants, and reminiscent in many respects of the 'religious experience' of William James, for all these things are obviously very closely connected. This 'religiosity' is taken by Bergson to be a superior kind of religion, for he thinks, like all those who follow the same tendencies, that he is 'sublimating' religion, whereas all he is

---

2. So far as morality is concerned, it is not of special interest here, but the explanation of it proposed by Bergson is of course parallel to his explanation of religion.

3. It is worthy of note that Bergson seems to avoid the use of the word 'truth', and that he almost always uses instead the word 'reality', a word that in his view signifies that which undergoes continual change.

doing is to empty it of all positive content, since there is nothing in religion compatible with his conceptions. Such notions are no doubt all that can be extracted from a psychological theory, for experience has failed to show that any such theory can get beyond 'religious feeling'—and that, once more, is not religion. In Bergson's eyes 'dynamic religion' finds its highest expression in 'mysticism', which however he does not understand and sees on its worst side, for he only praises it for whatever in it is 'individual', that is to say, vague, inconsistent, and in a sense 'anarchic'; and the best examples of this kind of mysticism, though he does not quote them, could be found in certain teachings of occultist and Theosophist inspiration. What really pleases him about the mystics, it must be stated categorically, is their tendency to 'divagation' in the etymological sense of the word, which they show only too readily when left to themselves. As for that which is the very foundation of true mysticism, leaving aside its more or less abnormal or 'eccentric' deviations (which may or may not strike one's fancy), its attachment to a 'static religion' he evidently regards as negligible; nevertheless one feels that there is something here that worries him, for his explanations concerning it are somewhat embarrassed; but a fuller examination of this question would lead too far away from what for present purposes are its essentials.

To return to 'static religion': so far as its supposed origins are concerned, it will be seen that Bergson trustfully accepts all the tales of the all too well known 'sociological school', including those that are most worthy of suspicion: 'magic', 'totemism', 'taboo', 'mana', 'animal worship', 'spirit worship', and 'primitive mentality', nothing being missing of the conventional jargon or of the accustomed trivialities, if such expressions may be allowed (as indeed they must be when discussing matters so grotesque in character). The only thing for which he is perhaps really responsible is the place he assigns to a so-called 'fable-making function', which seems to be much more fabulous than that which it seeks to explain: but he had to invent some sort of theory to allow of the comprehensive denial of the existence of any real foundation of those things that are commonly treated as 'superstitions', a 'civilized' philosophy, and more than that, a 'twentieth-century' philosophy, evidently considering that any other attitude would be unworthy of itself. In all this there is only one point of present interest, that concerning 'magic'; magic is a great resource for certain theorists, who clearly have no idea of what it really is, but who try to find in it the origin both of religion and of science. Bergson's position is not precisely that: he seeks for a 'psychological origin' in magic, and turns it into 'the exteriorization of a desire that fills the heart,' and he makes out that 'if one reconstitutes by an effort of introspection the natural reaction of man to his perception of things, one finds that magic and religion are connected, and that there is nothing in common between magic and science.' It is true that later on he wavers: if one adopts a certain point of view, 'magic evidently forms part of religion,' but from another point of view 'religion is opposed to magic'; he is clearer when he asserts that 'magic is the opposite of science' and that 'far from preparing for the coming of science, as has been supposed, magic has been the great obstacle against which methodical learning has had to contend.' All that is almost exactly the reverse of the truth, for magic has absolutely nothing to do with religion, and, while admittedly not the origin of all the sciences, it is simply a single science among the others; but Bergson is no doubt quite convinced that no sciences can exist other than those enumerated in modern 'classifications', established from the most narrowly profane point of view imaginable. Speaking of 'magical operations' with the imperturbable self-assurance of one who has never seen any,[4] he writes this remarkable sentence: 'If primitive intelligence had begun its dealings with such matters by conceiving principles, it

4. It is most regrettable that Bergson was on bad terms with his sister, Mrs S. S.L. MacGregor Mathers (alias 'Soror Vestigia Nulla Retrorsum') who might have been able to give him a little instruction in such matters. [S.S.L MacGregor Mathers, author of *The Kabbalah Unveiled*, was a leading figure in various occult organizations in the early twentieth century, primarily in England, and is known especially for his role in the founding of The Order of the Golden Dawn, whence the 'initiatic' name given for his wife derives. Mrs Mathers was herself very active in all these matters. For a time the Order of the Golden Dawn attracted a number of figures who became well-known in later years, including William Butler Yeats (on whom both of the Mathers exerted a strong influence for a time) and Arthur Edward Waite. ED.]

would soon have had to give way to experience, which would have demonstrated their falsity.' One can admire the intrepidity of this philosopher, shut into his private room, and well protected against the attacks of certain influences that undoubtedly would not hesitate to take advantage of him as an auxiliary no less valuable than unwitting, when he denies *a priori* everything that does not fit into the framework of his theories. How can he think that men were stupid enough to have repeated indefinitely, even without 'principles', 'operations' that were never successful, and what would he say if it should be found, on the contrary, that experience 'demonstrates the falsity' of his own assertions? Obviously he does not even imagine the possibility of anything of that kind; such is the strength of the preconceived ideas in him and in those like him that they do not doubt for a single instant that the world is strictly confined within the measure of their conceptions (this in fact being what allows them to construct 'systems'); and how can a philosopher be expected to understand that he ought to refrain, just like an ordinary mortal, from talking of things he knows nothing about?

Now it is particularly worthy of note, and highly significant as regards the reality of the connection between Bergsonian 'intuitionism' and the second phase of anti-traditional action, that magic, by an ironical turn of affairs, is now cruelly avenging the denials of our philosopher. It has reappeared in our days, through the recent 'fissures' in our world, in a form that is at once the lowest and the most rudimentary, in the disguise of 'psychic science' (the very thing that some people prefer to call, rather unfortunately, 'metapsychics'), and it succeeds in securing admission thereto, while avoiding recognition not only as something very real, but also as destined to play a leading part in the future of Bergson's 'dynamic religion'! This is no exaggeration: he speaks of 'survival' just like any common spiritist, and he believes in a 'deepening of the range of experiment' making it possible to come to a 'conclusion as to the possibility and even the probability of a survival of the soul' (what exactly does that mean, and is it not apparent that he is thinking of the phantasmagoria of 'psychic corpses'?), but without the possibility of knowing whether it will be 'for a time or for ever.' But this last annoying limitation does not prevent him from proclaiming in dithyrambic tones: 'No more than this is needed in order to turn into a living and active reality a belief in a life after death such as is met with in most men, though it is usually verbal, abstract, ineffective.... Indeed, if we were sure, absolutely sure, of survival we could no longer think of anything else.' The ancient magic was more 'scientific' than this, in the true sense of the word, if not in the profane sense, and it had not the same pretensions; but in order that some of its most elementary phenomena should give rise to interpretations of this kind it was necessary to wait for the invention of spiritualism, which could not come to birth until a late stage of the modern deviation had been reached. It is in fact the spiritualist theory concerning such phenomena, that and nothing else, that is finally accepted by Bergson, as it was by William James before him, with 'a joy' that makes 'all pleasures pale' (this incredible statement, with which his book ends, is quoted word for word). His 'joy' establishes for us the degree of discernment of which this philosopher is capable, for as far as his good faith is concerned, that certainly is not in question, and profane philosophers are usually not suited to act otherwise than as dupes in cases of this kind, thus serving as unconscious intermediaries for the hoaxing of many others: but apart from that, talking of 'superstition', never before has there been so good an example of it, and it is this fact that gives the best idea of the real worth of all the 'new philosophy', as its partisans are pleased to call it!

34

THE MISDEEDS
OF PSYCHOANALYSIS

IN PASSING FROM PHILOSOPHY TO PSYCHOLOGY it will be found
that identical tendencies appear once again in the latter, and in the
most recent schools of psychology they assume a far more dangerous aspect, for instead of taking the form of mere theoretical postulates they are given practical applications of a very disturbing
character; the most 'representative' of these new methods, from the
point of view of the present study, are those grouped under the general heading of 'psychoanalysis'. It may be noted that, by a curious
inconsistency, their handling of elements indubitably belonging to
the subtle order continues to be accompanied in many psychologists by a materialistic attitude, no doubt because of their earlier
training, as well as because of their present ignorance of the true
nature of the elements they are bringing into play;[1] is it not one of
the strangest characteristics of modern science that it never knows
exactly what the object of its studies really is, even when only the
forces of the corporeal domain are in question? It goes without saying too that there is a kind of 'laboratory psychology', the end-
point of the process of limitation and of materialization of which

---

1. The case of Freud himself, founder of 'psychoanalysis', is quite typical in this
respect, for he never ceased to declare himself a materialist. One further remark:
why is it that the principal representatives of the new tendencies, like Einstein in
physics, Bergson in philosophy, Freud in psychology, and many others of less
importance, are almost all of Jewish origin, unless it be because there is something
involved that is closely bound up with the 'malefic' and dissolving aspect of nomadism when it is deviated, and because that aspect must inevitably predominate in
Jews detached from their tradition?

the 'philosophico-literary' psychology of university teaching was but a less advanced stage, and now no more than a sort of accessory branch of psychology, which still continues to coexist with the new theories and methods; to this branch apply the preceding observations on the attempts that have been made to reduce psychology itself to a quantitative science.

There is certainly something more than a mere question of vocabulary in the fact, very significant in itself, that present-day psychology considers nothing but the 'subconscious', and never the 'superconscious', which ought logically to be its correlative; there is no doubt that this usage expresses the idea of an extension operating only in a downward direction, that is, toward the aspect of things that corresponds, both here in the human being and elsewhere in the cosmic environment, to the 'fissures' through which the most 'malefic' influences of the subtle world penetrate, influences having a character than can truthfully and literally be described as 'infernal'.[2] There are also some who adopt the term 'unconscious' as a synonym or equivalent of 'subconscious', and this term, taken literally, would seem to refer to an even lower level, but as a matter of fact it only corresponds less closely to reality; if the object of study were really unconscious it is difficult to see how it could be spoken of at all, especially in psychological terms; and besides, what good reason is there, other than mere materialistic and mechanistic prejudice, for assuming that anything unconscious really exists? However that may be, there is another thing worthy of note, and that is the strange illusion which leads psychologists to regard states as being more 'profound' when they are quite simply more inferior; is not this already an indication of the tendency to run counter to spirituality, which alone can be truly profound since it alone touches the principle and the very center of the being? Correspondingly, since the domain of psychology is not extended upward, the 'superconscious' naturally remains as strange to it and as cut off from it as ever; and when psychology happens to meet

2. It may be noted in this connection that Freud put at the head of his *The Interpretation of Dreams* the following very significant epigram: *Flectere si nequeo superos, Acheronta movebo* (Virgil, *Aeneid*, VII, 312).

anything related to the 'superconscious', it tries to annex it merely by assimilating it to the 'subconscious'. This particular procedure is almost invariably characteristic of its so-called explanations of such things as religion and mysticism, together with certain aspects of Eastern doctrine such as *Yoga*; there are therefore features in this confusion of the superior with the inferior that can properly be regarded as constituting a real subversion.

It should also be noted that psychology, as well as the 'new philosophy', tends in its appeal to the subconscious to approach more and more closely to 'metapsychics';[3] and in the same way it cannot avoid making an approach, though perhaps unwittingly (at least in the case of those of its representatives who are determined to remain materialists in spite of everything), to spiritualism and to other more or less similar things, all of which rely without doubt on the same obscure elements of a debased psychism. These same things, of which the origin and the character are more than suspect, thus appear in the guise of 'precursory' movements and as the allies of recent psychology, which introduces the elements in question into the contemporary purview of what is admitted to be 'official' science, and although it introduces them in a roundabout way (nonetheless by an easier way than that of 'metapsychics', the latter being still disputed in some quarters), it is very difficult to think that the part psychology is called upon to play in the present state of the world is other than one of active participation in the second phase of anti-traditional action. In this connection, the recently mentioned pretensions of ordinary psychology to annex, by forcible assimilation to the 'subconscious', certain things that by their very nature elude it, only belong to what may be called the 'childish' side of the affair, though they are fairly clearly subversive in tendency; for explanations of that sort, just like the 'sociological' explanations of the same things, are really of a 'simplistic' ingenuousness that sometimes reaches buffoonery; but in any case, that sort of thing is far less serious, so far as its real consequences are concerned, than the

3. Incidentally it was the 'psychist' Myers who invented the expression 'subliminal consciousness', which was later replaced in the psychological vocabulary for the sake of brevity by the word 'subconscious'.

truly 'satanic' side now to be examined more closely in relation to the new psychology.

A 'satanic' character is revealed with particular clarity in the psychoanalytic interpretations of symbolism, or of what is held rightly or wrongly to be symbolism, this last proviso being inserted because on this point as on many others, if the details were gone into, there would be many distinctions to make and many confusions to dissipate: thus, to take only one typical example, a vision in which is expressed some 'supra-human' inspiration is truly symbolic, whereas an ordinary dream is not so, whatever the outward appearances may be. Psychologists of earlier schools had of course themselves often tried to explain symbolism in their own way and to bring it within the range of their own conceptions; in any such case, if symbolism is really in question at all, explanations in terms of purely human elements fail to recognize anything that is essential, as indeed they do whenever affairs of a traditional order are concerned; if on the other hand human affairs alone are really in question, then it must be a case of false symbolism, but then the very fact of calling it by that name reveals once more the same mistake about the nature of true symbolism. This applies equally to the matters to which the psychoanalysts devote their attention, but with the difference that in their case the things to be taken into consideration are not simply human, but also to a great extent 'infra-human'; it is then that we come into the presence, not only of a debasement, but of a complete subversion; and every subversion, even if it only arises, at least in the first place, from incomprehension and ignorance (than which nothing is better adapted for exploitation to such ends), is always inherently 'satanic' in the true sense of the word. Besides this, the generally ignoble and repulsive character of psychoanalytical interpretations is an entirely reliable 'mark' in this connection; and it is particularly significant from our point of view, as has been shown elsewhere,[4] that this very same 'mark' appears again in certain spiritualist manifestations—anyone who sees in this no more than a mere 'coincidence' must surely have much good will, if indeed he is not completely blind. In most cases the psychoanalysts

4. See *The Spiritist Fallacy*, pt. 2, chap. 10.

may well be quite as unconscious as are the spiritualists of what is really involved in these matters; but the former no less than the latter appear to be 'guided' by a subversive will making use in each case of elements that are of the same order, if not precisely identical. This subversive will, whatever may be the beings in which it is incarnated, is certainly conscious enough, at least in those beings, and it is related to intentions that are doubtless very different from any that can be suspected by people who are only the unconscious instruments whereby those intentions are translated into action.

Under such conditions, it is all too clear that resort to psychoanalysis for purposes of therapy, this being the usual reason for its employment, cannot but be extremely dangerous for those who undergo it, and even to those who apply it, for they are concerned with things that can never be handled with impunity; it would not be taking an exaggerated view to see in this one of the means specially brought into play in order to increase to the greatest possible extent the disequilibrium of the modern world and to lead it on toward final dissolution.[5] Those who practice such methods are on the other hand without doubt convinced of the benefits afforded by the results they obtain; theirs is however the very delusion that makes the diffusion of these methods possible, and it marks the real difference subsisting between the intentions of the 'practitioners' and the intentions of the will that presides over the work in which the practitioners only collaborate blindly. In fact, the only effect of psychoanalysis must be to bring to the surface, by making it fully conscious, the whole content of those lower depths of the being that can properly be called the 'sub-conscious'; moreover, the individual concerned is already psychologically weak by hypothesis, for if he were otherwise he would experience no need to resort to treatment of this description; he is by so much the less able to resist 'subversion', and he is in grave danger of foundering irremediably in the chaos of dark forces thus imprudently let loose; even if he manages

5. Another example of such means is furnished by the comparable employment of 'radiaesthesia', for in this case also psychic elements of the same quality very often come into play, though it must be admitted that they do not appear under the 'hideous' aspect that is so conspicuous in psychoanalysis.

in spite of everything to escape, he will at least retain throughout the rest of his life an imprint like an ineradicable 'stain' within himself.

Someone may raise an objection here, based on a supposed analogy with the 'descent into hell' as is met with in the preliminary phases of the initiatic journey; but any such assimilation is completely false, for the two aims have nothing in common, nor have the conditions of the 'subject' in the two cases; there can be no question of anything other than a profane parody, and that idea alone is enough to impart to the whole affair a somewhat disturbing suggestion of 'counterfeit'. The truth is that this supposed 'descent into hell', which is not followed by any 're-ascent', is quite simply a 'fall into the mire', as it is called according to the symbolism of some of the ancient Mysteries. It is known that this 'mire' was figuratively represented as the road leading to Eleusis, and that those who fell into it were profane people who claimed initiation without being qualified to receive it, and so were only the victims of their own imprudence. It may be mentioned that such 'mires' really exist in the macrocosmic as well as in the microcosmic order; this is directly connected with the question of the 'outer darkness', [6] and certain relevant Gospel texts could be recalled, the meaning of which agrees exactly with what has just been explained. In the 'descent into hell' the being finally exhausts certain inferior possibilities in order to be able to rise thereafter to superior states; in the 'fall into the mire' on the other hand, the inferior possibilities take possession of him, dominate him, and end by submerging him completely.

There was occasion in the previous paragraph again to use the word 'counterfeit'; the impression it conveys is greatly strengthened by some other considerations, such as the denaturing of symbolism previously mentioned, and the same kind of denaturing tends to spread to everything that contains any element of a 'supra-human' order, as is shown by the attitude adopted toward religion,[7] and

6. The reader may be referred here to what has been said earlier about the symbolism of the 'Great Wall' and of the mountain *Lokāloka*.

7. Freud devoted a book specially to the psychoanalytical interpretation of religion, in which his own conceptions are combined with the 'totemism' of the 'sociological school'.

toward doctrines of a metaphysical and initiatic order such as *Yoga*. Even these last do not escape this new kind of interpretation, which is carried to such a point that some proceed to assimilate the methods of spiritual 'realization' to the therapeutical procedures of psychoanalysis. This is something even worse than the cruder deformations also current in the West, such as those in which the methods of *Yoga* are seen as a sort of 'physical culture' or as therapeutic methods of a purely physiological kind, for their very crudity makes such deformations less dangerous than those that appear in a more subtle guise. The subtler kind are the more dangerous not simply because they are liable to lead astray minds on which the less subtle could obtain no hold; they are certainly dangerous for that reason, but there is another reason affecting a much wider field, identical with that which has been described as making the materialistic conception less dangerous than conceptions involving recourse to an inferior psychism. Of course the purely spiritual aim, which alone constitutes the essentiality of *Yoga* as such, and without which the very use of the word becomes a mere absurdity, is no less completely unrecognized in the one case than in the other. *Yoga* is in fact no more a kind of psychic therapy than it is a kind of physiological therapy, and its methods are in no way and in no degree a treatment for people who are in any way ill or unbalanced; very far from that, they are on the contrary intended exclusively for those who must from the start and in their own natural dispositions be as perfectly balanced as possible if they are to realize the spiritual development which is the only object of the methods; but all these matters, as will readily be understood, are strictly linked up with the whole question of initiatic qualification.[8]

But this is not yet all, for one other thing under the heading of 'counterfeit' is perhaps even more worthy of note than anything mentioned so far, and that is the requirement imposed on anyone who wants to practise psychoanalysis as a profession of being first

---

8. On an attempt to apply psychoanalytical theories to the Taoist doctrine, which is of the same order as *Yoga*, see the study by André Préau, *La Fleur d'or et le Taoisme sans Tao* [Paris: Bibliotheque Chacornac, 1931], which contains an excellent refutation of the attempted application.

'psychoanalyzed' himself. This implies above all a recognition of the fact that the being who has undergone this operation is never again the same as he was before, in other words, to repeat an expression already used above, it leaves in him an ineradicable imprint, as does initiation, but as it were in an opposite sense, for what is here in question is not a spiritual development, but the development of an inferior psychism. In addition, there is an evident imitation of the initiatic transmission; but, bearing in mind the difference in the nature of the influences that intervene, and in view of the fact that the production of an effective result does not allow the practice to be regarded as nothing but a mere pretence without real significance, the psycho-analytic transmission is really more comparable to the transmission effected in a domain such as that of magic, or even more accurately that of sorcery. And there remains yet another very obscure point concerning the actual origin of the transmission: it is obviously impossible to give to anyone else what one does not possess oneself, and moreover the invention of psychoanalysis is quite recent; so from what source did the first psychoanalysts obtain the 'powers' that they communicate to their disciples, and by whom were they themselves 'psychoanalyzed' in the first place? To ask this question is only logical, at least for anyone capable of a little reflection, though it is probably highly indiscreet, and it is more than doubtful whether a satisfactory answer will ever be obtained; but even without any such answer this kind of psychic transmission reveals a truly sinister 'mark' in the resemblances it calls to mind: from this point of view psychoanalysis presents a rather terrifying likeness to certain 'sacraments of the devil'.

35

THE CONFUSION
OF THE PSYCHIC
AND THE SPIRITUAL

THE ACCOUNT GIVEN ABOVE, dealing with some of the psychological explanations that have been applied to traditional doctrines, covers only a particular case of a confusion that is very widespread in the modern world, namely, the confusion of the psychic and the spiritual domains. Even when it is not carried to such a point as to produce a subversion like that of psychoanalysis, this confusion assimilates the spiritual to all that is most inferior in the psychic order; it is therefore extremely serious in every case. In a sense it follows as a natural result of the fact that Westerners have for a very long time past no longer known how to distinguish the 'soul' from the 'spirit' (Cartesian dualism being to a great extent responsible for this, merging as it does into one and the same category everything that is not the body, and designating this one vague and ill-defined category indifferently by either name); and the confusion never ceases to be apparent even in current language: the word 'spirits' is popularly used for psychic entities that are anything but 'spiritual', and the very name 'spiritualism' is derived from that usage; this mistake, together with another consisting in using the word 'spirit' for something that is really only mental, will be enough by way of example for the present. It is all too easy to see the gravity of the consequences of any such state of affairs: anyone who propagates this confusion, whether intentionally or otherwise and especially under present conditions, is setting beings on the road to getting irremediably lost in the chaos of the 'intermediary world', and thereby, though often unconsciously, playing the game of the 'satanic' forces that rule over what has been called the 'counter-initiation'.

It is important at this point to be very precise if misunderstanding is to be avoided: it cannot be said that a particular development of the possibilities of a being, even in the comparatively low order represented by the psychic domain, is essentially 'malefic' in itself; but it is necessary not to forget that this domain is above all that of illusions, and it is also necessary to know how to situate each thing in the place to which it normally belongs; in short, everything depends on the use made of any such development; the first thing to be considered is therefore whether it is taken as an end in itself, or on the other hand as a mere means for the attainment of a goal of a superior order. Anything whatever can in fact serve, according to the circumstances of each case, as an opportunity or 'support' to one who has entered upon the way that is to lead him toward a spiritual 'realization'; this is particularly true at the start, because of the diversity of individual natures, which exercises its maximum influence at that point, but it is still true to a certain extent for so long as the limits of the individuality have not been completely left behind. But on the other hand, anything whatever can just as well be an obstacle as a 'support', if the being does not pass beyond it but allows itself to be deluded and led astray by appearances of realization that have no inherent value and are only accidental and contingent results—if indeed they can justifiably be regarded as results from any point of view. The danger of going astray is always present for exactly as long as the being is within the order of individual possibilities; it is without question greatest wherever psychic possibilities are involved, and is naturally greater still when those possibilities are of a very inferior order.

The danger is certainly much less when possibilities confined to the corporeal and physiological order alone are involved, as they are in the case of the aforementioned error of some Westerners who take *Yoga*, or at least the little they know of its preparatory procedures, to be a sort of method of 'physical culture'; in cases of that kind, almost the only risk incurred is that of obtaining, by 'practices' accomplished ill-advisedly and without control, exactly the opposite result to that desired, and of ruining one's health while seeking to improve it. Such things have no interest here save as examples of a crude deviation in the employment of these 'practices', for they are really designed for quite a different purpose, as remote as possible from the physiological domain, and natural repercussions occurring in that domain constitute but a mere 'accident' not to be credited with the smallest importance. Nevertheless it must be added that these same 'practices' can also have repercussions in the subtle modalities of the individual unsuspected by the ignorant person who undertakes them as he would a kind of 'gymnastics', and this considerably augments their danger. In this way the door may be quite unwittingly opened to all sorts of influences (those to take advantage of it in the first place being of course always of the lowest quality), and the less suspicion the victim has of the existence of anything of the kind the less is he prepared against them, and still less is he able to discern their real nature; there is in any event nothing in all this that can claim to be 'spiritual' in any sense.

The state of affairs is quite different in cases where there is a confusion of the psychic properly so called with the spiritual. This confusion moreover appears in two contrary forms: in the first, the spiritual is brought down to the level of the psychic, and this is what happens more particularly in the kind of psychological explanations already referred to; in the second, the psychic is on the other hand mistaken for the spiritual; of this the most popular example is spiritualism, though the other more complex forms of 'neo-spiritualism' all proceed from the very same error. In either case it is clearly the spiritual that is misconceived; but the first case concerns those who simply deny it, at least in practice if not always explicitly, whereas the second concerns those who are subject to the delusion of a false spirituality; and it is this second case that is now more particularly in view. The reason why so many people allow themselves to be led astray by this delusion is fundamentally quite simple: some of them seek above all for imagined 'powers', or broadly speaking and in one form or another, for the production of more or less extraordinary 'phenomena'; others constrain themselves to 'centralize' their consciousness on inferior 'prolongations' of the human individuality, mistaking them for superior states simply because they are outside the limits within which the activities of the 'average' man are generally enclosed, the limits in question being, in the state corresponding to the profane point of view of the present period, those of what is commonly called 'ordinary life', into which no possibility of an extra-corporeal order can enter. Even within the latter group it is the lure of the 'phenomenon', that is to say in the final analysis the 'experimental' tendency in the modern spirit, which is most frequently at the root of the error; what these people are in fact trying to obtain is always results that are in some way 'sensational', and they mistake such results for 'realization'; but this again amounts to saying that everything belonging to the spiritual order escapes them completely, that they are unable even to conceive of anything of the kind, however remotely; and it would be very much better for them, since they are entirely lacking in spiritual 'qualification', if they were content to remain enclosed in the commonplace and mediocre security of 'ordinary life'. Of course there can be no question of denying the reality as such of the 'phenomena' concerned; in fact they can be said to be only too real, and for that reason all the more dangerous. What is now being formally contested is their value and their interest, particularly from the point of view of spiritual development, and the delusion itself concerns the very nature of spiritual development. Again, if no more than a mere waste of time and effort were involved, the harm would not after all be so very great, but generally speaking the being that becomes attached to such things soon becomes incapable of releasing itself from them or passing beyond them, and its deviation is then beyond remedy; the occurrence of cases of this kind is well known in all the Eastern traditions, where the individuals affected become mere producers of 'phenomena' and will never attain the least degree of spirituality. But there is still something more, for a sort of 'inverted' development can take place, not only conferring no useful advantage, but taking the being ever further away from spiritual 'realization', until it is irretrievably astray in the inferior 'prolongations' of its individuality recently mentioned, and through these it can only come into contact with the 'infra-human'. There is then no escape from its situation, or at least there is only one, and that is the total disintegration of the conscious being; such a disintegration is strictly equivalent in the case of the individual to final dissolution in the case of the totality of the manifested 'cosmos'.

For this reason, perhaps more than for any other, it is impossible to be too mistrustful of every appeal to the 'subconscious', to 'instinct', and to sub-rational 'intuition', no less than to a more or less ill-defined 'vital force'—in a word to all those vague and obscure things that tend to exalt the new philosophy and psychology, yet lead more or less directly to a contact with inferior states. There is therefore all the more reason to exercise extreme vigilance (for the enemy knows only too well how to take on the most insidious disguises) against anything that may lead the being to become 'fused' or preferably and more accurately 'confused' or even 'dissolved' in a sort of 'cosmic consciousness' that shuts out all 'transcendence' and so also shuts out all effective spirituality. This is the ultimate consequence of all the anti-metaphysical errors known more especially in their philosophical aspect by such names as 'pantheism', 'immanentism', and 'naturalism', all of which are closely interrelated, and many people would doubtless recoil before such a consequence if they could know what it is that they are really talking about. These things do indeed quite literally amount to an 'inversion' of spirituality, to a substitution for it of what is truly its opposite, since they inevitably lead to its final loss, and this constitutes 'satanism' properly so called. Whether it be conscious or unconscious in any particular case makes little difference to the result, for it must not be forgotten that the 'unconscious satanism' of some people, who are more numerous than ever in this period in which disorder has spread into every domain, is really in the end no more than an instrument in the service of the 'conscious satanism' of those who represent the 'counter-initiation'.

There has been occasion elsewhere to call attention to the initiatic symbolism of a 'navigation' across the ocean (representing the psychic domain), which must be crossed while avoiding all its dangers in order to reach the goal;[1] but what is to be said of someone who flings himself into the ocean and has no aspiration but to drown himself in it? This is very precisely the significance of a so-called 'fusion' with a 'cosmic consciousness' that is really nothing but the

---

1. See *The King of the World* and *Spiritual Authority & Temporal Power*.

confused and indistinct assemblage of all the psychic influences; and, whatever some people may imagine, these influences have absolutely nothing in common with spiritual influences, even if they may happen to imitate them to a certain extent in some of their outward manifestations (for in this domain 'counterfeit' comes into play in all its fullness, and this is why the 'phenomenal' manifestations so eagerly sought for never by themselves prove anything, for they can be very much the same in a saint as in a sorcerer). Those who make this fatal mistake either forget about or are unaware of the distinction between the 'upper waters' and the 'lower waters'; instead of raising themselves toward the 'ocean above', they plunge into the abyss of the 'ocean below'; instead of concentrating all their powers so as to direct them toward the formless world, which alone can be called 'spiritual', they disperse them in the endlessly changeable and fugitive diversity of the forms of subtle manifestation (this diversity corresponding as nearly as possible to the Bergsonian conception of 'reality') with no suspicion that they are mistaking for a fullness of 'life' something that is in truth the realm of death and of a dissolution without hope of return.

36

PSEUDO-INITIATION

THE ANTI-TRADITIONAL ACTIVITY now being studied in its various aspects has been called 'satanic', but it must be clearly understood that this word is used quite independently of any particular idea that anyone may have formed, whether in conformity with some theological outlook or otherwise, of any so-called 'Satan'; it is superfluous to say that 'personifications' have no importance from the present point of view and can have nothing to do with the matter in hand. What has to be taken into account is, on the one hand, the spirit of negation and of subversion into which 'Satan' is resolved metaphysically, whatever may be the special forms assumed by that spirit in order to be manifested in one domain or another, and, on the other hand, the thing that can properly be held to represent it and so to speak to 'incarnate' it in the terrestrial world, in which its action is being studied—and this thing is precisely what has been called the 'counter-initiation'. It should be noted that the expression 'counter-initiation' has been used here, and not 'pseudo-initiation', for the two are quite different, and it is important moreover not to confuse the counterfeiter with the counterfeit. 'Pseudo-initiation' as it exists today in numerous organizations, many of them attached to some form of 'neo-spiritualism', is but one of many examples of counterfeit, comparable to others to which attention has already been directed in their various orders; nevertheless, as a counterfeit of initiation, 'pseudo-initiation' has perhaps an importance even more considerable than that of the counterfeit of anything else. It is really only one of the products of the state of disorder and confusion brought about in the modern period by the 'satanic' activity that has its conscious starting-point in the 'counter-initiation'; it can also be, although unconsciously, an instrument of the latter, though this is no less true in the end of all the other counterfeits, whatever their degree, in the sense that they are all just so many means contributing to the realization of the same plan of subversion, so that each plays exactly the part, whether it be of greater or of lesser importance, that is assigned to it within the whole, this state of affairs itself constituting moreover a sort of counterfeit of the very order and harmony against which the whole plan is directed.

As for the 'counter-initiation', it is certainly not a mere illusory counterfeit, but on the contrary something very real in its own order, as the effectiveness of its action shows only too well; at least, it is not a counterfeit except in the sense that it necessarily imitates initiation like an inverted shadow, although its real intention is not to imitate but to oppose. This intention is inevitably doomed to failure, for the metaphysical and spiritual domain is completely closed to it, being inherently outside all oppositions; all it can do is to ignore or to deny that domain, and it can in no case get beyond the 'intermediary world'; the psychic domain is indeed in all respects the privileged sphere of influence of 'Satan' in the human order and even in the cosmic order;[1] but the intention exists nonetheless, and it implies a policy of working consistently in direct opposition to initiation. As for 'pseudo-initiation', it is no more than a mere parody, and this is as much as to say that it is nothing in itself, that it is devoid of all profound reality, or, if preferred, that its intrinsic value is neither positive like that of initiation nor negative like that of 'counter-initiation', but is quite simply nil. That being the case, one might be tempted to think that it is nothing but a more or less harmless amusement, but it is not merely that, for reasons that have been stated in the general explanations given of the true character of counterfeits and the part they are destined to play—and with the additional reason in this particular case that rites, by virtue of their nature, which is 'sacred' in the strictest sense of the word, are such that they can never be imitated with impunity. It can be said too

---

1. According to the Islamic doctrine it is through the *nafs* (soul) that *Shayṭān* can obtain a hold on man, whereas the *rūḥ* (spirit), of which the essence is pure light, is beyond the reach of his endeavors.

that the 'pseudo-traditional' counterfeits, to which belong all the denaturings of the idea of tradition dealt with hitherto, take their most dangerous form in 'pseudo-initiation', first because in it they are translated into effective action instead of remaining in the form of more or less vague conceptions, and secondly because they make their attack on tradition from the inside, on what is its very spirit, namely, the esoteric and initiatic domain.

It may be remarked that the 'counter-initiation' works with a view to introducing its agents into 'pseudo-initiatic' organizations, using the agents to 'inspire' the organizations, unperceived by the ordinary members and usually also by the ostensible heads, who are no more aware than the rank-and-file of the purpose they are really serving; but it is as well to add that such agents are in fact introduced in a similar way and wherever possible into all the more exterior 'movements' of the contemporary world, political or otherwise, and even, as was mentioned earlier, into authentically initiatic or religious organizations, but only when their traditional spirit is so weakened that they can no longer resist so insidious a penetration. Nevertheless, except for the last-named case, in which there is the most direct application possible of dissolutionary activity, the 'pseudo-initiatic' organizations doubtless furnish the field of action most worthy of the attention of the 'counter-initiation', and they must be the object of special efforts on its part for the very reason that the work it undertakes is above all anti-traditional, and that it is wholly concentrated on that work and on nothing else. This is the probable reason for the existence of numerous links between 'pseudo-initiatic' manifestations and all sorts of other things that at first sight might appear to have no connection whatever with them, but that are all representative of the modern spirit in one or another of its most fully developed forms;[2] why indeed, if it were not so, should 'pseudo-initiates' constantly play so important a part in such affairs? It could be said that, among all the instruments or measures of all kinds employed in this sort of way, 'pseudo-initiation' must from its very nature logically take first place; it is of course but a cog

---

2. A number of examples of activities of this kind have been given in *Theosophy: History of a Pseudo-Religion*.

in the machine, but a cog that controls many others, and one with which the others become engaged, as it were, in such a way that they derive their movement from it. Here again counterfeit makes its appearance: 'pseudo-initiation' imitates in this way the function of an invisible prime mover [*moteur invisible*], properly belonging in a normal order to initiation; but great care must be taken not to forget that initiation truly and legitimately represents the spirit, principal animator of all things, whereas so far as 'pseudo-initiation' is concerned the spirit is obviously absent. The immediate result is that action instigated through such channels, instead of being truly 'organic', can only have a purely 'mechanical' character, and this fact fully justifies the analogy with cogs used above; moreover, as we have already seen, is it not obvious that the most striking feature of everything we meet with in the world today is its mechanical character, this world where day by day the machine invades new fields, and where the human being himself is reduced to being more and more like an automaton in all his activities, because all spirituality has been taken away from him? That is where all the inferiority of artificial productions is most blatant, even if a 'satanic' cleverness has presided over their elaboration; machines can be manufactured, but not living beings, because, once more, it is the spirit that is bound to be missing and must always remain so.

An 'invisible prime mover' has been mentioned, and in addition to the imitative tendency that is again in evidence from this point of view, 'pseudo-initiation' derives for the purpose it has in view an incontestable advantage over anything that is more 'public' in character from its comparative 'invisibility', however relative it may be. It is not as if 'pseudo-initiatic' organizations for the most part took much trouble to hide their existence, many of them indeed going so far as openly to indulge in a propaganda totally incompatible with their esoteric pretensions, but in spite of this they continue as organizations to be among the least apparent, and to be those that best lend themselves to the exercise of a 'discreet' action, so that the 'counter-initiation' can get more directly into contact with them than with anything else, without having to fear that its intervention will be unmasked, and all the more so because in any such environment it is always possible to find some means of escape from the consequences of an indiscretion or a lack of prudence. Moreover the greater part of the general public, while it is more or less aware of the existence of 'pseudo-initiatic' organizations, is by no means clear as to what they are and is not inclined to attach much importance to them, as it sees nothing in them but mere 'eccentricities' without serious significance; and the very indifference of the public serves the same purpose, albeit unwittingly, as could be attained by strict secrecy.

So far, an attempt has been made to describe as clearly as possible the real, though unconscious, part played by 'pseudo-initiation' and the true nature of its relations with the 'counter-initiation'; and it should be added that the latter may in certain cases find in the former a field of observation and selection for recruitment to its own ranks, but that aspect of the matter need not be pursued here. There is also something of which not even an approximate idea can be conveyed, and that is the unbelievable multiplicity and complexity of the ramifications that in fact subsist between all these things, for they are indeed such that they could only be clarified by a direct and detailed study; but it will probably be agreed that only the 'principle', if that is the right word, is of interest for the present. Nevertheless this is not all: a broad view has been given of the reason for the counterfeiting of the traditional idea by 'pseudo-initiation'; it remains to be shown more precisely how this is achieved, so that the treatment of the matter may not appear to have been too exclusively 'theoretical'.

One of the simplest means at the disposal of 'pseudo-initiatic' organizations for the fabrication of a false tradition for the use of their adherents is undoubtedly 'syncretism', which consists in assembling in a more or less convincing manner elements borrowed from almost anywhere, and in putting them together as it were 'from the outside', without any genuine understanding of what they really represent in the various traditions to which they properly belong. As any such more or less shapeless assemblage must be given some appearance of unity so that it can be presented as a 'doctrine', its elements must somehow be grouped around one or more 'directing ideas', and these last will not be of traditional origin, but, quite the contrary, will usually be wholly profane and modern conceptions, and so inherently anti-traditional; it has already been remarked that in 'neo-spiritualism' the idea of 'evolution' in particular plays a preponderant part in this capacity. It is easy to understand that any such procedure greatly enhances the gravity of the situation; under such conditions it is no longer a question of making a sort of 'mosaic' of traditional odds and ends, which might after all provide no more than a perfectly useless but fairly inoffensive amusement; it becomes a question of denaturing, and it could be described as a 'perversion' of traditional elements, since people will be led to attribute to them a meaning altered so as to agree with the 'directing idea', until finally it runs directly counter to the traditional meaning. Of course those who do this sort of thing may not be acting with any clear consciousness, for the modern mentality that is theirs can be the cause of a real blindness in such matters, in all of which due account must always be taken, first of the simple incomprehension arising from that very mentality, and then, or rather perhaps especially, of the 'suggestions' victimizing in the first place the 'pseudo-initiates' themselves, so that they may in their turn join in inculcating the same suggestions into other people. This kind of unconsciousness in no way alters the results or diminishes the danger of such things, nor does it make them any less suited to serve, even if only 'after the event', the ends at which the 'counter-initiation' is aiming. There are of course cases in which agents of the 'counter-initiation' may have promoted or inspired the formation of 'pseudo-traditions' of the kind described by a more or less direct intervention; a few examples could no doubt be found, but it should not be assumed that even in these cases the conscious agents have themselves been the known and apparent creators of the 'pseudo-initiatic' forms in question, for it is clear that prudence demands that they should always hide as much as possible behind mere unconscious instruments.

The word 'unconsciousness' as used above is intended to mean that those who thus elaborate a 'pseudo-tradition' are usually totally unaware of the purpose it is really serving. Concerning the character and value of any such production, it is more difficult to admit the purity of their good faith, though even in that respect it is possible that they delude themselves to some extent, or that they may be deceived in the manner outlined at the end of the previous paragraph. Account must also be taken fairly frequently of 'anomalies' of a psychic nature, which again complicate matters and incidentally provide particularly favorable conditions for influences and suggestions of all sorts to produce their maximum effect; attention need only be called, without pursuing the matter further, to the anything but negligible part frequently played in such affairs by 'clairvoyants' and other 'sensitives'. But in spite of everything, there almost always comes a point at which conscious trickery and charlatanism become a sort of necessity for the directors of a 'pseudo-initiatic' organization: for instance, if someone happens to notice borrowings made more or less clumsily from a particular tradition—and it is not very difficult to do so—how could the directors admit the fact without being obliged to confess themselves to be no better than ordinary profane people? They do not usually hesitate in a case of that kind to reverse the true relations and boldly declare that it is their own 'tradition' that is the common 'source' of all those they have robbed; and if they do not manage to convince everyone, at least there are always some innocents who will take them at their word, and in numbers sufficient to ensure that their position as 'heads of schools', to which they usually cling above everything else, is not in danger of being seriously compromised, all the more so because they do not pay much attention to the quality of their 'disciples', for, in conformity with the modern mentality, quantity seems to them much more important; and this alone is enough to show how very far they are from having even the most elementary notion of the real nature of esoterism and initiation.

It is scarcely necessary to say that all that has been described so far is no mere matter of more or less hypothetical possibilities, but is a matter of real and properly established fact; if all the facts had to be specified there would be no end to it, and to attempt the task would serve no very useful purpose: a few characteristic examples will suffice. For instance, the procedure of 'syncretism' recently mentioned has been followed in the setting up of a sham 'Oriental tradition', that of the Theosophists, comprising nothing oriental but a terminology misunderstood and misapplied; and as the world of such affairs is always 'divided against itself' in accordance with the

Gospel saying, French occultists in a spirit of opposition and rivalry constructed in their turn a so-called 'Western tradition' of the same kind, in which many of the elements, notably those drawn from the Kabbalah, can hardly be said to be Western with respect to their origin, though they are Western enough with respect to the special manner of their interpretation. The first-named presented their 'tradition' as the very expression of 'ancient wisdom', the second, perhaps a little more modest in their pretensions, sought more particularly to pass off their 'syncretism' as a 'synthesis', and few people have misused this last word so badly. If the first-named showed more ambition it is perhaps because there were present at the origins of their 'movement' some rather enigmatic influences, the true nature of which they themselves would no doubt have been quite unable to determine; so far as the second group is concerned, they knew only too well that there was nothing behind them, that their work was only that of a few individuals with nothing but themselves to rely on, and if nevertheless it so happened that 'something' else effected an entry, that certainly did not happen till much later; these two cases, considered in relation to the circumstances outlined, could without difficulty be taken as applications of what was said earlier, but the task of deducing the consequences that may seem to the reader to arise logically can be left to his own efforts.

The truth is that there has never existed anything that could rightly be called either an 'Oriental tradition' or a 'Western tradition', any such denomination being obviously much too vague to be applied to a defined traditional form, since, unless one goes back to the primordial tradition, which is here not in question for very easily understandable reasons, and which is anyhow neither Eastern nor Western, there are and there always have been diverse and multiple traditional forms both in the East and in the West. Others have thought to do better and to inspire confidence more easily by appropriating to themselves the name of some tradition that really existed at some more or less distant date, and using it as a label for a structure that is no less incongruous than the others, for although they naturally make some use of what they can manage to find out about the tradition on which they have staked their claim, they are forced to reinforce their few facts, always very fragmentary and often even partly hypothetical, by recourse to other elements either borrowed from a different source or wholly imaginary. In every case, a cursory examination of these productions is enough to make apparent the specifically modern spirit that has presided over their formation, and it is invariably betrayed by the presence of one or more of the 'directive ideas' alluded to above; after that there is no object in further researches nor in taking the trouble to determine exactly and in detail the real source of any one element of the mixture, since the first discovery shows clearly enough, and without leaving room for the smallest doubt, that one is in the presence of nothing but a pure counterfeit.

One of the best examples that can be given of the last-named case is that of the many organizations that at the present time call themselves 'Rosicrucian'; needless to say, they do not fail to be mutually contradictory, and even to quarrel more or less openly, while all claim to be the representatives of one and the same 'tradition'. In fact any one of them, without a single exception, can be admitted to be perfectly right when it denounces its rivals as being illegitimate and fraudulent; never have there been as many people calling themselves 'Rosicrucian', or even 'Brothers of the Rose-Cross', as can be found now that there are no authentic ones left! There is anyhow very little danger in passing oneself off as the continuation of something that belongs entirely to the past, especially when the danger of exposure is further reduced by the fact that the organization in question has, as in this case, always been enveloped in some obscurity, so much so that its end is as obscure as its origin; is there anyone among the profane public or even among the 'pseudo-initiates' who can say exactly what the tradition that was known for a time as Rosicrucian really was? It should be mentioned that these remarks on the usurpation of the name of an initiatic organization do not apply to a case such as that of the imaginary 'Great White Lodge', of which oddly enough more and more is being heard in many quarters, and no longer only among the Theosophists: at no time and in no place has this name ever had an authentically traditional connotation; and if it is used as the conventional 'mask' for something that has some degree of reality, then that thing should certainly not be sought for in the initiatic domain.

The fact that some people choose to locate the 'Masters' to whom they profess adherence in some highly inaccessible region of central Asia or elsewhere has often aroused comment; this is a fairly easy way of ensuring that their assertions are unverifiable, but it is not the only way, because remoteness in time can serve the same purpose in this respect as remoteness in space. Others do not hesitate to claim to be attached to some tradition that has entirely disappeared and has been extinct for centuries, even for thousands of years. However, unless they are bold enough to assert that their chosen tradition has been perpetuated for that length of time in a manner so secret and so well concealed that nobody but themselves has been able to discover the smallest trace of it, they are admittedly deprived of the appreciable advantage of being able to claim a direct and continuous filiation, for in their case the claim cannot even present an appearance of plausibility such as it can still present when of a fairly recent form such as that of the Rosicrucian tradition is chosen; but this defect does not seem to have much importance in their eyes, for they are so ignorant of the true conditions of initiation that they readily imagine that a mere 'ideal' attachment, without any regular transmission, can take the place of an effective attachment. It is moreover clear that a tradition will lend itself the more readily to any fantastic 'reconstitution' the more completely it is lost and forgotten, and that it is then all the more difficult to be sure about the real significance of its remaining vestiges, which can therefore be made to mean almost anything desired, each person naturally putting into it whatever may conform to his own ideas. There is doubtless no need to look for any other explanation of the fact that the Egyptian tradition is specially 'exploited' in this way, and that so many 'pseudo-initiates' of very different schools show a preference for it that would otherwise be difficult to understand. It must be made clear, in order to avoid any mistaken application of what has been said, that these observations in no way concern references to Egypt or to other things of the same kind such as may sometimes be met with in certain initiatic organizations, where however their character is only that of symbolical 'legends', with no pretension to a superior value based on their initiatic origin. The question now at issue is that of alleged restorations, purporting to be valid as such, of traditions or initiations that no longer exist; but no such restoration, even on the impossible supposition that it could be exact and complete in all respects, would in any case possess any inherent interest, except as a mere archaeological curiosity.

Here this already long discussion must be brought to a close; it has amply sufficed to indicate in a general way the nature of the many 'pseudo-initiatic' counterfeits of the traditional idea that are so characteristic of our times: a mixture, more or less coherent but rather less than more so, of elements partly borrowed and partly invented, the whole dominated by anti-traditional conceptions such as are peculiar to the modern spirit, and for this reason serving no purpose other than the further spread of these same conceptions by making them pass with some people as traditional, not to mention the manifest deceit that consists in giving, in place of 'initiation', not only something purely profane in itself, but also something that makes for 'profanation'. Should anyone now put forward the suggestion, as a sort of extenuating circumstance, that there are always in these affairs, despite all their faults, some elements derived from genuinely traditional sources, the answer would be this: in order to get itself accepted, every imitation must take on at least some of the features of the thing imitated, but that is just what makes it so dangerous; is not the cleverest lie, as well as the most deadly, precisely the lie that mixes most inextricably the true and the false, thus contriving to press the true into service in order to promote the triumph of the false?

37

THE DECEPTIVENESS OF 'PROPHECIES'

THE MIXTURE OF TRUTH AND FALSEHOOD met with in the 'pseudo-traditions' of modern manufacture is found again in the so-called 'prophecies' that have been propagated and exploited in every way, especially in the last few years, for ends of which the least that can be said is that they are highly enigmatic. They are described as 'so-called' prophecies because the word 'prophecy' can only be properly used of the announcements of future events contained in the sacred books of the various traditions and proceeding from an inspiration of a purely spiritual order; any other use of the word is entirely misleading, 'prediction' being the proper word to use in all other cases. Predictions may come from quite varied sources; at least some have been a result of the application of certain secondary tra-ditional sciences, and these are certainly the most valid, but only on condition that their meaning can really be understood, and this is not always very easy, because for many reasons they are usually for-mulated in rather obscure terms, which often do not become clear until after the events to which they relate have taken place; it is there-fore always as well to be mistrustful, not of the predictions them-selves, but of the erroneous or 'tendentious' interpretations that may be made of them. As for the rest, insofar as there is anything authen-tic in them, it emanates almost exclusively from 'seers'—sincere no doubt, though only very partially 'enlightened'—who have experi-enced certain confused perceptions related more or less accurately to a future that is usually not at all clearly determined, particularly as to the date and the order of succession of events, and who have unconsciously mixed those perceptions with their own ideas and consequently expressed them still more confusedly, so much so that it becomes possible to find in their statements almost anything one wants to find.

It is easy to see what purpose this sort of thing can serve under present conditions: such predictions almost always present everything in a distressing or even in a terrifying light, because that is the aspect of events that has naturally struck the 'seers', it is therefore enough, in order to disturb the mentality of the public, merely to spread them about, accompanied if necessary by commentaries that will emphasize their threatening aspect and will treat the events they are concerned with as imminent.[1] If one prediction agrees with another their effect will be reinforced, and if they contradict one another, as often happens, they will only produce all the more disorder; in either case there will be so much the more gained by the forces of subversion. It must be added too that all these things, proceeding as they generally do from fairly low regions in the psychic domain, carry with them for that reason unbalancing and dissolving influences that add considerably to their danger, this no doubt being why even those who put no faith in them experience, in many cases, a kind of discomfort in their presence, comparable to that induced even in people who are not at all 'sensitive' by the presence of subtle forces of an inferior order. One would scarcely believe, for example, how many people have become seriously and perhaps irremediably unbalanced through the numerous predictions connected with the 'Great Pope' or the 'Grand Monarch'. These predictions do contain a few traces of certain truths, but strangely distorted by the 'mirrors' of an inferior psychism, and in addition brought down to the measure of the mentality of the 'seers' who have to some extent 'materialized' them and have 'localized' them more or less narrowly

---

1. The announcement of the destruction of Paris by fire, for example, has been promulgated several times in this way, the exact dates being specified, although nothing has ever happened, except for the impression of terror invariably aroused in many people, and never growing any less with the repeated failure of the predictions.

so as to force them into the framework of their own preconceived ideas.[2] The way in which this group of predictions is presented by the 'seers' in question, who are very often the subjects of 'suggestions',[3] makes a near approach to certain very dark and 'underground' matters, the astonishing ramifications of which, at least since the beginning of the nineteenth century, would be particularly interesting to follow for anyone who wanted to write a history of those times, a history would certainly be very different from the one that is taught 'officially'. But needless to say there can be no question of going into the detail of these matters, and it must suffice simply to have mentioned this very complex affair, which has obviously been intentionally confused in all its aspects;[4] for it could not have been passed over in silence without leaving too big a blank in the list of the principal elements characteristic of the modern period, since it constitutes one of the most significant symptoms of the second phase of anti-traditional action.

Moreover, the mere propagation of predictions such as those alluded to is only the most elementary part of the work now going on in this field, for almost all the propagation that needs to be done has already been done, though unwittingly, by the 'seers' themselves; other parts of the work demand the elaboration of subtler interpretations if the predictions are to be made to serve the desired ends. The predictions used in this way are more particularly those that are based on certain forms of traditional knowledge, and then it is their obscurity that is chiefly taken advantage of for the purpose

2. The relatively valid part of the predictions in question seems to be related chiefly to the function of the *Mahdi* and that of the tenth *Avatāra*; these matters, which directly concern the preparation for the final 'rectification', are outside the subject of this book; all that need be mentioned now is that their very deformation lends itself to an 'inverted' exploitation leading toward subversion.

3. It must be clearly understood that this in no way means that they are the subjects of 'hallucinations': the difference between the meaning of the two terms is the difference between seeing things that have been consciously and voluntarily imagined by others, and imagining them oneself 'subconsciously'.

4. For example, a little thought about all that has been done to throw the question of the survival of Louis XVII into inextricable confusion will give an idea of what is meant here.

in view;[5] some of the Biblical prophecies themselves are for the same reason the objects of this kind of 'tendentious' interpretation, the authors of which are incidentally often acting in good faith, but can only be regarded as the victims of 'suggestion' and as being made use of to apply 'suggestion' to others. It is as if there were a sort of highly contagious psychic 'epidemic', but it fits too neatly into the plan of subversion to be 'spontaneous'; on the contrary, like all other manifestations of the modern disorder (including the revolutions, which the ingenuous also believe to be 'spontaneous') it necessarily presupposes a conscious will at its starting-point. The worst form of blindness would be to see nothing more in all this but a mere question of 'fashion' without real importance;[6] and the same could be said of the growing diffusion of certain 'divinatory arts', which are certainly not as inoffensive as people who do not get to the bottom of things may suppose: they are generally the uncomprehended residues of ancient traditional sciences now almost entirely lost, and, apart from the danger already attached to them by virtue of their 'residual' character, they are arranged and combined in such a way that their employment opens the door, under the pretext of 'intuition' (and this approach to the 'new philosophy' is in itself rather remarkable), to the intervention of all those psychic influences that are most dubious in character.[7]

Use is also made, along with appropriate interpretations, of predictions more suspect in origin but nonetheless fairly old; these

5. The predictions of Nostradamus provide the most typical and the most important example; the more or less extraordinary interpretations assigned to them, particularly in the last few years, are almost numberless.

6. 'Fashion' itself, an essentially modern invention, is in its real significance something not entirely devoid of importance: it represents unceasing and aimless change, in contrast to the stability and order that reign in traditional civilizations.

7. Much could be said in this connection about the use of the Tarot in particular. It contains vestiges of an undeniably traditional science, whatever may have been its real origin, but it also has some very tenebrous aspects; no allusion is intended here to the many occultist fantasies to which the Tarot has given rise, for they are mostly negligible; the concern is with something much more effective, making its handling really dangerous for anyone not sufficiently protected against the action of the 'underground forces'.

were perhaps not originally made in order to be of use in present circumstances, although the powers of subversion had evidently acquired some considerable influence at the time of their origin (the time in question being that at which the modern deviation may be said to have begun, from the fourteenth to the sixteenth centuries), and it is not impossible that those powers then had in view, not only some more special and immediate objective, but also the preparation for a work not intended to be accomplished until after a long interval.[8] This preparation has in fact never ceased: it has been carried out in other modalities, of which the 'suggestion' applied to modern 'seers' and the organization of 'apparitions' of a very unorthodox kind represent an aspect in which the direct intervention of subtle influences is most clearly shown; but this aspect is not the only one, and, even when it is a question of predictions apparently manufactured 'from start to finish', similar influences may very well come into play to no less an extent, firstly for the very reason that their original inspiration emanates from a 'counter-initiatic' source, and secondly because of the nature of the elements that are taken to serve as 'supports' to their elaboration.

These last words are written with an example in mind that is quite astonishing, as much in itself as in the success it has had in many quarters; for those reasons it deserves rather more than a mere mention: the example is that of the so-called 'prophecies of the Great Pyramid', widely disseminated in England and thence to the whole world for ends that are perhaps in part political, but which certainly go beyond politics in the ordinary sense of the word. They

8. Anyone who may be desirous of learning some details of this aspect of the question might usefully consult, in spite of the reservations that would have to be made on certain points, a book called *Autour de la Tiare* by Roger Duquet, the posthumous work of a man who had been fairly closely involved in some of the 'underground' work referred to above, and who wanted at the end of his life to give his 'testimony', as he himself says, and to contribute to some extent to the unmasking of these mysterious undercurrents; the 'personal' reasons he may have had for doing this have no importance, and in any case clearly do not detract in any way from the interest of his 'revelations'. [Full reference: Roger Duquet, *Autour de la Tiare: Essai sur les prophéties concernant la succession des papes du XIIIe siècle à la fin des temps: Joachim de Fiore, Anselma de Marsico, St. Malachie, le 'Moine de Padoue',* etc. (Paris: Nouvelle éditions latine, 1997). ED.]

are closely linked to another piece of work undertaken in order to persuade the English that they are the descendants of the 'lost tribes of Israel'; but here again it would be impossible to go into details without getting involved in developments that would be out of place here. However that may be, here is the gist of the matter in a few words: by measuring, in a manner not wholly free from arbitrariness (all the more so because nobody is in fact quite sure about the measures actually used by the ancient Egyptians), the various parts of the corridors and chambers of the Great Pyramid,[9] an attempt has been made to discover 'prophecies' in the form of correspondences between the numbers thus obtained and the dates of history. There is in this an absurdity so manifest that one cannot but wonder how it is that nobody seems to notice it; it only shows the extent to which our contemporaries are victims of 'suggestion', for even supposing that the constructors of the Pyramid really did build some sort of 'prophecies' into it, there are two things that would on the whole be plausible: either that the 'prophecies', which would necessarily have to be based on some knowledge of cyclic laws, should be related to the history of the world in general and of humanity, or that they should be adapted so as to deal more particularly with Egypt; but in fact neither turns out to be the case, for all the information extracted is in a form related to the point of view of Judaism in the first place, and of Christianity in the second, so that the only logical conclusion would be that the Pyramid is not an Egyptian monument at all, but a 'Judeo-Christian' monument! This alone should be enough to put this unlikely story into its proper place; but it is worth adding that the whole is conceived in accordance with a so-called 'chronology' of the Bible that is highly contestable

---

9. The Great Pyramid is in truth not so very much bigger than the two others, especially than its nearest neighbor, so that the difference is not very striking; but without any very evident reason all the modern 'seekers' have been as it were 'hypnotized' almost exclusively by this one; to it are always related all their most fanciful hypotheses, many of which could better be described as 'fantastic', including, to give only two of the queerest examples, one that attempts to find in its interior arrangements a map of the sources of the Nile, and another that makes out that the 'Book of the Dead' is no more than an explanatory description of those same arrangements.

and conforms to the narrowest and most Protestant 'literalism', doubtless because the material had to be adapted to the special mentality of the environment in which it was to be chiefly circulated in the first place. Many other curious features could be noted: thus it appears that no date since the beginning of the Christian era can have been of sufficient interest to be recorded before that of the invention of railways; if that were so one would have to believe that these ancient builders brought a very modern perspective to bear on their appreciation of the importance of events; in this appears the element of the grotesque never lacking in that sort of thing, and it is precisely that which betrays their real origin: the devil is no doubt very clever, but he can never help being ridiculous in one way or another![10]

But this is still not all: from time to time, on the strength of the 'prophecies of the Great Pyramid' or of other predictions, and as a result of calculations of which the basis is never very clearly defined, it is announced that such and such an exact date will mark 'the entry

10. Before leaving the subject of the Great Pyramid, attention should be drawn to another modern fantasy connected with it: some people attach much importance to the fact that it was never finished; the summit is in fact missing, but all that can be said for certain about it is that the most ancient authors whose evidence is available, but who are nevertheless relatively recent, all describe it as truncated, as it is today; but it is a long step from this to the claim, as expressed word for word by an occultist, that 'the hidden symbolism of the Hebrew and Christian Scriptures is directly related to events that took place in the course of the building of the Great Pyramid'; indeed, this is another assertion that seems singularly lacking in plausibility on all counts! It is a strange fact that the official seal of the United States bears the truncated pyramid, and over it is a triangle with rays, separated and isolated from it by a surrounding circle of clouds, but apparently intended to replace the summit. There are other decidedly strange details in this seal as well, and the 'pseudo-initiatic' organizations rampant in America try to make good use of them by interpreting them in conformity with their own 'doctrines'; they certainly seem to indicate an intervention by suspicious influences: thus, the number of the courses of the Pyramid is thirteen (this number reappearing somewhat insistently in other features, notably that of the letters of which the motto E pluribus unum is composed) and is alleged to correspond to the number of the tribes of Israel (the two half-tribes of the sons of Joseph being counted separately), and no doubt this has some connection with the real origin of the 'prophecies of the Great Pyramid', which, as we have seen, tend to treat the Pyramid as a sort of 'Judeo-Christian' monument, for reasons that are somewhat obscure.

of humanity into a new era' or else 'the coming of a spiritual renewal' (we shall see later on how this must really be understood); several of these dates are already past, and it does not appear that anything very notable has happened; but what does all that sort of thing really signify? In fact, it is just another way of making use of predictions (additional, that is, to their use for increasing the disorder of our times by broadcasting seeds of trouble and disorganization), and perhaps not the least important, for it turns them into an instrument of direct suggestion, thus contributing to the effective determination of the course of certain future events; for instance, to take a simple and easily understood example, does anyone believe that the repeated announcement of a revolution in a particular country at a particular time will not assist those who have an interest in its breaking out at that time? Underlying the present situation is the fact that certain people want to create a 'state of mind' favorable to the realization of 'something' that is part of their plans; this 'something' can no doubt be modified by the action of contrary influences, but they hope that their methods will serve to bring it about a little sooner or a little later. It remains to be shown more exactly to what this 'pseudo-spiritual' enterprise is leading, and it is necessary to say, without meaning to be in any way 'pessimistic' (all the more so because, as has been explained on other occasions, 'optimism' and 'pessimism' are opposed sentimental attitudes which as such, must remain wholly outside the strictly traditional point of view adopted here), that the outlook for the fairly near future is anything but reassuring.

38

FROM
ANTI-TRADITION
TO
COUNTER-TRADITION

THE PREVIOUS CHAPTER was concerned with matters that, like everything else belonging essentially to the modern world, are radically anti-traditional; but in a sense they go even further than 'anti-tradition', understood as being pure negation and nothing more, for they lead toward the setting up of something that can more appropriately be called a 'counter-tradition'. The distinction between the two is similar to that made earlier between deviation and subversion, and it corresponds to the same two phases of anti-traditional action considered as a whole. 'Anti-tradition' found its most complete expression in the kind of materialism that could be called 'integral', such as that which prevailed toward the end of the last century; as for the 'counter-tradition', we can still only see the preliminary signs of it, in the form of all the things that are striving to become counterfeits in one way or another of the traditional idea itself. It is as well to point out at once that, just as the tendency to 'solidification', expressing itself as 'anti-tradition', has not been able to reach its extreme limit—since that limit would have been outside and beneath all possible existence—it may be expected that the same will apply to the tendency to dissolution, expressing itself in its turn in the 'counter-tradition'. The very conditions of manifestation, so long as the cycle is not entirely completed, obviously demand that this should be so; and as far as the actual end of the cycle is concerned, it presupposes the 'rectification' whereby the 'malefic' tendencies will be 'transmuted' to produce a definitely 'benefic' result, as has already been explained above. Moreover, all the prophecies (the word is of course used here in its rightful sense) indicate that the apparent triumph of the 'counter-tradition' will only be a passing one, and that at the very moment when it seems most complete it will be destroyed by the action of spiritual influences which will intervene at that point to prepare for the final 'rectification'.[1] Nothing less than a direct intervention of this kind would in fact suffice to bring to an end, at the chosen time, the most formidable and the most truly 'satanic' of all the possibilities included in cyclical manifestation; but that is enough by way of anticipation, and it is now necessary to continue with a more careful examination of the real nature of the 'counter-tradition'.

For this purpose, the part to be played by the 'counter-initiation' must again be referred to: after having worked always in the shadows to inspire and direct invisibly all modern movements, it will in the end contrive to 'exteriorize', if that is the right word, something that will be as it were the counterpart of a true tradition, at least as completely and as exactly as it can be so within the limitations necessarily inherent in all possible counterfeits as such. Just as initiation is, as explained, the thing that effectively represents the spirit of a tradition, so will the 'counter-initiation' play a comparable part with respect to the 'counter-tradition'; but obviously it would be quite wrong and improper to speak of the spirit in the second case, since it concerns that from which the spirit is most completely absent, that which would even be its opposite if the spirit were not essentially beyond all opposition; nevertheless opposition is undoubtedly attempted, and is accompanied by imitation in the manner of the inverted shadow previously referred to on more than

---

1. To this truth is really related the formula 'when everything seems lost, then it is that everything will be saved', repeated in a sort of mechanical way by a considerable number of 'seers', each of whom has of course applied it to something he can understand, usually to events of comparatively minor importance, even to such as are quite secondary and merely 'local', by virtue of the 'minimizing' tendency already mentioned in connection with the stories about the 'Grand Monarch', leading to his being seen as no more than a future king of France; needless to say, real prophecies are concerned with affairs of quite different dimensions.

one occasion. That is why the 'counter-tradition', however far it carries the imitation, will never succeed in being anything but a parody, but it will be the most extreme and the most gigantic of all parodies, and we have only so far seen, despite all the falsification of the modern world, some very partial 'trials' and some very pale 'prefigurations' of it; something much more formidable is in preparation for a future considered by some to be near, the growing rapidity of the succession of events today being an indication of its proximity. Needless to say, no attempt will be made here to fix on more or less precise dates, after the fashion of the followers of the so-called 'prophecies'; and even if it were possible to do so through a knowledge of the exact length of cyclical periods (the main difficulty in such cases lying always in the establishment of the right starting-point to take as a basis of calculation), it would nevertheless be proper to maintain the strictest reserve about the results, and that for reasons exactly contrary to those that actuate the conscious or unconscious propagators of denatured predictions, that is to say, in order not to run the risk of contributing to a further growth of the anxiety and disorder now reigning in our world.

However that may be, the thing that makes it possible for affairs to reach such a point is that the 'counter-initiation' (and this is something that must be said) cannot be regarded as a purely human invention, such as would be in no way distinguishable by its nature from plain 'pseudo-initiation'; in fact it is much more than that, and, in order that it may really be so, it must in a certain sense, so far as its actual origin is concerned, proceed from the unique source to which all initiation is attached, the very source from which, speaking more generally, everything in our world that manifests a 'non-human' element proceeds; but the 'counter-initiation' proceeds from that source by a degeneration carried to its extreme limit, and that limit is represented by the 'inversion' that constitutes 'satanism' properly so called. A degeneration of this kind is obviously much more profound than is that of a tradition merely deviated to a certain extent, or even truncated and left with only its lower part; something more is involved even than in cases of dead traditions so completely abandoned by the spirit that the 'counter-initiation' itself can make use of their 'residues' for its own purposes, as explained earlier. This leads logically to the thought that this extreme degeneration must go a very long way back into the past; and, however obscure the question of its origins may be, there is some plausibility in the idea that it may be connected with the perversion of one of the ancient civilizations belonging to one or another of the continents that have disappeared in cataclysms occurring in the course of the present *Manvantara*.[2] In any case it is scarcely necessary to say that as soon as the spirit has withdrawn itself it is no longer possible to speak of initiation; the representatives of the 'counter-initiation' are in fact as completely ignorant as ordinary profane people, and more irremediably ignorant, of the essential, in other words, of all truth of a spiritual and metaphysical order, for this truth has become completely strange to them, even in its most elementary principles, ever since 'heaven was closed' to them.[3] Since it can neither lead beings toward 'supra-human' states as can initiation, nor confine itself exclusively to the human domain, the 'counter-initiation' inevitably leads them toward the 'infra-human', and the power to do so is precisely the only effective power left to it; it is only too easy to see that this is something quite different from the comedy of 'pseudo-initiation'. In Islamic esoterism it is said that one who presents himself at a certain 'gate', without having reached it by a normal and legitimate way, sees it shut in his face and is obliged to turn back, but not as a mere profane person, for he can never be such again, but as a *sāher* (a sorcerer or a magician working in the domain of subtle possibilities of an inferior order).[4] It would be impossible to put the position more clearly; it is a question of the 'infernal' way trying to oppose the 'celestial' way, and actually achieving the outward appearances of

---

2. The sixth chapter of Genesis might perhaps provide, in a symbolical form, some indications relating to the distant origins of the 'counter-initiation'.

3. The symbolism of the 'fall of the angels' can be applied analogically to the matter in hand, which corresponds exactly thereto in the human order; and that is why the word 'satanic' can be used in its most precise sense in this connection.

4. The last degree of the 'counter-initiatic' hierarchy is occupied by what are called the 'saints of Satan' (*awliyā' al-shayṭān*) who are in a sense the inverse of the true saints (*awliyā' al-Raḥmān*), thus manifesting the most complete expression possible of 'inverted spirituality' (cf. *The Symbolism of the Cross*).

opposition, although such appearances can only be illusory; and, as was pointed out earlier when speaking of the false spirituality in which some beings, who are engaged in a sort of 'inverted realization', lose themselves, this way can only end at last in the total 'disintegration' of the conscious being and in its final dissolution.[5]

Naturally, in order that the imitation by inverted reflection may be as complete as possible, centers are likely to be established to which the organizations appertaining to the 'counter-initiation' will be attached. These centers will of course be purely 'psychic', like the influences they use and transmit, and in no sense spiritual, like the centers of initiation and of the true tradition, but they will be able, for the reasons given, to assume up to a point the outward appearance of spiritual centers, thus producing the illusion characteristic of 'inverted spirituality'. But there need be no cause for surprise if these centers themselves, and not merely some of the organizations that are more or less directly subordinated to them, are found to be engaged in struggles one with another, for the domain in which they are placed is the nearest domain of all to 'chaotic' dissolution, and therefore all oppositions are given free rein in it, and are not harmonized and reconciled by the direct action of a superior principle, necessarily lacking in such case. The result often is an impression of confusion and incoherence in everything connected with the manifestations of these centers and their offshoots, and that impression is certainly not illusory; it is even a characteristic 'mark' of such things; they can only agree as it were negatively, in the common struggle against the true spiritual centers, insofar as the latter are situated on a level at which such a struggle can take place, that is to say only insofar as they are concerned with a domain that does not extend beyond the limits of our individual state.[6] It is here that what

5. A finality so conclusive of course represents only an exceptional case, which is that of the *awliyā' al-shayṭān*; the fate of those who have gone less far in the same direction is only that of being abandoned on a road that leads nowhere, to which they may be confined for the indefinity of an 'aeon' or cycle.

6. From the initiatic point of view this domain is that of what are known as the 'lesser mysteries'; on the other hand, everything connected with the 'greater mysteries' is essentially of a 'supra-human' order, and is thereby out of range of any

can properly be called the 'stupidity of the devil' becomes apparent: the representatives of the 'counter-initiation' who act in this way are deluded into thinking that they are opposing the spirit itself, though nothing can really be opposed to it; but at the same time, in spite of themselves and unknown to themselves, they are really subordinated to it and can never cease to be so, just as everything that exists is submitted, albeit unconsciously and involuntarily, to the divine Will, from which nothing can escape. Thus they too are in fact being made use of, though against their will, and though they may themselves hold an exactly contrary belief, for the realization of 'the divine plan in the human domain';[7] like all other beings they take the part in that plan that suits their nature, but instead of being effectively conscious of that part, as are the true initiates, they are only conscious of its negative and inverse aspect. Thus they themselves are dupes, and in a way that is much worse for them than is the mere ignorance of the profane, since, instead of keeping them as it were at the same point, it has the effect of driving them ever further away from the principial center, until finally they fall into 'outer darkness'. But if the affair is looked at, not in relation to these beings themselves, but in relation to the world as a whole, it must be allowed that they are necessary in the place they occupy as elements in that whole, like all other beings, and as 'providential' instruments (to use theological language) in the passage of the world through its cycle of manifestation, for all partial disorders, even when they appear in a certain sense to be the supreme disorder, must nonetheless necessarily contribute in some way to the total order.

These few considerations should make it easier to understand why the constitution of a 'counter-tradition' is possible, but also why it can never be otherwise than eminently unstable and almost ephemeral, but this does not prevent its actually being in itself, as was said earlier, the most redoubtable of all possibilities. It will also

such opposition, since it belongs to the domain which is by its very nature absolutely closed and inaccessible to the 'counter-initiation' and to its representatives at all levels.

7. *Al-Tadāb r al-ilāhiyyah fi'l-mamlakat al-insāniyyah*, title of a treatise of Muḥyi' d-Dīn ibn al-'Arabī.

be understood that this is the goal at which the 'counter-initiation' really aims and has always aimed throughout the whole course of its activity, and that the merely negative 'anti-tradition' only represented a necessary preparation. It now only remains to investigate rather more closely what can be foreseen, with the help of various concordant indications, of the modalities in which the 'counter-tradition' is likely to be realized in the future.

39

THE GREAT PARODY:
OR SPIRITUALITY
INVERTED

FROM EVERYTHING THAT HAS BEEN SAID so far it is easy to deduce that the setting up of the 'counter-tradition' and its apparent momentary triumph will in effect be the reign of what has been called 'inverted spirituality'; this last is of course only a parody of spirituality, imitating it so to speak in an inverse sense, so as to appear to be its very opposite; it appears to be its opposite, but is not really so, for whatever may be its pretensions no symmetry or equivalence between the one and the other is possible. This point must be insisted on, for many people allow themselves to be deceived by appearances, and imagine that there exist in the world two contrary principles contesting against one another for supremacy; this is an erroneous conception, identical to that commonly attributed, rightly or wrongly, to the Manicheans, and consisting, to use theological language, in putting Satan on the same level as God. There are certainly nowadays many people who are 'Manicheans' in this sense without knowing it, and this too is the effect of a 'suggestion' as pernicious as any. The conception concerned amounts to the affirmation of a fundamentally irreducible principial duality, or in other words, to a denial of the supreme Unity that is beyond all oppositions and all antagonisms; that such a denial should be made by adherents of the 'counter-initiation' need cause no surprise, and it may even be sincere on their part, since the metaphysical domain is completely closed to them: it is therefore all the more evidently necessary for them to propagate the conception and to impose it on others, for in no other way can they succeed in getting themselves taken for what they are not and what they can never really be, namely, representatives of something that could be put on a level with spirituality and might eventually prevail over it.

This 'inverted spirituality' is thus in very truth only a false spirituality, but it is false to the most extreme degree conceivable; false spirituality can be spoken of in every case in which, for example, the psychic is mistaken for the spiritual, without necessarily going as far as total subversion, and that is why the expression 'inverted spirituality' is certainly best suited for designating total subversion, provided that the way in which it must be understood is precisely specified. It is in fact identifiable with the 'spiritual renewal' the near approach of which is persistently announced by people who are often quite unaware of its real nature; or again, it is the 'new age', into which the present humanity is being driven by all available means,[1] and the general state of 'expectation' created by the diffusion of the predictions alluded to above may well contribute effectively toward hastening its arrival. The attraction of 'phenomena', already taken account of as one of the determining factors in the confusion of the psychic and the spiritual, may also play a very important part, for most men will be caught and deceived by it in the time of the 'counter-tradition', since it is said that the 'false prophets' who will arise at that time shall 'show great signs and wonders, so as to lead astray, if possible, even the elect.'[2]

It is particularly in this connection that the manifestations of 'metapsychics' and of the various forms of 'neo-spiritualism' may even now be taken as a sort of 'prefiguration' of what must happen later, though they only give a very slight idea of it. In principle, the action of the same inferior subtle forces will be involved, but those forces will be set to work with incomparably greater strength; and when one sees how many people are always ready blindly to place

---

1. The extent to which the expression 'new age' has in these days been spread about and repeated in all quarters is almost unbelievable, with a significance that can often appear to be different in different cases, but it always tends positively to the establishment of the same persuasion in the mentality of the public.

2. Matt. 24:24.

complete confidence in all the divagations of a mere 'medium', simply because they are supported by 'phenomena', it is not surprising that seduction will then be more general. That is why it can never be said often enough that 'phenomena' by themselves prove absolutely nothing where the truth of a doctrine or of any sort of teaching is concerned, and that 'phenomena' are the special domain of the 'great illusion', wherein everything that people so readily take to be signs of 'spirituality' can always be simulated and counterfeited by the play of the inferior forces in question. This is perhaps the only field in which the imitation may be really perfect, because the very same 'phenomena' (the word being taken in its proper sense of outward appearances), will in fact be produced in both cases, the difference lying only in the nature of the causes engaged in each. The great majority of men are inevitably unable to determine the nature of these causes, so that there is no doubt that the best thing to do is not to attach the slightest importance to anything 'phenomenal', or perhaps better still to regard it *a priori* as an unfavorable sign; but how can this be made comprehensible to the 'experimental' mentality of our contemporaries, a mentality first fashioned by the 'scientistic' point of view of the 'anti-tradition', and finally becoming one of the most potentially effective contributing factors in the success of the 'counter-tradition'?

'Neo-spiritualism' and the 'pseudo-initiation' proceeding from it are also from another point of view as it were a partial 'prefiguration' of the 'counter-tradition'. Reference has already been made to the utilization of elements authentically traditional in origin, perverted from their true meaning, and then to some extent brought into the service of error; this perversion is only a move in the direction of the complete reversal that must characterize the 'counter-tradition' (the case of the intentional reversal of symbols dealt with earlier being a significant example); but at that time there will no longer be only a few fragmentary and scattered elements involved, because it will be necessary to produce the illusion of something comparable, indeed of something intended by its authors to be equivalent, to that which constitutes the integrality of a real tradition, including its outward applications in all domains. It may be observed in this connection that the 'counter-initiation', although it invented and propagated for its own purposes all the modern ideas that together represent the merely negative 'anti-tradition', is perfectly conscious of the falsity of those ideas, and obviously knows all too well what attitude to adopt with respect to them; but that in itself indicates that the intention in propagating them can only have been the accomplishment of a transitory and preliminary phase, for no such enterprise of conscious falsehood could be in itself the true and only aim in view; it was only intended to prepare for the ultimate coming of something different, something that should appear to constitute a more 'positive' accomplishment, namely, the 'counter-tradition' itself. This is why one can already see sketched out, in various productions of indubitably 'counter-initiatic' origin or inspiration, the idea of an organization that would be like the counterpart, but by the same token also the counterfeit, of a traditional conception such as that of the 'Holy Empire', and some such organization must become the expression of the 'counter-tradition' in the social order; and for similar reasons the Antichrist must appear like something that could be called, using the language of the Hindu tradition, an inverted *Chakravartī*.[3]

The reign of the 'counter-tradition' is in fact precisely what is known as the 'reign of Antichrist', and the Antichrist, independently of all possible preconceptions, is in any case that which will concentrate and synthesize in itself for this final task all the powers of the 'counter-initiation', whether it be conceived as an individual or as a collectivity. It could even, in a certain sense, be both at the same time, for there must be a collectivity that will be as it were the

---

3. On the subject of the *Chakravartī* or 'universal monarch' see *The Esoterism of Dante*, and *The King of the World*. The *Chakravartī* is literally 'he who makes the wheel turn', and this implies that he is situated at the center of all things, whereas the Antichrist is on the contrary the being who will be situated furthest from that center; he will nevertheless claim to 'make the wheel turn', but in a direction opposite to that of the normal cyclic movement (incidentally, this is 'prefigured' unconsciously in the modern idea of 'progress'), whereas in fact no change in the rotation is possible before the 'reversal of the poles', that is before the 'rectification' that can only be brought about by the intervention of the tenth *Avatāra*; moreover the Antichrist will parody in his own way the very function of the final *Avatāra*, who is represented as the 'second coming of Christ' in the Christian tradition.

THE GREAT PARODY: OR SPIRITUALITY INVERTED 271

'exteriorization' of the 'counter-initiatic' organization itself when it finally appears in the light of day, and there must also be a person who will be at the head of the collectivity, and as such be the most complete expression and even the very 'incarnation' of what it will represent, if only in the capacity of 'support' to all the malefic influences that he will first concentrate in himself and then project onto the world.[4] He will obviously be an 'imposter' (this is the meaning of the word *dajjāl* by which he is usually designated in Arabic) since his reign will be nothing other than the 'Great Parody' in its completest form, the 'satanic' imitation and caricature of everything that is truly traditional and spiritual; nevertheless he will be made in such a way, so to speak, that it will be entirely impossible for him not to play that part. His time will certainly no longer be the 'reign of quantity', which was itself only the end-point of the 'anti-tradition'; it will on the contrary be marked, under the pretext of a false 'spiritual restoration', by a sort of reintroduction of quality in all things, but of quality inverted with respect to its normal and legitimate significance.[5] After the 'egalitarianism' of our times there will again be a visibly established hierarchy, but an inverted hierarchy, indeed a real 'counter-hierarchy', the summit of which will be occupied by the being who will in reality be situated nearer than any other being to the very bottom of the 'pit of hell'.

This being, even if he appears in the form of a particular single human being, will really be less an individual than a symbol, and he will be as it were the synthesis of all the symbolism that has been inverted for the purposes of the 'counter-initiation', and he will

---

4. He can therefore be regarded as the chief of the *awliyā al-shayṭān*, and as he will be the last to fulfill that function, and at the same time his function will then have its most manifest importance in the world, it can be said that he will be as it were their 'seal' (*khātim*), according to the terminology of Islamic esoterism; it is not difficult to see from this to what point the parody of the tradition will be carried in all its aspects.

5. Money itself, or whatever may take its place, will once more possess a qualitative character of this sort, for it is said that 'no one can buy or sell unless he has the mark, that is, the name of the beast or the number of its name' (Rev. 13:17), and this implies the actual use in connection with money of the inverted symbols of the 'counter-tradition'.

manifest it all the more completely in himself because he will have
neither predecessor nor successor. In order to express the false carried to its extreme he will have to be so to speak 'falsified' from every
point of view, and to be like an incarnation of falsity itself.[6] In order
that this may be possible, and by reason of his extreme opposition
to the true in all its aspects, the Antichrist can adopt the very symbols of the Messiah, using them of course in an inverted sense;[7] and
the predominance accorded to the 'malefic' aspect, or, more accurately, its substitution for the 'benefic' aspect by the subversion of
the double meaning of symbols, is what constitutes his characteristic mark. In the same way there can be and must be a strange resemblance between the designations of the Messiah (*al-masīḥ* in
Arabic) and of the Antichrist (*al-masīkh*);[8] but the latter are really
only deformations of the former, just as the Antichrist is represented as deformed in all the more or less symbolical descriptions
that have been given of him, and this again is very significant. These
descriptions indeed particularly emphasize the bodily asymmetries,
and this implies essentially that they are the visible signs of the
actual nature of the being to whom they are attributed, for such
things are in fact always signs of some interior disequilibrium; this
is why certain deformities constitute 'disqualifications' from the
initiatic point of view, but at the same time it can easily be imagined
that they are 'qualifications' in the opposite sense, that is, from the
point of view of 'counter-initiation'. The very name of the latter

6. Thus he will be the antithesis of the Christ saying 'I am the Truth', or of a *wali*
like al-Ḥallāj saying in the same way '*ana'l-Ḥaqq*'.

7. 'The analogy existing between the true doctrine and the false has perhaps not
received sufficient attention: St. Hippolytus, in his little work on the Antichrist
gives a memorable example of it which will not be surprising to people who have
studied symbolism: the Messiah and the Antichrist both have as their emblem the
lion.' (P. Vulliaud, *La Kabbale Juive*, vol. II, p373) The profound reason from the
kabbalistic point of view lies in the consideration of the two faces, luminous and
obscure, of *Metatron*; it is also why the Apocalyptic number 666, the 'number of the
Beast', is also a solar number (cf. *The King of the World*).

8. Here there is an untranslatable double meaning: *Masīkh* can be taken as a
deformation of *Masīha*, by the mere addition of a dot to the final letter; but at the
same time the first word means 'deformed', which correctly expresses the character
of the Antichrist.

implies that it moves in opposition to initiation, consequently in the direction of an increase in the disequilibrium of beings, leading finally to the 'dissolution' or 'disintegration' previously referred to. The Antichrist must evidently be as near as it is possible to be to 'disintegration', so that one could say that his individuality, while it is developed in a monstrous fashion, is nevertheless at the same time almost annihilated, thus realizing the inverse of the effacement of the 'ego' before the 'Self', or in other words, realizing confusion in 'chaos' as against fusion in principial Unity; and this state, as represented by the very deformity and disproportion of his bodily shape, is actually at the lower limit of the possibilities of our individual state, so that the summit of the 'counter-hierarchy' is indeed the place that really befits him in the 'world upside down' that will be his. Furthermore, even from a purely symbolical point of view, and inasmuch as he represents the 'counter-tradition', the Antichrist is no less necessarily deformed: it has been explained that the 'counter-tradition' can only be a caricature of the tradition, and caricature implies deformation; moreover, if it were otherwise, there would be no outward means of distinguishing the 'counter-tradition' from the true tradition, but the former must bear in itself the 'mark of the devil', so that at least the 'elect' may not be seduced. Besides this, the false is necessarily also the 'artificial', and in this respect the 'counter-tradition' cannot fail, despite its other characteristics, to retain the 'mechanical' character appertaining to all the productions of the modern world, of which it will itself be the last; still more exactly, there will be something in it comparable to the automatism of the 'psychic corpses' spoken of earlier, and like them it will be constituted of 'residues' animated artificially and momentarily, and this again explains why it can contain nothing durable; a heap of 'residues', galvanized, so to speak, by an 'infernal' will: surely nothing could give a clearer idea of what it is to have reached the very edge of dissolution.

There seems to be no occasion to dwell further on these matters; it would be of little use in the end to seek to foresee in detail how the 'counter-tradition' will be constituted, and the general indications already given should be almost enough for anyone who wants to devise for himself their application to particular points and any such attempt being in any case beyond the scope of the present enquiry. That enquiry has now been extended to the final stage of the anti-traditional action that must lead this world toward its end; between the fleeting reign of the 'counter-tradition' and the final moment of the present cycle there can only be the 'rectification', which will suddenly put back all things into their normal place at the very moment when subversion seems complete, thus at one stroke preparing for the 'golden age' of the future cycle.

40

THE END
OF A WORLD

THE VARIOUS MATTERS DEALT WITH in the course of this study together constitute what may, in a general way, be called the 'signs of the times' in the Gospel sense, in other words, the precursory signs of the 'end of a world' or of a cycle. This end only appears to be the 'end of the world', without any reservation or specification of any kind, to those who see nothing beyond the limits of this particular cycle; a very excusable error of perspective it is true, but one that has nonetheless some regrettable consequences in the excessive and unjustified terrors to which it gives rise in those who are not sufficiently detached from terrestrial existence; and naturally they are the very people who form this erroneous conception most easily, just because of the narrowness of their point of view. In truth there can be many 'ends of the world', because there are cycles of very varied duration, contained as it were one within another, and also because this same notion can always be applied analogically at all degrees and at all levels; but it is obvious that these 'ends' are of very unequal importance, as are the cycles themselves to which they belong; and in this connection it must be acknowledged that the end now under consideration is undeniably of considerably greater importance than many others, for it is the end of a whole *Manvantara*, and so of the temporal existence of what may rightly be called a humanity, but this, it must be said once more, in no way implies that it is the end of the terrestrial world itself, because, through the 'rectification' that takes place at the final instant, this end will itself immediately become the beginning of another *Manvantara*.

While on this subject, there is yet one more point needing to be explained more precisely: the partisans of 'progress' have a habit of saying that the 'golden age' is not in the past but in the future; nevertheless the truth is that so far as our own *Manvantara* is concerned it is in the past, for it is nothing other than the 'primordial state' itself. There is a sense however in which it is both in the past and in the future, but only on condition that attention is not confined to the present *Manvantara* but is extended to include the succession of terrestrial cycles, for insofar as the future is concerned nothing but the 'golden age' of another *Manvantara* can possibly be in question; it is therefore separated from our period by a 'barrier' completely insurmountable to the profane people who say that sort of thing, and they have no idea what they are talking about when they announce the near approach of a 'new age' as being one with which the existing humanity will be concerned. Their error, in its most extreme form, will be that of the Antichrist himself when he claims to bring the 'golden age' into being through the reign of the 'counter-tradition', and when he even gives it an appearance of authenticity, purely deceitful and ephemeral though it be, by means of a counterfeit of the traditional idea of the *Sanctum Regnum*; this makes clear the reason for the aforesaid preponderant part played by 'evolutionist' conceptions in all the 'pseudo-traditions', and although these 'pseudo-traditions' are still but very partial and very feeble 'prefigurations' of the 'counter-tradition', yet they are no doubt unconsciously contributing more directly than anything else to the preparations for its arrival. The 'barrier' recently alluded to, which in a sense compels those for whom it exists to confine themselves entirely to the interior of the present cycle, is of course a still more insuperable obstacle to the representatives of the 'counter-initiation' than it is to those who are merely profane, for the former are oriented wholly toward dissolution, and so they above all are those for whom nothing can exist outside the present cycle, and it is therefore more particularly for them that the end of the cycle must really be the 'end of the world' in the most complete sense that the expression can bear.

This raises another related question on which a few words should be said, although an answer is really contained implicitly in some of the considerations previously dealt with, and it is this: to what extent are the people who most fully represent the 'counter-initiation' effectively conscious of the part they are playing, and to what extent are they on the other hand but the tools of a will surpassing their own and therefore hidden from them, though they be inescapably subordinated to it? In accordance with what has been said above, the limits between the two points of view from which their action can be envisaged is necessarily determined by the limits of the spiritual world, into which they can in no way penetrate; they may possess a knowledge of the possibilities of the 'intermediary world' as extensive as anyone cares to think, but this knowledge will nevertheless always be irremediably falsified by the absence of the spirit, which alone could give it its true meaning. Obviously such beings can never be mechanists or materialists, nor even partisans of 'progress' or 'evolutionists' in the popular sense of the words, and when they promulgate in the world the ideas which these words express, they are practicing a conscious deceit; but these ideas concern only the merely negative 'anti-tradition', which for them is but a means and not an end, and they could, just like anyone else, seek to excuse their deception by saying that 'the end justifies the means'. Their error is of a much more profound order than that of the men whom they influence and to whom they apply 'suggestion' by means of those ideas, for it arises in no other way than as the consequence of their total and invincible ignorance of the true nature of all spirituality; this makes it much more difficult to say exactly up to what point they may be conscious of the falsity of the 'counter-tradition' they aim at setting up, for they may really believe that in doing so they are opposing the spirit as manifested in every normal and regular tradition, and that they are situated on the same level as those who represent it in this world; and in this sense the Antichrist must surely be the most 'deluded' of all beings. This delusion has its root in the 'dualist' error referred to earlier; dualism is found in one form or another in all beings whose horizon does not extend beyond certain limits even if the limits are those of the entire manifested world; such people cannot resolve the duality they see in all things lying within those limits by referring it to a superior principle, and so they think that it is really irreducible and are thereby led to a denial of the Supreme Unity, which indeed for them is as if it were not. For this reason it has been possible to say that the representatives of the 'counter-initiation' are in the end the dupes of the part they themselves are playing, and that their delusion is in truth the worst delusion of all, since it is positively the only one whereby a being can be not merely led more or less seriously astray, but actually irremediably lost; nonetheless, if they were not so deluded they would clearly not be fulfilling a function that must be fulfilled, like every other function, so that the Divine plan may be accomplished in this world.

This leads back to the consideration of the twofold, or 'benefic' and 'malefic' aspect of the whole history of the world, seen as a cyclic manifestation; and this is really the 'key' to all traditional explanations of the conditions under which this manifestation is developed, especially when it is being considered, as at present, in the period leading directly to its end. On the one hand, if this manifestation is simply taken by itself, without relating it to a much greater whole, the entire process from its beginning to its end is clearly a progressive 'descent' or 'degradation', and this is what may be called its 'malefic' aspect; but, on the other hand, the same manifestation, when put back into the whole of which it is a part, produces results that have a truly 'positive' result in universal existence; and its development must be carried right to the end, so as to include a development of the inferior possibilities of the 'dark age', in order that the 'integration' of those results may become possible and may become the immediate principle of another cycle of manifestation; this is what constitutes its 'benefic' aspect. The same applies when the very end of the cycle is considered: from the special point of view of that which must then be destroyed because its manifestation is finished and as it were exhausted, the end is naturally 'catastrophic' in the etymological sense, in which the word evokes the idea of a sudden and irretrievable 'fall'; but, on the other hand, from the point of view according to which manifestation, in disappearing as such, is brought back to its principle so far as all that is positive in its existence is concerned, this same end appears on the contrary as the 'rectification' whereby, as explained, all things are no less suddenly re-established in their 'primordial state'. Moreover this can be applied analogically to all degrees, whether a being or a world is in question: in short, it is always the partial point of view that is 'malefic', and the point of view that is total, or relatively total with respect to the other, that is 'benefic', because all possible disorders are only disorders when they are considered in themselves and 'separatively', and because these partial disorders are completely effaced in the presence of the total order into which they are finally merged, constituting, when stripped of their 'negative' aspect, elements in that order comparable to all others; there is indeed nothing that is 'malefic' except the limitation that necessarily conditions all contingent existence, and this limitation as such has in reality but a purely negative existence. The two points of view, respectively 'benefic' and 'malefic', have been spoken of earlier as if they were in some way symmetrical; but it is easy to understand that they are nothing of the kind, and that the second signifies only something that is unstable and transitory, whereas only that which the first represents has a permanent and positive character, so that the 'benefic' aspect cannot but prevail in the end, while the 'malefic' aspect vanishes completely because it was in reality only an illusion inherent in 'separativity'. Nevertheless, the truth is that it then becomes no longer proper to use the word 'benefic' any more than the word 'malefic', for the two terms are essentially correlative and cannot properly be used to indicate an opposition when it no longer exists, for it belongs, like all oppositions, exclusively to a particular relative and limited domain; as soon as the limits of that domain are overstepped, there is only that which is, and which cannot not be, or be other than it is; and so it comes about that, if one does not stop short of the most profound order of reality, it can be said in all truth that the 'end of a world' never is and never can be anything but the end of an illusion.

INDEX

Great Pyramid 256–258
Great Triad 140 n10
Great White Lodge 249
Greek(s) 12 n1, 27, 30, 92

al-Ḥallāj 272 n6
Hebrew 28, 75 n2, 147, 152–153,
    258 n10
Hermetic 139–140
Hermetism 168
Hindu:
    doctrine 11, 15, 57, 66, 140
    tradition 1, 12, 25, 28, 30 n10,
    139 n7, 142, 148 n10, 160 n1,
    172–3, 270
Holy Empire 270
humanism 103, 193, 197, 212
hypergeometry 126

individualism 8, 62, 90
immanentism 239
Iran 146
Islamic:
    civilization 56
    doctrine 242 n1
    esoterism 263, 271 n4
    rites 157 n9
    tradition 139 ns6 and 7, 160 n1,
    173
Israel 147, 153, 257–258

James, William 220, 222, 226
Jerusalem 147, 153
Jews 145 n2, 227 n1
Judaism 257
Judeo-Christian 257–258

Ka'bah 139 n7
Kabbalah 28, 139 n7, 157 n10, 168
    n2, 248
Kabires 154–155, 157

Kali-Yuga 1, 84, 132, 174
Kant 36, 126 n2
Kether 139 n7

Leibnitz 30, 34 n4, 50–51, 76 n3,
    96–97,121
Locke 92
Lokāloka 172 n1, 232 n6
Louis XVII 254 n4
lycanthropy 183

MacGregor Mathers, S.S.L. 224
    n4
magic(ian) 153, 168, 181–183, 185–
    187, 206, 223–226, 234, 263
magnetism 125, 169
Mahdi 254 n2
Manicheans 267
mantra(s) 148 n10, 206
Manvantara(s) 3, 42, 128, 132, 143,
    168 n2, 263, 275–276
materialism 20–21, 96–101, 103–
    104, 106, 113, 117–118, 124, 149
    n12, 165, 169–171, 173, 180, 194–
    195, 197, 201, 215, 217, 219, 221,
    260
Melchizedek 150 n14
metapsychic(s) 170, 217–219, 229,
    268
Metatron 272 n7
Moksha 64
Montsalvat 160 n2
Muḥyi'd-Dīn ibn al-Arabī 63 n1,
    265 n7
mūla 16 n1
mūlādhāra 139 n7
Myers 229 n3

nāma 12, 66
nāma-rūpa 24, 63
naturalism 239